How to Be an Intellectual

How to Be an Intellectual

Essays on Criticism, Culture, and the University

Jeffrey J. Williams

FORDHAM UNIVERSITY PRESS

NEW YORK 2014

Library of Congress Cataloging-in-Publication Data

Williams, Jeffrey, 1958 – author.
  How to be an intellectual : essays on criticism, culture, and the university / Jeffrey J. Williams. — First edition.
    pages cm
  Summary: "This book sheds academic obscurity to tell the story of trends in contemporary literary and cultural criticism and the state of the American university. It collects noted and new essays by Jeffrey J. Williams, who regularly publishes in Dissent, the Chronicle of Higher Education, and LARB, as well as major academic venues" — Provided by publisher.
  ISBN 978-0-8232-6380-6 (hardback) — ISBN 978-0-8232-6381-3 (paper)
  1. Criticism—United States. 2. Intellectuals—United States. 3. Literature—Study and teaching (Higher)—United States. I. Title.
  PN99.U5W55 2014
  801'.950973—dc23

                                                                    2014008676

Printed in the United States of America

16 15 14   5 4 3 2 1

First edition

CONTENTS

ACKNOWLEDGMENTS

If I thanked all the people that there are to thank, the acknowledgments would threaten to be endless. Let me note, first, the editors who suggested, commissioned, or edited these essays in earlier versions. I am especially grateful to Liz McMillen at the *Chronicle of Higher Education* for getting me started there, and to Karen Winkler for keeping me going. I would also like to thank the people at *Dissent*, a good journal for criticism between academic and glossy, in particular Maxine Phillips and Michael Walzer. And I should thank Evan Kindley at *Los Angeles Review of Books* for prompting me to write on "liberal bias," as well as Eyal Amiran, longtime stalwart at *Postmodern Culture*.

I am grateful for comments and encouragement from colleagues, particularly from Kathy Newman, Victor Cohen, David Shumway, Jon Klancher, and my students at CMU; Katie Hogan nearby at Carlow; Noah Heringman and Devoney Looser at Missouri; and Hap Veeser, whose gracious remarks came at a good time.

Several people deserve special thanks: Heather Steffen, who helped at key stages getting the book together; Frank Donoghue, who understood the project and wrote a helpful reader's report; Luke Menand, whose encouragement helped; Joel Woller, who offers kind comments about my writing after beating me at backgammon; Marc Bousquet, who handles the criticism of academic labor so that I don't have to; David Downing, who has been a constant support in the neighborhood; and John Fried, who tapped the journalistic experience he has been trying to hide to give excellent comments.

Finally, I would like to thank Bruce Robbins, who fortunately paid attention to my arguments even when I was a cheeky grad student and has given a boost to this project all along; my daughter, Virginia Williams, who

I suspect has had to quell rolling her eyes when Dad sent her essays, to which she gave perceptive comments; and Vince Leitch, who not only read but, channeling *American Idol*, rated every essay. I owe him a huge debt of gratitude for reading the first version of this manuscript over a weekend and FedExing it back, and for his constant concern. Fortunately, though such a debt is impossible to repay, he seems to accept wine.

"Criticism without Footnotes," "Credibility and Criticism," and "Bellwether" appear here for the first time. Other essays first appeared in the following places, sometimes with different titles (titles in journalism are assigned by editors). All of them have been revised for this volume, some quite substantially.

Chronicle of Higher Education: "Book Angst"; "The Critic as Wanderer (Terry Eagleton)"; "The Editor as Broker (Gordon Hutner)"; "From Cyborgs to Animals (Donna Haraway)"; "Gaga Feminism (Judith Halberstam)"; "How Critics Became Smart"; "Intellectuals and Politics (Stefan Collini)"; "A Life in Criticism (M.H. Abrams)"; "My Life as Editor"; "Other People's Words"; "The Pedagogy of Prison"; "Prodigal Critics (Bloom, Fish, and Greenblatt)"; "The Political Theory License (Michael Walzer)"; "The Retrospective Tenor of Recent Theory"; "The Rise of the Theory Journal"; "Shelf Life"; "The Statistical Turn in Literary Criticism"; "The Thrill Is Gone"; "The University on Film"; "Unlucky Jim."

Dissent: "The Academic Devolution"; "How to Be an Intellectual"; "The Pedagogy of Debt"; "Student Debt and the Spirit of Indenture."

Inside Higher Ed "Academic Opportunities Unlimited."

LARB/Salon: "The Neoliberal Bias of Higher Education."

minnesota review: "Teacher."

PMC: "The Ubiquity of Culture."

VLS: "Publicist Intellectuals."

The Critical Pulse: Credos from Thirty-Six Contemporary Critics, ed. Jeffrey J. Williams and Heather Steffen (Columbia University Press, 2012): "Long Island Intellectual."

How to Be an Intellectual

Introduction: Criticism without Footnotes

This book represents my effort to write a different kind of criticism from the academic mainstream. It fuses the techniques of literary journalism with scholarship to report on contemporary theory, intellectual life and culture, politics, and the university. One way to put it is that this book offers criticism without footnotes.

Journalism and scholarship usually inhabit different planets, with different gods, languages, and forums. Journalism pays homage to Hermes, favoring speed over the lumbering pace of academe, the timely report over the arcane investigation, the straightforward account over tedious elaboration. Its language is colloquial and direct, and it typically appears in the newspaper, magazine, or blog. Scholarship looks to Apollo, favoring rumination over snap judgments, careful qualifications over broad generalizations, and time-consuming research over the quick surmise. Its language is often hieratic, employing specialized terms specific to those in its particular fields, and it resides in small circulation academic journals or books. There is occasional commerce between the two planets, but rarely dual citizenship, and there is the constant suspicion that one violates precisely what the other values, academics thinking that journalism yields superficial over serious knowledge, and journalists thinking that academia opts for its own obscure cubbyholes over actual relevance.

If a fundamental task of criticism is to explain our culture, I think that scholarship needs better means of exposition than it usually employs and that enjoins an audience beyond a narrow academic field. (We often hear about interdisciplinarity, but most scholarship does not reach an audience outside of its field or period, so perhaps we should start with interfieldarity.) Conversely, we need journalistic accounts that filter from the deep well of scholarship and do not condescend to academe nor make it sound like a distant planet called Geek. So I have tried to develop a kind of writing that resides between the two, tapping into the scholarly but taking the form of the reportorial or exploratory essay. To that end, this book collects thirty-two relatively short essays, at least by academic standards, some five or so pages, drawing a portrait or giving my angle on a topic, and others ten or twelve pages, elaborating on a comparison or larger issue.

We sometimes call critical articles "essays," but as a kind of writing they have more in common with the social scientific article or research report. Think of how they look: usually twenty-five or thirty pages, with full academic paraphernalia. The critical article is a curious development in the history of the literary essay, occurring only in the last fifty years, when criticism not only moved to academic quarters but also adopted the protocols and measures of advanced academic research (a story I tell here, in "The Rise of the Theory Journal" and elsewhere). The very form of the article, I think, broaches a contradiction: while many critics claim to question normative practices and problematize received opinion, most of their writing follows this staid form unthinkingly and is slavish to authority, intoning "as Deleuze argues," "as Butler has written," "in Foucauldian terms."

It is easy to complain about academic writing, but part of my point throughout this book is that much in academe is valuable, particularly its scholarly core, building the reservoir of what we know, and its protocols, testing what we know and resisting venal pressures. However, there is a difference between scholarship and scholasticism, and too much contemporary criticism tends toward scholasticism, toward the worst traits of the word "academic," so that it is overly technical, hermetic, and without much use—except, as the saying goes, for a CV line. Rather than the conventional distinction between academic and journalistic criticism, perhaps the more salient distinction is between scholasticism and criticism, and we should militate against scholasticism.

It's also easy to complain about journalism—that it's shallow, reproduces received opinion, and so on—but we can learn lessons from the tautness and pointedness with which good journalists write. However, Edmund Wilson, often held up as the paragon of the public intellectual because he lived by literary journalism, actually had some cautionary words about it, remarking in "Thoughts on Being Bibliographed" (1943) that even serious journalism "involves its own special problems," such as trying to put "solid matter into notices of ephemeral happenings" and avoiding the dictates of editors and their "over-anxious intentness on the fashions of the month or the week." In other words, there was not a halcyon time before our own to which we should return. My point instead is that journalism presents one solution for responding to the particular problems we have now, serving to bridge the distance and difficulty of contemporary theory and research, to dispel canards about the university and defend its public purpose, and to renew literary culture.

A more modest way to put this is that we should consider criticism a craft like other forms of literary writing. This does not mean that criticism vies with fiction or poetry, although it might aspire to the literary essay. Or perhaps its role is similar to translation. The pieces in this book translate the work of critics and other writers as well as the recent history of the university so that people not fully embedded in it might understand it, and so that people more versed in it might see it afresh. A work of literary translation is not to popularize its topic or to dumb it down, but to convey it in a way that is both faithful to the material and legible to a reader who has a different idiom.

This is as much a corrective to some of my own habits and to my own training as to anything else. I was drawn to criticism through the power of the essay, reading those of Orwell, Wilson, and Susan Sontag early on, intrigued by their voices, seeing things differently through their observations, and admiring the confidence of their views. They were not afraid to make generalizations and to judge the material they discussed, and they conveyed a commitment to the importance of literature, culture, and politics. Through graduate school, I was taught to write very differently, avoiding generalizations and judgments, instead inventorying previous sources, "reading" passages in laborious detail, and making statements that followed the theory I had read. The results sometimes felt forced, not quite getting at what I really cared about or thought. But I do not want to make it sound as if I experienced a conversion, as some critics testified during the 1990s, renouncing theory for the unmediated enjoyment of literature, or something like that. Rather, I have tried to bring it a step farther, to synthesize the analytic edge of theory with the exposition of journalism, to distill the scholarly into essential points, and to tell stories about ideas so that other people might gain a handle to grasp and use them.

The short essay lends itself to distillation, like a snapshot offering a focused foray on an idea, writer, book, or issue. Perhaps I lack patience, but

I am disposed to the short form that can be read in one concentrated sitting, that carries its points on its sleeve, and that sticks in mind. (I have to add, somewhat defensively, that to make essays read easily does not mean they are easy to write.) I don't mean to say that all criticism should adopt this form—obviously some inquiries or issues require much more space, and I myself have long essays on criticism, contemporary fiction, and the university—but there is a good deal of critical writing that takes far too many liberties with our time and attention. Most likely it was written not to be read but to be measured, filling the quantum of the twenty-five-page article.

Of course, I am not the only one who works the space between literary journalism and scholarship. Louis Menand is a master of it, one of the few who is a genuine scholar as well as a high-level journalist, and I take notes from him. As is the British critic Stefan Collini, whom I profile here. (There is a tradition of academics who occasionally do reviewing, but it is usually moonlighting from academic work, and I am talking about those who make crossing over a regular if not fundamental part of their work.) Still, Menand is relatively anomalous among his academic cohort, which took up literary theory. In my surmise, the tendency to cross over has gained momentum over the past two decades, particularly since the culture wars of the late 1980s and early 1990s, and it has enlisted a number of critics of my academic generation, born around 1960, slightly after the Sixties Generation but not quite Generation X, did their graduate training in the 1980s, and began their academic careers around 1990. For instance, my contemporary, Michael Bérubé, issued an apt call for "public access" in the mid-1990s and has written indefatigably for a variety of audiences, especially on politics, academic and otherwise. Another contemporary, Laura Kipnis, has developed an arch but deeply intellectual style as a prominent cultural commentator on sex and politics. Likewise, Andrew Ross, Michael Warner, Judith "Jack" Halberstam, and Eric Lott each cross over to public venues, as I discuss in some of the essays here.

Generations are one of those concepts that everyone recognizes but no one quite agrees on, but I think that generations give us some traction to understand how historical change affects culture. Change arises not just from a lone figure who puts forth a new theory—the heroic model that often rules histories of criticism—but also from our social and cultural circumstances and institutions, which we experience in concert and which shape us. To talk about the shifts in contemporary criticism, I have marked off "the theory generation," those born in the late 1930s through early 1950s and coming through the expanding American university, who forged the new discourses of theory in the late 1960s and 1970s that revolutionized the study of literature and culture, shifting from explication and the affirmation of universal human values to theoretical speculation, investigating signs and structures.

Things were different for my generation. We entered the scene *after* the revolution, so theory was part of the groundwater, there when we got there. I have called my cohort "the posttheory generation" to indicate our lateness, signaling not the death of theory but our revisionary stance toward it. The change in feeling, I suspect, is similar to Lionel Trilling's description, in "On the Teaching of Modern Literature," of his students' reaction to modernism, taking its shock for granted; for us, theory was ordinary, and we took the ideas that everything was constructed, or disciplined and contained by power, or indeterminate, for granted. We also entered the scene, as I mentioned, during the fraught days of the culture wars, and we experienced the increasing squeeze on public higher education and academic jobs— coordinates that seemed to demand a more public response. For many of us, it was no longer enough to have effect only on "the level of theory," and rather than the theory guru, who disseminates a major paradigm or approach, like Paul de Man, the most influential American critic of the 1970s, our model moved to the public critic, who aims to reach a larger public, often in magazines or for trade presses (each of the people I noted before has at least one trade book).

The shift to literary theory in the 1960s and 1970s was sometimes encapsulated as "the linguistic turn," and I am tempted to summarize the tendency now as "the public turn," in criticism and in the humanities more generally. (At least I hope it is, although I can unfortunately imagine different outcomes, for instance its doppelganger, "the commercial turn," as the humanities are reconfigured along the line of Big Data and customer tastes, or simply "the archival turn," as criticism tacks toward literary history over theory.) One can see a turn in the heightened attention to the concept of "the public" as well as in the effort to cross over to wider audiences. The concept of the "public" runs through a good deal of contemporary scholarship, both historical and theoretical, for instance in examining the creation of the public sphere in Europe and America in the eighteenth century, its expansion in the nineteenth, and its fragmentation in the twentieth, in the work of critics such as Warner, Lauren Berlant, Amanda Anderson, and many others. And, while most critics remain on the scholarly track, an active squad of contemporary critics, of my generation as well as the succeeding generation, like those clustered around the magazine *n + 1*, deliberately seek a public role and speak in a public voice.

Among my cohort, the beat I cover is criticism and theory itself. Other than sussing out its trends and directions, I have tried to build a material history of it, deciphering its formation in the American university through the twentieth century, as it served general education in midcentury and pure research in the post-Sputnik era. In addition, I try to give a lived sense of doing criticism, drawing on a series of interviews I have conducted that I hope build an oral history of criticism in our time. Another beat I cover, more than most of my cohort, is the state of higher education in the United States, how it has transformed over the past forty years from a flagship of the postwar welfare state to a privatized enterprise, oriented toward business and its own self-accumulation. Thus, I have focused attention on and analyzed the casualization of academic labor and the indebtedness of students, higher education no longer a respite but an induction into a kind of indenture. Last, I have probably been more self-consciously aware of adapting the literary model of the essay, particularly in the essays in the closing section of this volume.

While these essays traverse topics from Richard Rorty to working in prison, I would like to think that the book is not a grab bag but hangs together like an album of pictures that clearly come from the same eye. In general, I take an institutional perspective. A common metaphor for the operation of criticism is "a conversation," which is a hopeful metaphor, presumably welcoming all into the field, but it also suggests that literature, culture, and criticism are self-contained lines of discourse. Instead, I look to see how our institutions make us, framing the way that we do literature, culture, and criticism, as well as how we in turn make our institutions.

Thinking about institutions is a self-conscious habit, and I am drawn to questions about why we do what we do, what it means to be a critic and intellectual, and what it means to participate in academe. Hence the title of the volume, *How to Be an Intellectual*. Alas, it might disappoint those looking for a guidebook if it were shelved in a self-help section, or it might seem rather grand, but the phrase is more a constant question than a prescription, and many of the essays depict the various ways that people have fashioned themselves as intellectuals. The title comes from the first essay, which looks at Rorty's "Intellectuals in Politics." For Rorty, the critic has a special position as an intellectual and a special obligation to engage the politics of our society. I think that Rorty is finally unfair in his essay—he attacks Andrew Ross for his merely cultural politics—but it foregrounds the tensions of our role, and it also illustrates the shifting idea of what it means to be a critic, for his generation and ours. While I primarily write about those in literary and cultural studies, like Rorty I use the extensive sense of the critic, nearly synonymous with "intellectual." This view contrasts with that of someone like Stanley Fish, who asserts a narrow definition, holding that literary critics should stick to literature and that politics is outside their job description. I think that Fish's argument relies on a disingenuous nominalism—if a "literary" critic, the critic should only deal with literature—and is historically shallow, as criticism has always had fuzzy borders and critics have often talked about larger issues of culture, society, and politics. Even the traditionalist T. S. Eliot remarked, in his first editorial in *The Criterion* (1926), that criticism should deal with "general ideas," "not merely on literature, but on what we may suppose to be the interests of any intelligent person with literary taste." This capaciousness invites confusion about literary criticism, particularly compared to other disciplines of thought, which seem to nail down a tidier object of study. Through this book I take criticism as the kind of writing that deals not just with intra-academic conversations but also with public education—that is, with educating as broad a public as possible and with public issues, as well as with literature and culture.

For the sake of some guideposts, I have grouped the essays in four sections, each with a brief preface. The first section, "The Politics of Criticism," centers on battles, trends, and turns in contemporary criticism. We have not lacked for "historicizing" literature, but we usually see criticism as a march of statements or approaches. Rather than seeing criticism as a disembodied line of discourse, I focus on the institutional and social pressures that have shaped it and changed it.

The second section, "Profiles in Criticism," offers short tours of the work of a number of notable critics, recounting how they have fashioned their careers, through accident and intention, in the midst of postwar American culture. Since the New Critics issued a prohibition against the "intentional fallacy," there has been a tendency to discount talk of an author's life. But I think we need to see critics in their time and place. In addition, we tend to deal with a critic's work piecemeal, whereas I try to take account of someone's work over a long span. I also try to dispel some received opinions about contemporary criticism—for instance, that the rise of theory was an import of "French theory." Rather, in the cases of a number of American critics, it was a homegrown development.

While I consider the formative influence that the university has had on contemporary American criticism, in the third section, "The Predicament of the University," I turn full attention to it, analyzing the predicament of students, conscripted into debt, and academic labor, deskilled into contingent positions. The university is not just a physical institution but also a cultural idea, and I also look at representations of it in recent fiction and film. Higher education is said to stand apart from "the real world," but given that about 70 percent of Americans travel through higher education, it has a leading role in American experience and speaks directly to the way that we apportion opportunity and rights in our society and culture.

Before it became a front-page issue, I wrote about student debt because it was something I confronted, and even more disturbingly something I saw my daughter and my students facing. It just didn't seem right that twenty-one- and twenty-two-year-olds had $30,000, $50,000 or even $100,000 in debt before they entered a full adult franchise, and in fact impeded their opportunity to a franchise. Though you don't have to wear it on your sleeve, I think that criticism comes from a personal root, from something that touches you, or the people around you, which in turn obligates you to say and do something about it. That is, criticism carries an obligation to work against injustice.

Still, criticism for me is not generated from a "position" but comes from the alchemy of training and accident, scholarly grounding and curiosity, political views and individual interests. The last section, "The Personal and the Critical," gathers essays that reflect on some of my experiences in and out of the world of books, from working as a correction officer in a New York State prison in the early 1980s to working in some of the nooks and crannies of the literary world, such as a used bookstore or editing a literary and critical journal. These experiences no doubt tint the filter through which I glean the world—for instance, working in prison gave me a little more worldly perspective than being a scholarship boy—and do criticism. Criticism is one way we have to reflect on how we live, what we have learned from it, and whether we should live differently.

PART ONE

The Politics of Criticism

Criticism in our time seems subject to frequent change. This section looks at some of the turns in contemporary criticism, such as the rise and fall of literary theory, the institutionalization of cultural studies, the resurrection of the public intellectual, and the embrace of quantitative methods. One question that runs through it is the political relevance, or irrelevance, of culture.

Sometimes the history of criticism is framed as a kind of relay race, with a topic handed from one runner to the next (the focus on the sign, for instance, passed from Saussure to Lévi-Strauss to Derrida to Butler). It is a history without history. In contrast, I focus especially on the institutional conditions of criticism, the material circumstances within which it is embedded and that make it possible, permitting certain work to be done or not done and inflecting its form. Since the 1940s, that history has had a lot to do with higher education, first with the aims of general education and more recently with the protocols of advanced research.

To examine that history, in several essays I look at some of the peripheral objects and vehicles of criticism, for instance the theory journal. Such entities usually recede to the mute background, like an Amazon.com box irrelevant to the book inside, but they shape criticism in their own distinctive ways. A great deal has been written about "the little magazine," but almost nothing on this newer, albeit more academic, genre. Or I look at the path of modern criticism through its keywords of approbation, shifting over the past century from "soundness" to "rigor" to the current "smart."

I begin with a longer essay that I originally wrote for *Dissent* comparing Richard Rorty and Andrew Ross. The pragmatist philosopher and the avatar of cultural studies might seem strange bedfellows, but their 1991 debate in *Dissent* foregrounds the question of the politics of criticism, illustrating the culture wars then and now. My take is that it also encapsulates the difference between intellectual generations, and the concept of generations helps us understand contemporary criticism and, more generally, academic culture. Generations are fuzzy around the edges, but they provide a way to locate critics and intellectuals historically, formed not as singular geniuses but as part of their historical cohorts.

Rorty's original essay was called "Intellectuals in Politics" and he has rather strict advice for what intellectuals should do (hence the title of my essay). Throughout this book, the intellectuals I talk about hail primarily from my disciplinary neck of the woods, literary and cultural studies. But for Rorty and in common usage, "critic" is often interchangeable with "intellectual," particularly with the critic who reaches outside his or her academic corner to take up the charge of politics.

ONE

How to Be an Intellectual: *Rorty v. Ross*

In the fall of 1991, Richard Rorty published an essay in *Dissent* magazine called "Intellectuals in Politics." It was not a profile of model figures but something of a jeremiad, castigating intellectuals in order to bring them back to their proper purpose. It upbraided American intellectuals for their disconnection from politics, standing by while the rich ripped off the poor, especially in the wake of the savings and loan crisis and recession of 1990–91. Rorty indicted two groups in particular: journalists and literature professors. Of journalists he charged that they failed the tradition of Lincoln Steffens by not properly educating the electorate. Of literature professors he charged that they failed to "remind voters of their ideals" and had given up on ordinary politics; instead they were intent on internecine pursuits like "advanced literary theory."

Such charges were not entirely new, but Rorty went an extra step and named names. In the larger media sphere, he cited a *Newsweek* editor, Larry Martz, but it was his accusation in the academic sphere that he himself inhabited that drew blood, or at least some attention. He took to task a young Princeton professor, Andrew Ross, finding him guilty of celebrating popular culture indiscriminately, embracing postmodern theory rather than the concrete conditions of those downtrodden, and switching "attention from electoral to cultural politics" or real to academic politics. This switch, in Rorty's eyes, was characteristic of the "contemporary academic left" and "represents attitudes that are widespread in American literature departments."

The Spring 1992 issue of *Dissent* carried a response from Ross and a rejoinder by Rorty. Ross pointed out the relevance of culture to politics (cultural factors like gender and race help "explain how structures of wealth and power are maintained and reproduced from day to day") and noted Rorty's skewed depiction of his work (about his representing literary theory, he remarked "I am not Rorty's man"). Rorty conceded that culture does have some import, but observed that the exchange demonstrated a "fairly sharp generational difference." His side represented the Old Left and people like "Lionel Trilling, John Dewey, Paul Goodman, Sidney Hook, and Daniel Bell"—in other words, the New York Intellectuals, and what Rorty took as the traditional readership of *Dissent*. A key difference with the newer generation was its position on the Cold War, which older intellectuals thought was a good war, whereas younger ones did not. Rorty's reply helped explain some of his animus: Ross's 1989 book *No Respect: Intellectuals and Popular Culture* had taken the New York Intellectuals down a peg, criticizing their ignoring a range of cultural injustices as well as their cheering along the Cold War imperium.

The early 1990s were of course the height of the culture wars, and the exchange played out the Left version of them, split along the trench lines of traditional versus cultural or identity politics. I return to it now, though, not to resuscitate those quarrels, but to look at Rorty and Ross and their respective careers. The exchange, like most such exchanges, probably served to entrench each side rather than persuade the other, but it also brought to center stage two of the more prominent humanities intellectuals in the United States of the last two decades. What models of the intellectual do they each present? While one might debate the merits of cultural politics, Rorty was accurate in observing that he and Ross represented different intellectual generations, a difference that has become clearer in the interim.

Given his passing in 2007, it is fitting to take stock of Rorty's career and how he fashioned himself, moving from an academic philosopher to public intellectual. It is also a good point to consider Andrew Ross's career since he was only starting out in 1991 but has subsequently built a sizeable body of work. Especially over the last decade, Ross has become a kind of social reporter. To put it more contentiously, if Rorty was throwing stones, what kind of house did he live in? And has Ross borne out or absolved himself of Rorty's charges?

By the early 1990s, Richard Rorty was widely regarded as the leading philosopher in the United States. Ironically a good part of his reputation derived from his walking away from philosophy, or at least the mainstream of philosophy departments in the postwar era. The dominant current was analytic philosophy, focused on technical issues, largely of language, and fields like formal logic, rather than large existential questions or the history of philosophy, as those in the discipline strove for the precision of a science. Doing graduate work and taking his first academic job in the 1950s, Rorty earned a reputation in analytic philosophy with articles elucidating distinctions like the mind-body problem. Though he had yet to publish a monograph, he cemented his reputation with an influential anthology, *The Linguistic Turn: Recent Essays in Philosophical Method* (1967). But through the 1970s he underwent a metamorphosis, investigating Continental figures like Nietzsche, Heidegger, and Derrida, who were not considered seriously in the analytic tradition, and returning to the American pragmatists, especially John Dewey, who were considered quaint or outmoded. His 1979 *Philosophy and the Mirror of Nature* announced Rorty's pragmatist turn, arguing that philosophy had been misguided in creating a theory of mind based on reflection. That assumed a metaphysical foundation: there was a core Truth that philosophy attempted to divine. For Rorty, it should instead present useful "redescriptions." Philosophy was not systematic but a conversation, and its value not that it might reveal Truth but that it might be edifying.

Seeing philosophy this way prompted two things. Rorty became more of a historicist, reworking the conversation of philosophy, and he found a renewed value in literature. In place of philosophy providing Truth, literature provided inspiration. His historical perspective prompted a steady stream of essays looking at figures from both Anglo-American and Continental philosophy, many of them gathered in *Consequences of Pragmatism: Essays, 1972–1980* (1982) and the four volumes of his *Philosophical Papers* (1991–2007). His gravitation toward literature culminated in his 1989 book *Contingency, Irony, and Solidarity*, which argued for the power of narrative over logic to deal with problems like human suffering, and found models in writers like George Orwell.

Contingency, Irony, and Solidarity was also Rorty's bid to become more of a public figure, commenting on our common lot. As Neil Gross shows in his biographical study *Richard Rorty: The Making of an American Philosopher* (2008), Rorty deliberately set out to refashion himself from the late 1970s on. His move in 1982 from Princeton, where he was a mainstay of the philosophy department, to the University of Virginia as an at-large professor of the humanities symbolized his evolution. By the late 1980s and through the 1990s, he embraced a role as a public intellectual, with pieces in the *London Review of Books*, the *New York Times*, and *Dissent*. He also published *Achieving Our Country* (1998), praising American democracy and urging intellectuals to take more pride in their country, and a collection of his more public essays, *Philosophy and Social Hope* (1999), in a Penguin paperback. The philosopher was reborn.

Rorty's writings on politics have a refreshingly straightforward stance and plainspoken style, boiling down an issue to its basic terms, like the rich "ripping us off" in "Intellectuals in Politics." They also, in their pragmatist habit, do not hold out a utopia for which to strive or an absolute case from which to measure; rather, they give examples that one can use or from which to draw inspiration. Rorty typically held out the better hope of American democracy, which led to one of his most controversial statements in the late 1990s, when he scolded American intellectuals for not being patriotic in a *Times* op-ed piece (reprinted in *Achieving Our Country*). Part of his argument followed from *Contingency, Irony, and Solidarity*: It is less useful to appeal to broad if not metaphysical categories like "the human." Rather, it is more persuasive to argue that Americans should not suffer hunger, for instance, than that humans shouldn't suffer hunger. But he also excoriated American intellectuals for their lack of patriotism. It is hard to separate this latter view from the American exceptionalism that gave credence to our subsequent wars.

In some ways Rorty became a man of letters and, though he debunked the special status of philosophy, he asserted a distinctive status for criticism. He gives it this estimable genealogy in "Professionalized Philosophy and Transcendentalist Culture" (collected in *Consequences of Pragmatism*): "Beginning in the days of Goethe and Macauley and Carlyle and Emerson, a kind of writing has developed which is neither the evaluation of the relative merits of literary productions, nor intellectual history, nor moral philosophy, nor epistemology, nor social prophecy, but all these things mingled into a new genre. This genre is often still called 'literary criticism.'" That is why he singled out literature professors in particular in "Intellectuals in Politics," rather than philosophy or sociology or political science professors. They had a special obligation, conferred by this tradition, to provide moral perspective on and imaginative vision of politics.

To this genealogy Rorty added, nearer to our time, the "New York intellectuals," and he maintained a high regard for figures like Lionel Trilling and Irving Howe, whose criticism balanced among literary, moral, and political reflection. His choice of the New York intellectuals was something of a return, since his parents had been involved in Left circles in New York, his father, James Rorty, a founding editor of *New Masses* and involved in Communist Party and Trotskyist politics in the early 1930s. (His father was also a poet, which might explain some of Rorty's residual regard for literature, as he suggested in an essay in *Poetry Magazine* before he died.) Rorty had walked away from this heritage while building his academic career, but his later eschewal of philosophy was a kind of prodigal return.

Rorty's connection to the New York intellectuals explains some of the heightened charge of "Intellectuals in Politics." He typically argued in a matter-of-fact, unruffled tone (in person, his signature gesture was the shrug), but part of his crossness, I would speculate, was because Ross's book *No Respect* hit close to home. In the last chapter, Ross criticizes the New York intellectuals for their disconnection from popular concerns, citing James Rorty among a group of better-known names. The contest, then, was not only over the importance of culture but over who controlled the legacy of the New York intellectuals.

In "Intellectuals in Politics" Rorty identifies with the Old Left, or those who cut their political teeth in the 1930s and had a palpable sense of how the rich rip off the poor, but he himself, born in the 1930s and whisked to college in 1946 at the age of fifteen, was very much an academic product, and his authority came not from his political work or experience but his academic work and standing. Though he went against the grain of philosophy, he was in many ways typical of his academic generation, one buoyed on the rich waters of the postwar university. After attending the University of Chicago (B.A., 1950; M.A., 1952), he went to Yale for his Ph.D. (1958). Other than a brief ellipsis in the military in 1957–58 (he was assigned to the Signal Corps and evidently bored), he was on the academic fast track, teaching and earning tenure at Princeton. (Gross cites several letters from Rorty's parents commenting on his absorption in his academic career.) He was typical of his generation, too, insofar as he attained academic reputation and position on relatively few publications, and no monograph before *Philosophy and the Mirror to Nature.*

The postwar years produced a new cohort of intellectuals. They were not like the earlier and scrappier generation of New York Intellectuals, who argued in the legendary lunchroom of City College, often held a variety of jobs in journalism and elsewhere before landing in academe, and traveled the fraught path of Left politics of the 1930s. Rather, they benefited from what I have called the welfare state university, when there was relatively opulent funding for research as well as tuition, they were often trained at elite universities, and they adopted the pro-American liberalism of the 1950s without the tendrils of a communist past. They were fast-tracked into a booming academic world. It is often remarked that the Sixties generation revolutionized academe, but it was actually an earlier generation that first reaped the benefits of enhanced intellectual leisure and created most of the new discourse and terms of criticism, theory, and philosophy.

Rorty's generation was the one that created "advanced literary theory." For instance, many of its leading members, such as Harold Bloom, Fredric Jameson, and Stanley Fish, were born in the 1930s and whisked through academe in similar ways. Rorty probably had more influence on those who did "advanced literary theory" than on those in his home discipline, philosophy, and by the 1980s was taken as an exemplar of postmodern theory in his debunking of "foundational" concepts. Thus, in "Intellectuals in Politics," it was odd that Rorty, himself subject to many attacks on his postmodern or relativist position, would throw a similar kind of paint on someone else, with whom, on paper, he would otherwise be allied. (In his reply, he notes that he and Ross would likely vote the same on many issues.)

Along with the culture wars, the 1990s also saw the celebration of the figure of the public intellectual. What was usually meant by it, though, was not someone like Irving Howe or Michael Harrington, whose statements arose from a long engagement in political work, but an academic who made a foray to the public sphere, and in my view that is the weakness of the model Rorty represents. Rorty attained his public position primarily from his academic work and was not notably involved in party politics, as, say, those who built DSA (Democratic Socialists of America), or as Howe was involved in various enterprises, including the founding of *Dissent*, and he did not write on class or politics before the late 1980s. (The recent work of Walter Benn Michaels exhibits a similar tendency. Like Rorty, Michaels has attacked the focus on cultural or identity politics at the expense of class, but his argument did not arise from his connection to any actual political group; rather, it is literally an academic argument, over terminology and perceived academic trends, rather than an argument for actual policy or a report of what the working class experience.) Though Rorty castigated the "academic left," he was a creature of it, and he imagined his audience as something called "the academic left." And though he eschewed the top-down nature of foundational thinking, Rorty's rhetoric in "Intellectual Politics" is top-down. The genre of "Intellectuals in Politics" is that of the bully pulpit, leading by upbraiding rather than example.

The strength of Rorty's model is his incisive clarity. In a late essay he remarks that the customary distinction between analytic and Continental philosophy is the wrong one; it should be between analytic and conversational philosophy, or between "scholasticism . . . controversies that have no interest to anyone outside the philosophical profession," and that which builds a new vocabulary "to make us happier, freer, and more flexible." Reduction is often derided in contemporary criticism and complication praised, but Rorty's gift was his ability to reduce complicated issues to useable, conversational distinctions, like "rich and poor." He resisted the mire of academic qualification and quibble, and he reinfused intellectual conversation with a colloquial American idiom. The contribution that he is most known for is reinserting pragmatism in the anthology of philosophy, but perhaps his most striking intellectual contribution is his style. In a hyper-specialized time, he crafted a pragmatic style that speaks to those outside the quadrants of a discipline or field and offers conversational distinctions with which to understand obscure concepts and disparate traditions.

In 1991, Andrew Ross was an untenured assistant professor. But, even though he was in his mid-thirties, he had published five books and written on a wide range of topics, many of them outside the traditional bandwidth of literary studies. He had also gained a good bit of celebrity, including his picture in the *New York Times Magazine*. It did not hurt that he was young and hip, wore a few earrings, and lived in New York.

Ross had started in a standard way for an English professor, as a critic of modern poetry. His first book, *The Failure of Modernism: Symptoms of American Poetry* (1986), for instance, offers interpretations of major poets from T. S. Eliot to John Ashbery through the lens of psychoanalytic theory. But Ross quickly left literary studies behind, moving on to write about intellectuals, technology, ecology, and other topics, in a string of books including *No Respect, Strange Weather: Culture, Science, and Technology in the Age of Limits* (1991), *The Chicago Gangster Theory of Life: Nature's Debt to Society* (1994), and *Real Love: In Pursuit of Cultural Justice* (1998), and a ceaseless stream of articles. These gave Ross a reputation as a purveyor of cultural studies, a movement that had appeared in Britain in the 1970s but only gained a toehold on these shores around 1990. Ross was quickly taken up as a representative for his academic generation, as it migrated from literary to cultural studies through the 1990s. (That migration, though it brought along the dictionary of theory, was also a departure of sorts from the "advanced literary theory" that had dominated literary studies in the 1970s and early 1980s.) Ross's departure from literary studies was confirmed by his move to the American studies department at NYU in 1993, and later to help found a department of "social and cultural analysis" there.

Cultural studies is often seen as synonymous with popular culture, but actually much of Ross's early work focused on science and technology rather than, say, television and videos. It has also been seen as an embrace of the popular, but Ross's stance toward the popular has been more analytical than fanlike. For instance, *No Respect* is more about intellectual positions toward popular culture than popular culture itself, and his central argument a correction of New York and other intellectuals, who typically assume a "legislative posture in the name of the popular," seeing it as what Rorty in his reply calls "schlock." Ross argues instead that intellectuals should "learn from the forms and discourses of the popular." It is a kind of democratic argument, and follows Raymond Williams's redefinition of culture as "a whole way of life" rather than the rarefied sense of "the best that has been known and thought." Ross pitched his tent with Williams's sense rather than the Arnoldian sense of the New York intellectuals.

Ross's work on science figured in a later chapter of the culture wars, and in the mid-1990s he was again attacked, this time because of his editing a special issue of the journal *Social Text* on the role of science. One of the articles accepted was a postmodern account of physics, claiming, among other things, that gravity is a social construction. The day the issue came out, the article was exposed as a hoax, which spurred a stream of attacks on the vacuity of postmodern theory and cultural studies. The article was obviously poorly vetted, and Ross's defensive response, complaining of a breach of academic faith on the part of the author, merely lent ballast to charges of cultural studies' shaky scholarly grounding. The controversy tarnished Ross's reputation; however, it should be noted that, in his own writing, Ross does not make arguments about science per se, but comments on the social uses of science. As he observes in a 1996 essay, "Cultural Studies and the

Challenge of Science," the funding and development of fighter planes (and also commercial aviation) derive from social institutions, public policy, and political decisions, not objective, scientific ones.

It is a paradox that most people who come to be seen as examples of a field, discipline, or critical movement are anomalies. Ross's career did not proceed on a predictable track, and his work is unusually prolific and varied. Scottish-born, he settled in the United States in 1980 because of the Thatcher cutbacks to higher education. His route was not the standard one through the Ivies nor Oxbridge (Aberdeen, M.A., 1978; Kent, Ph.D., 1984), and he held a visiting position at Illinois State University before landing a more prestigious berth at Princeton in 1985. Though taken as representing cultural studies, he has moved across various fields, most recently urban studies and labor. Even with the increasing publication expectations of the current university, his seventeen books (ten are monographs, the rest edited collections) in two decades after graduate school are extraordinary. He has also regularly made forays, since early in his career, to public venues, for instance writing for the *Nation* or a column for *Artforum* through the 1990s. He seems to beckon a new image of the academic-intellectual, that one can do it all. To be an academic no longer means a life of leisure and contemplation but one of compulsory hyperproductivity.

Ross's generation has experienced markedly different conditions than those in the postwar era. Coming of professional age during the 1980s, it encountered the terms of the post–welfare state university—shrinking state and federal funding, greater focus on private funding and research, higher tuitions and unprecedented debt, and dwindling full-time professorial jobs. It is often remarked that the supply of Ph.D.'s has outstripped demand, but that is a shibboleth: enrollments of students have continued to increase at a relatively constant rate, and faculty has expanded. The difference is that academic jobs have been casualized: now, a majority of those teaching are part-time (over 50 percent in 2007, according to the U.S. Department of Education; according to MLA statistics, over 67 percent in English by 2009). This has changed the experience of working as an academic: the relaxed, privileged aura is gone, whereby one got a job because one's advisor made a phone call, or one would receive tenure on the basis of a couple of articles and have a decade to mull over a book. With heightened competition for jobs, there has been greater stress on and a speedup of publications, and a general ethos of pressure and insecurity rather than leisurely reflection.

The postwar generation seemed a golden generation, but it grew under golden conditions; subsequent generations have been squeezed between the poles of overwork and underemployment. While there are regular complaints about academic overpublication, there has been little consideration of how these conditions affect contemporary thought.

These conditions, however, have spurred a wave of activism as well as critical analysis of "academic labor." Much of the activism has centered on the graduate student union movement, notably the Yale graduate student strike in 1995–96 and more recent strikes, such as the NYU strike in 2005. Ross, to his credit, has been involved in these strikes, supporting in various ways the Yale and the NYU graduate students, with whom he coedited the collection *The University Against Itself: The NYU Strike and the Future of the Academic Workplace* (2008). In one of his essays in *Dissent*, and to my mind his most elegant political essay, "Back to Class Politics" (1997), Rorty tells the heroic story of the American labor movement in the twentieth century, its split with intellectuals in the 1960s, and urges "academics to get back into the class struggle." Which is good advice, but in fact many academics had already done that during the 1990s around the issue of academic labor. Those of the earlier generation, like Rorty, have difficulty recognizing academe as a site of labor; they see it from the perspective of their training and job search, when graduate students were ushered into decent jobs, rather than fodder for the part-time mill. While I have little patience, like Rorty, for much academic posturing, academic politics is not a world apart from real politics, and particularly since the 1990s it is frequently union politics.

Over the last decade Ross has come to focus especially on labor, arising from his participation in the anti-sweatshop movement, for which he edited the collection *No Sweat: Fashion, Free Trade, and the Rights of Garment Workers* (1997), as well as the academic labor movement. In a sequence of books, including *No-Collar: The Humane Workplace and Its Hidden Costs* (2003), *Low Pay, High Profile: The Global Push for Fair Labor* (2004), *Fast Boat to China: Corporate Flight and the Consequences of Free Trade—Lessons from Shanghai* (2006), and *Nice Work If You Can Get It: Life and Labor in Precarious Times* (2009), he has reported on the high-tech workplace and the effects of globalization. They depart from the usual purview of cultural studies to more sociological terrain, but they emphasize the culture of work and how it has changed.

They investigate two trends in particular. The first is the way that the workplace has been reconfigured, celebrated in books like Richard Florida's

The Rise of the Creative Class that promote the freedom and progressive nature of the new knowledge industries—you don't have to be tied to a desk but can do your work in your pajamas, at any hour! Ross is a good deal less sanguine, noting how these new arrangements function to allow work to permeate all one's time. They draw a more far-reaching contract, as he describes it in *Nice Work:* "In return for ceding freedom of movement to workers . . . employers can claim ownership of ideas that germinate in the most free, and downtime, moments of their employees' lives." Curiously, he observes that "no-collar employees emulate the work mentality and flexible schedules of disinterested research academics," or, as he shows in an influential essay included in *Low Pay,* "The Mental Labor Problem," of artists and musicians.

The second trend is the globalization of labor, celebrated in books like Thomas Friedman's *The World Is Flat,* which promotes its inevitability as well as its modernizing effects. Instead, after researching in China for a year, Ross found it "a much more insidious process, especially for employees who are expected to collude in the effort to upload the contents of their brains," as he writes in *Fast Boat.* Such "knowledge transfer" allows outsourcing, driving wages down and making jobs constitutively insecure. This creates a precarious way of life for workers, even previously secure professional workers, and Ross predicts that it augurs the future of work, when most jobs will be short-term and people will have many through their lives. To meet this, rather than having nostalgia for the old model of a job with one firm over a career, he advocates "a guaranteed income or social wage, decoupled from the circumstances of employment."

This latter phase of Ross's work crystallizes a distinctive blend of social and cultural criticism that he calls "scholarly reporting." It has affinities with investigative journalism and ethnography, drawing on in-depth interviews as well as other kinds of research. For *No-Collar,* Ross set up shop at two high-tech companies in New York for a year and a half, and for *Fast Boat to China* he studied Mandarin and moved to China for a year. On one hand, this is consistent with his view in *No Respect,* that intellectuals should attend to the popular. On the other hand, it departs from his earlier work in focusing less on academic argument and engaging more directly the actual experience of those working. While one cannot ascribe his shift to Rorty's advice, in a recent essay, "The Case for Scholarly Reporting," Ross recounts retraining himself to listen to people. He has crafted a way to bridge the academic and the everyday, using scholarship not only to speak to scholarly conversations but to issues in the world, like labor.

While Ross began by criticizing the New York intellectuals, he has more in common with them than one might expect. Rather than Trilling, in his range and some of his concerns he resembles less staid New York figures like Paul Goodman. Goodman was trained in literature, his dissertation, subsequently published as *The Structure of Literature* (1954), bearing the theoretical stamp of the Chicago critics prominent at midcentury. But Goodman turned to a range of social and cultural issues, most notably in *Growing Up Absurd: Problems of Youth in the Organized Society* (1960), as well as in collections like *Utopian Essays and Practical Proposals* (1962). Goodman represents an alternative strand of the New York line, less resolutely literary and focused on modernist high culture and more oriented toward social commentary and activism. One way to characterize their difference might be that Rorty tacked toward Trilling's model of the liberal literary critic and his tone of moral seriousness, whereas Ross has tacked toward less buttoned-up and more radical figures like Goodman or C. Wright Mills.

Goodman, like Ross, was responsive to the pulse of his time and inordinately productive, writing a range of literary, cultural, and social criticism, as well as fiction and poetry. The price of such a disposition, though, is sometimes durability, and that is a weakness of the model Ross represents. It is the downside of reporting. With the exception of "The Mental Labor Problem," it is hard to find a signature essay that encapsulates his view or crystallizes his style. And, unlike Rorty's style, which has a crisp brevity, Ross's style can be winding rather than direct; "The Mental Labor Problem," for instance, proceeds more by accumulating instances than by distilling and clarifying its view.

The strength of Ross's model is the original way he has fashioned a criticism that engages concrete social issues and problems. Academic work sometimes seems schizophrenic, a sphere apart from one's politics or real world concerns. But Ross has found a way to bridge those spheres, and his version of scholarly reporting brings criticism down from the heights of theory to the kinds of experience people have every day. He exemplifies one way contemporary critics might organically deal with politics in their work.

I have a distinct memory of reading "Intellectuals in Politics" when it first appeared because it seemed Rorty was talking about me. I was a new literature professor, in my second year at East Carolina University, a second-tier but large campus in the University of North Carolina system. What is more, I was hired to teach theory, so I might have been sent from central casting to fit Rorty's bill. But he wasn't quite right. I was also a socialist, a dues-paying member of the party of Debs, and worked with Committees of Correspondence there to do things like protest the first Gulf War or ally with janitors in their struggle to organize. Especially in the new South, one of the lessons I learned was that politics are humble rather than heroic.

Rorty's scheme placed me in something called "the academic left." It was the first time I had heard the phrase, and it has always mystified me. It seems an obvious category error: one might be of the socialist left, or the liberal left, or the Maoist left, but I know of no Academic Party that might generate political positions. (Academics probably tend toward the culturally liberal segment of the spectrum, typical of the professional-managerial class, although it is questionable whether they are socially liberal—consider that, demographically, the largest major is now business, with nearly a quarter of all students.) Moreover, the attribution of an "academic left" played into the hands of archconservatives of the time, confirming their frequently revived anthem of "God and Man at Yale." As a fan of George Orwell's "Politics and the English Language," I would ban "the academic left" from good English.

While Rorty had a gift for crisp discriminations, his dividing real and academic politics also seemed an obvious straw man. Who would claim the latter, effectively saying he or she did fake politics? A better distinction might be between abstract and practical politics. To that end, we should keep in mind both clauses of Goodman's title "Utopian Essays and Practical Proposals." Rorty took the high ground but he had no practical proposals. Ross provides a concrete description of labor but does not focus on practical proposals. I think that we need to turn more to policy, to offer practical proposals to approach the utopias we might theorize. Jeremiads occasionally have their use, but I favor examples like Adolph Reed's proposal for free tuition at public universities, as part of the Labor Party campaign "Free Higher Ed."

In contemporary criticism, we are typically trained to spot the error or the contradiction in a writer's thought. We pounce on what we find "problematic." But I think that problems are for solving, and I prefer criticism that is useful. From Rorty we can take his style and focus, the way he had of boiling points down to a graspable distinction. From Ross we can take his keen sense of observation and his forging criticism that engages people on the ground. To both I would add the imperative of practical proposals. While it is heady to legislate from above, our job is more modest.

TWO

The Retrospective Tenor of Recent Theory

Literary theory seems caught in a holding pattern. Instead of the heady manifestos and rampant invention of the late 1960s through the early 1980s, it now has turned retrospective, still set on the theoretical platforms of poststructuralism and the work of its major figures, like Foucault, Lacan, Derrida, and so on. Once discursive bomb-throwers and banes of traditionalists, they are now standard authorities to be cited in due course.

One sign of this retrospective stance is a recent wave of reprints and anniversary editions. Two of them provide bookends for the heyday of theory. In 2007 Johns Hopkins University Press reissued the fortieth-anniversary edition of *The Structuralist Controversy: The Languages of Criticism and the Sciences of Man*, a collection of papers from a legendary 1966 conference at Hopkins (really the forty-first anniversary, but that would be clunky). The conference is often cited as inaugurating the theoretical turn in American criticism, bringing the new developments in French theory to these shores. The speakers included a who's who of major semiotic, structuralist, Marxist, and psychoanalytic critics. It also introduced a young philosopher named Jacques Derrida to the American scene, and his paper asserted that the premises of structuralism contradicted or deconstructed themselves. Ten years later, the American translation of Derrida's *Of Grammatology* (1976; rev. ed. 1998), expanding on his idea of deconstruction, changed the way that literary scholars responded to works and wrote criticism. It argued, among other things, that signs do not point to stable meanings but spin off into indeterminacy, and it was pitched in a difficult, speculative idiom. That idiom and the preoccupation with indeterminacy inflected American criticism for the next two decades.

In 2007 as well, the University of Chicago Press reissued the twentieth-anniversary edition of Gerald Graff's *Professing Literature: An Institutional History*, which was quickly deemed the standard history of the discipline after it appeared in 1987. Graff traced the formation of English departments from the late nineteenth century up to the theory era and showed how literary studies developed through conflicts between traditional practitioners of scholarship and advocates of new kinds of criticism. If *The Structuralist Controversy* took the role of the Declaration of Literary Theory, *Professing Literature* served more like Washington's memoirs, recounting the success of the revolution.

Alongside these, over the past few years there has been a stream of revamped editions, individually or in series such as Routledge Classics or Verso's Radical Thinkers. They include the thirtieth-anniversary edition of Terry Eagleton's template for Marxist criticism and his most concerted theoretical statement, *Criticism and Ideology: A Study in Marxist Literary Theory* (1976; 2006); Jonathan Culler's groundbreaking survey, *Structuralist Poetics: Structuralism, Linguistics, and the Study of Literature* (1975; 2002), which provided a basic introduction for a generation of graduate students; Fredric Jameson's restoration of Marxism to American criticism, *The Political Unconscious: Narrative as a Socially Symbolic Act* (1981; 2002), which issued his famous call to "always historicize"; and Gayatri Spivak's *In Other Worlds: Essays in Cultural Politics* (1987; 2006), which brought a postcolonial and feminist perspective to poststructuralism. A score of other books accompanied this wave.

It is not unusual that some critical books are reissued or see new editions, but they are usually ones that have sustained course adoptions and crossover appeal, like Eagleton's *Literary Theory: An Introduction* (1983; 2nd ed. 1996; 3rd ed. 2008) or Edward W. Said's *Orientalism* (1978; 1995; 2003). The current crop of reprints is different. Those I have mentioned were all noteworthy books when they came out, so it is not entirely surprising that they remain in print, at least for their historical value. What is surprising is that most of them were decidedly academic, not crossover works, and they bear the marks of their moment. It is especially surprising that they remain relatively unsupplanted, given the short life cycle of academic scholarship. For example, Culler's *Structuralist Poetics* harks back to methods that were displaced by deconstruction (seven years later, he himself published *On Deconstruction: Theory and Criticism After Structuralism* [1982; twenty-fifth anniversary ed. 2007]), and Eagleton distanced himself from the impulse of *Criticism and Ideology*, remarking in 1990 that it reflected the fetish of the 1970s for finding an overarching method. Many of the recent reissues feel dated.

The retrospective turn is particularly ironic compared to the stance that the new theorists took toward criticism of the previous era. They consciously superseded it, rarely dealing with it substantively, consigning it to the dustbin of history. By the 1970s, critical classics that ruled a decade or two before, like Cleanth Brooks's *The Well-Wrought Urn: Studies in the Structure of Poetry* (1947) and William K. Wimsatt's *The Verbal Icon: Studies in the Meaning of Poetry* (1954), were barely read, except perhaps as examples of the limitations of their authors' generation. In the phrase of the influential deconstructive critic, Paul de Man, they represented "the deadend of formalist criticism." The central book of the more politically cognizant New York intellectuals, Lionel Trilling's *The Liberal Imagination: Essays on Literature and Society* (1950), went out of print.

Previous critics might have been recognized as part of the history of criticism, like Samuel Johnson or Matthew Arnold, but they had little bearing on the excited present of theory. When I was in graduate school in the late 1980s, for instance, we did not read Trilling or his fellow New Yorker Irving Howe on politics and the novel, but Jameson and Eve Kosofsky Sedgwick. The era of theory was presentist, its stance forward-looking, whereas now it seems to have shifted to memorializing its own past.

The case is like that of contemporary music, and one explanation for it might be the zeitgeist. Arising in the 1960s, literary theory was the rock and roll of criticism, dispensing with the Guy Lombardos of the previous generation. Cleanth Brooks and company were the music of your parents, pleasant, humane, respectful of tradition; theory wanted to blow things up. It was loud, pitched against the straitjacket of the canon, Western metaphysics, phallocentrism, racial stereotypes, and normative sex.

Now theory is more like the eclectic mix one might find on an iPod, disregarding set genres and combining in ways that the original theory loyalists would not, to suit your mood at the moment: some Jameson along with Andrew Ross, maybe an oldie from Arnold along with Judith Butler, and a classic like Aristotle for background music. (I would speculate that a key reason for the success of Slavoj Žižek, the indefatigable Slovenian theorist, is his talent as a deejay, sampling a wide itinerary of theory.) In this frame, the stream of reprints is like the remastered boxed sets of the Beatles or Ramones. No doubt it's better to have them than not, and often they come in crisp new packages (the Verso reissues are particularly striking in design and feel), but they are no longer the events they were when they were published.

The zeitgeist now seems perceptibly different, less heady and with less sense of possibility and more weight of the past. But that gives only a very broad explanation: the zeitgeist is like a mist that hangs over the landscape, tinting everything in its path but hard to see close up. It might characterize a cultural mood, but it doesn't explain the concrete circumstances.

A more scholarly explanation might look to the sociology of knowledge and see the stasis of criticism in terms of Thomas Kuhn's *Structure of Scientific Revolutions*. According to Kuhn, science does not proceed by a steady progress, as we tend to assume; most practice at any one time is relatively static, operating according to a general framework or "paradigm." Rather than a stream, intellectual work plateaus and ponds; it changes only when too much pressure builds, and then it breaks in a waterfall. The plateaus Kuhn calls "normal science," and the waterfalls "scientific revolutions."

Perhaps we are in a period of "normal science," after the cascade of theory. That makes some sense, but one reservation is that the sciences have different protocols of evidence, testing, and proof, and different histories of advancement, than literary criticism. They are ahistorical disciplines (you don't see many physicists building their arguments from Aristotle), while criticism is still a historical discipline. The main textbooks, for example, are compendia of past work, whereas in the sciences they are synopses of the present state of knowledge. That is because you can usually pinpoint an underlying paradigm at any given point in a science, whereas literary studies draws on a concatenation of theoretical models. It would be as if some physicists were Newtonian, some Einsteinian, some theosophists, some string theorists, and some just stubborn.

Kuhn's insight was to point out the way science progresses through the work of groups of scientists rather than just individuals. Paradigms are the premises that those in a scientific field hold in common. This adds a social dimension to the study of science, but it primarily explains how ideas work within a discipline. It doesn't address the social factors that make the institutions that house disciplines, and it begs the question of what puts the scientists (or critics) there.

———————

There is a revealing throwaway comment in the new preface to *The Structuralist Controversy*, noting that the 1966 Hopkins conference occurred thanks to a $30,000 grant from the Ford Foundation. That would be more than $200,000 in 2012 dollars. Excluding the lottery, it is hard to imagine that one could garner a $30,000 grant, much less six digits, in our current environment for a conference on the latest developments in criticism.

The support from the Ford Foundation was not a blip but the result of the policy and practice of the post–World War II university, and I think it points to a more concrete explanation for the rise of theory. Particularly after Sputnik and the enactment of the National Defense Education Act of 1958 (NDEA), the university experienced what historians call its "Golden Age." It received unprecedented support, in spirit as well as funding, and its charge tipped from teaching to producing research to bolster America's position as a leader in the world.

Flush new money went not only to the sciences in the race to build rockets, but also to the humanities. "One of the primary purposes of the NDEA was to stimulate the study of modern foreign languages," the American Council on Education reported in 1962. In this milieu, English and particularly comparative literature departments experienced unprecedented plenty and encouraged speculative research. They in turn hired and trained scholars positioned to embrace the new intellectual currents from Europe.

This is not to say that theory was an inevitable result, but federal, state, and foundation funds created the conditions for theory to flourish. Theory provided a rationale for advanced research, beyond the previous generation's orientation toward "practical criticism"—doing "readings" of individual works—which had its roots in teaching. Ideas might have their own history, but they also ebb and flow according to their material situation. Criticism, like the arts and most other species of culture, ebbs and flows with the tides of its patronage.

The retrospective turn fits our time of shrunken support for the humanities. Some in the theory generation, like Stanley Fish, have suggested that the present conceptual shrinkage has come about because no worthy heirs have appeared to take the place of the intellectual giants of his generation. But the current generation subsists on pinched diets, with less than a third of those in languages and literatures holding secure, tenure-line jobs, according to a recent Modern Language Association report. It is a somewhat bitter irony that, for all their radical panache, those in the theory generation rarely turned their revolutionary fervor and relentless interrogations to the situation of academic labor.

Departing from the wild speculation and heady pronouncements of the theory years, one of the few distinctive new strands in recent criticism focuses on academic labor. Criticism is constrained by its material conditions, but sometimes it can bite back. Especially if you don't feed it.

THREE

The Rise of the Theory Journal

In the 1970s, the journals in literary studies underwent a tidal shift. Before that, the major organs had been "little magazines," like the legendary *Partisan Review* and *Kenyon Review*, or scholarly journals, such as *JEGP* (*Journal of English and Germanic Philology*) and *Speculum*, a journal of medieval studies. But the 1970s brought a wave of new journals.

In roughly a decade, more than twenty journals were founded in the United States, among them *New Literary History* (1969), *diacritics* (1971), *SubStance* (1971), *boundary 2* (1972), *Feminist Studies* (1972), *New German Critique* (1973), *Critical Inquiry* (1974), *Semiotext(e)* (1974), *Signs* (1975), *Enclitic* (1977), *Glyph* (1977), *Structuralist Review* (1978), *Discourse* (1979), and *Social Text* (1979). They were joined by several established journals that retooled themselves along similar lines, including *Georgia Review*, *MLN* (*Modern Language Notes*), and *Yale French Studies*, as well as new entries in neighboring fields, such as the art-based *October* (1976). They constituted a new genre: the theory journal.

By 1970 the little magazine, which had been a flagship of American culture of the 1950s, was waning as critical arbiter (*Kenyon Review*, for instance, ceased publication in 1969). The major scholarly journals were still marching along, although they were staid and traditional, focused for the most part on early periods, notably medieval and Renaissance eras.

Theory journals represented a new focus. Rather than scholarly desiderata or close readings, they had bigger fish to fry, taking the wide-angle lens of concepts like language, society, gender, or interpretation, and they promoted theoretical systems that dealt with them, such as structuralism, Marxism, feminism, and deconstruction. They were less narrowly wedded to literature and often questioned the aims and boundaries of literary studies, as well as the role of criticism itself. And they were adversarial, especially in their first decade, self-consciously announcing the new.

The theory journal also announced a new kind of professor. For earlier standards like *JEGP*, *Studies in Philology*, or *Medium Aevum*, one pictured a tweed-jacketed Anglophile who pored over old manuscripts with a magnifying glass as reader or contributor. For the theory journal, one instead imagined a mini-skirted or blue-jeaned rabble-rouser passionately arguing about the signifier, ideology, patriarchy, or aporias. It wasn't your father's literary studies, or his literary journal.

The rise of the theory journal, so different and so numerous in such a short time, probably reflects the flourishing of a new cultural sensibility. However, journals are not just buoyed by ideas; they also depend on an institutional infrastructure. The theory journal rose on the crest of the postwar infrastructure of higher education. It was a good time to be a professor and to do criticism, and it was a good time for journals.

Just as that moment was remarkable for fostering an armada of journals, our current moment is remarkable for its relative paucity of new journals. Though some who entered academe during the 1960s bemoan the lack of critical imagination now, that paucity is not from lack of intelligence; rather, it is because of the draining of support for the humanities. Infrastructure seems tertiary, but it provides possibilities for certain kinds of work to be done, or not done.

The theory journal was a hybrid of the "little magazine" and the scholarly journal. The little magazine itself arose from a split in the family tree of the literary journal, with one sizable branch bearing, in the late nineteenth and early twentieth centuries in the United States, mass commercial magazines like *The Saturday Evening Post* and the *Atlantic*, and a much more delicate branch bearing entries such as *The Dial* and *Hound and Horn*. The latter were "little magazines" because they had small circulations, and, often featuring modernist literature, they pitched themselves against the commercialism of the big magazines. They were short-lived, often with uneven support and editorship, but the nail in the coffin was the Great Depression of the 1930s.

The next major wave of literary journals occurred in midcentury, with what a British historian called "The American Big Four"—*Partisan Review*, *Kenyon Review*, *Hudson Review*, and *Sewanee Review*. They were the flagships of the criticism of their era—of the New Criticism, as well as that of the New York Intellectuals—and pitched themselves against traditional academic journals, foregrounding modernism and American as well as European literature. They are often celebrated as a high point of American public culture, but they were for the most part academic productions, their editors academics, housed in literature departments and supported by universities, and with circulations of one or two thousand.

The learned or scholarly journal also arose during the late nineteenth and early twentieth centuries in the United States. It was a byproduct of the system of higher education that developed after the Civil War. In England scholarly journals often evolved from amateur or royal societies; in the United States, learned journals derived from the rise of the major research universities, like Johns Hopkins University (1876), which sired *MLN* in 1886, and the University of Chicago (1892), which created *Modern Philology* in 1903. Early scholarly journals in literature were oriented toward philology, the method imported from the German research university that influenced their American cousins of the time.

By midcentury, the little magazine took center stage in literary studies. It was oriented toward criticism over historical scholarship, favored the essay over the technical article, and carried few if any footnotes. It also published poetry and fiction. Scholarly journals generally covered early periods of British literature—*Studies in Philology* the Renaissance, *Speculum* medieval, and so on—whereas the little magazine leaned toward the modern, staking out literary culture for a rising, college-educated audience.

By the 1970s, the little magazine largely divested itself of criticism. Instead it turned toward creative writing, following the model of the 1950s startup *Paris Review* (1953). The next decade saw the founding of a wave of little magazines devoted to creative writing, such as *Triquarterly* (1964), *New American Review* (1967), *Iowa Review* (1971), and *Ploughshares* (1975). (Similarly, *The Kenyon Review* was reborn in 1979 and continues today as a creative writing journal.) They conjoined with the development of creative writing programs, as departments separated creative and critical functions and filled them with different faculty. In the earlier era, a single person, like John Crowe Ransom, founding editor of *Kenyon Review*, or T. S. Eliot, editor of *Criterion*, was a poet and critic, as well as an editor.

The theory journal adopted the tendency toward critical and cultural commentary of the little magazine, grafted to the edifice of the scholarly journal. From the little magazine it embraced reporting on contemporary trends in thought, and it also brought politics into literary studies. From the scholarly journal it adopted scholarly protocols and style; it grafted the formal rules of scholarship onto the speculative literary essay, promulgating a form of the twenty-page academic article. Like the scholarly journal, its goal was to produce knowledge, but it was oriented toward generating new knowledge rather than preserving old. It also divested itself of creative writing. Also like the scholarly journal, it addressed an academic audience rather than the more general, educated audience of the little magazine.

The conditions of the 1960s gave impetus to the theory journal, but not quite in the way that most explanations assume. The politics of the time and the foment of European philosophy inflected literary theory, but the theory journal developed under the auspices of the contemporary American research university. It called for a new organ of scientific knowledge of literature, one that spurred innovations rather than merely the preservation of knowledge.

Higher education was one of the jewels in the crown of postwar American society, and in 1968 Christopher Jencks and David Riesman declared its success in their book *The Academic Revolution*. The revolution was that of professors, whose positions morphed from overworked schoolteachers to autonomous experts. By the late 1960s, Jencks and Riesman observed that, for the first time in American history, professors concentrated more on research than teaching, on their disciplines than their particular campuses, and on graduate education than undergraduate. The theory journal was an outgrowth of these shifts.

The midcentury little magazine carried out the aims of general education and flourished under the immediate postwar regime. It was not directed to a coterie audience, as the earlier, modernist little magazine had been, but to those newly attending college, an educated audience hungry for the wares of culture. Its aim was not research; like much criticism of the time, its role was pedagogical and expository.

The theory journal carried out the aims of advanced research and flourished under the terms of the academic revolution. It set its coordinates toward the discipline, graduate education, and professional advance. It adverted to disciplinary topics, like signs or discourse or social texts; the little magazine hailed those who had an undergraduate education, whereas the theory journal was directed to graduate students or professors; the little magazine was humanistic, whereas the theory journal reached toward the scientistic, in its turn toward the human sciences, as they were called, and theory. Though it adopted the format of the scholarly journal, it fostered a revolution against traditional approaches; rather than preserving tradition brick by scholarly brick, its goal was to produce new knowledge through theoretical surmises.

Its material backing provides one way to explain the shifts in the literary journal over the course of the last century. The early little magazine was funded primarily by patrons; like the American university at the turn of the century, it was backed by philanthropy. That granted it independence from the market, but also prompted an elitist bearing of the connoisseur. That crumbled during the Great Depression, and the midcentury little magazine adopted a more democratic, and perhaps striving, tenor. It was financed more impersonally by foundations, whose goal was to promote American culture. For instance, *Kenyon Review* received substantial grants from the Rockefeller Foundation, including a five-year grant in 1947 for $22,500 ($218,000 in 2012 dollars). The foundation was a central institution in the immediate postwar period, as policy makers used it to build the new meritocracy they wanted, as well as to mobilize culture in the service of the Cold War.

By the 1960s, funding came more concertedly from state and federal government, not only for specific research projects but also for institutions. The theory journal thrived on university funds. For instance, *New Literary History* received $14,000 a year ($86,000 in 2012 dollars) its first five years from the University of Virginia. This was on top of other kinds of support, notably for libraries that would subscribe to most new journals, a practice that had come to an end by the 1990s. The enhanced research university fostered the tendency toward technical specialization, although it also allowed for a good deal of intellectual freedom, experiment, and exploration.

This genealogy prompts the question: What new kind of journal is looming now? One might identify a turn toward cultural studies in criticism, but there is no comparable wave of cultural studies journals. Rather, cultural studies has been absorbed into the format of the theory journal. One obvious answer is online journals, but most existing online journals, like *Postmodern Culture* (1990), are in the lineage of the theory journal, although we probably cannot yet tell the form that online journals will finally take. One bleak hypothesis is that a new kind of journal has not appeared because of the shrinkage of support for the humanities.

The question of the future is the question of material backing. Without the capacious funding for higher education, I predict that the theory journal, and most literary journals, will return to being philanthropic enterprises, like the early little magazine, subject to private support. They will also be subject to the tastes and vicissitudes of that support. And they will become more rarefied as their readership shrinks—as the number of full-time faculty, who might publish in them and read them, winnows down. One cannot live by bread alone, but one cannot live without bread either.

FOUR

How Critics Became Smart

It was recently recommended to me to read someone's work: "You have to read it, it's really *smart*." And one typically hears things like, "I didn't agree with anything she said in that book, but it's really smart," or, less flatteringly, "How did he get that job? He's not very smart." Imagine how damning a comment on an official evaluation would be that said, "Not especially smart, but competent." In my observation, "smart" is the highest form of praise one can now receive in academe. While it has colloquial currency, "smart" carries a special status in contemporary academic culture.

But why this preponderance of smart? Why not competent? Or knowledgeable? Or conscientious? We might value these qualities as well, but they seem pedestrian, without the panache of being smart.

Historically, "smart" has only taken an approbative sense relatively recently. Deriving from the Germanic *smerten*, "to strike," smart designated the sharp pain from a blow during the Middle Ages. Beginning in the eighteenth century, it stretched to indicate a quality of mind, albeit one with an edge. For instance, the *Oxford English Dictionary* notes Frances Burney's 1778 use in her novel *Evelina*, "You're so smart, there's no speaking to you." (We still retain this sense, notably in the expression "smartass.") Smart suggested a facility and manner rather than a deeper quality. Its sense of immediacy eventually migrated to describe fashion—one might wear a smart suit. Of late, it seems that "smart" has progressed to being the term of art of quality of mind, in fact that has supplanted "intelligent."

In literary studies—I take examples from the history of criticism, which I know, although I expect there are parallels in other disciplines—the keyword of approbation during the early part of the twentieth century was "sound." Literary scholars of the time strove for sound scholarship that patiently added bits of knowledge rather than asserting a smart new way of thinking. They were seeking to establish a new discipline and emulated the classics, adopting the erudite method of philology, so that they might ferret out, for instance, the French root of a word in one of Chaucer's *Canterbury Tales*. They sought historical accuracy, the soundness of which conferred a kind of scientific legitimacy on their nascent discipline.

During midcentury the keyword shifted to "intelligent," indicating mental ability as well as discerning judgment. Lionel Trilling observed in a 1964 lecture that John Erskine, a legendary Columbia professor, had "provided a kind of slogan" for Trilling's generation with the title of his essay, "The Moral Obligation to Be Intelligent." Trilling reported that he was "seduced into bucking to be intelligent by the assumption . . . that intelligence was connected to literature, that it was advanced by literature." Midcentury critics strove to decipher this essential element of literature, and their predominant method was interpretive, in both the New Critics (of particular poems) and the New York intellectuals (of broader cultural currents).

The stress on intelligence conjoined with the imperatives of the post–World War II American university. Rather than a rarefied institution of the privileged, the university became a mass institution fully integrated with the welfare state, both in how it was financed and in the influx of students it welcomed. As Louis Menand recounts in "The Marketplace of Ideas," the leaders of the postwar university, such as James B. Conant of Harvard, strategically transformed the student body. To meet the challenge of the Cold War as well as the industrial and technological burgeoning of the United States, they inducted the best and the brightest from all classes—as long as they demonstrated their potential for intelligence. Conant was instrumental in founding the Educational Testing Service, which put in place exams like the SATs to do so.

In the latter part of the century, during the heyday of literary theory (roughly 1970–90), the keyword shifted to "rigor," designating the logical consistency and force of investigation. Literary critics claimed the rigor of theoretical description of rising social sciences like linguistics and sought to remake literary studies as a "human science" rather than one of the humanities. The distinctive quality of Paul de Man, the most influential American critic of the era, was widely held to be his rigor. In his 1979 critical classic *Allegories of Reading*, de Man himself pronounced that literature advanced not intelligence but rigor: "Literature as well as criticism is . . . the most rigorous and, consequently, the most unreliable language in terms of which man names and transforms himself."

The stress on rigor dovetailed with the development of the multiversity, as Clark Kerr named the expanding university of the era, and its research imperative, which had become entrenched by 1970. That was when, according to the sociologists Christopher Jencks and David Riesman, professors first defined themselves foremost as researchers rather than as teachers. Intelligence was more a pedagogical imperative oriented toward bringing up the level of the masses through cultural literacy, both for the New Critics in training students to read poems and for the New York intellectuals in purveying art and ideas to a general public, whereas rigor was more a professional imperative oriented toward producing expert knowledge within the multiversity.

Since around 1990 rigor has less currency, and now critics, to paraphrase Trilling, are bucking to be smart. This shift responds to changes in literary studies as well as the university. One explanation is that "rigor" responded to a more organized field, whereas "smart" responds to a progressively more disorganized field. In the era of theory, literary studies expanded and critics embraced a set of theoretical paradigms, such as structuralism, deconstruction, Marxism, and feminism. However, while the paradigms were multiple, one could attribute a standard of methodological consistency to each of them that was confirmed within each "school." Now there is no corresponding standard. Through the 1990s, literary studies ballooned to encompass low as well as high literary texts, world literatures as well as British works, and "cultural texts" like eighteenth-century gardens and punk fashion. At the same time, method loosened from the moorings of "schools" to more eclectic variations and admixtures gathered under the umbrella of cultural studies. Rather than a rigorous application of a theory, the value has shifted to the strikingness of a particular effort. We aim to make smart surmises among the plethora of studies of culture.

Another factor explaining the rise of smart is the change in the tenor of higher education since the 1980s, when universities were forced to operate more as self-sustaining entities than as subsidized public ones. (The multiversity was a primary arm of the welfare state; I have called this new incarnation "the post–welfare state university.") This shift has taken a number of paths, including greater pressure for business "partnerships," patents, and other sources of direct funding; the steep increase of tuition; and the wide-spread use of adjuncts and temporary teachers. Without the fiscal cushion of the state, the university has more fully internalized the protocols of the free market, selling goods, serving consumers, and downsizing labor. It has also internalized the chief protocol of the market, competition. Smart expresses the ethos of the new academic market. It grafts a sense of fashionable innovation onto intellectual work, and it emphasizes the sharpness of the individual practitioner, as an autonomous entrepreneur in the market.

One reason for the multiplicity of our pursuits is not simply our fecundity nor our fickleness but the scarcity of permanent, full-time academic jobs, starting in the 1970s but reaching crisis proportions in the 1990s. The competition for jobs has prompted an explosion of publications. At the same time, academic publishing has shed most of its firewall and become more market-oriented. In the research era, it was heavily subsidized, but in the post–welfare state university, its mandate is to be self-sufficient, and most university presses now depend primarily on sales. Consequently, the criterion for publication is not solely sound disciplinary knowledge or rigorous theoretical argument but commercial viability.

The current provenance of smart emphasizes novelty and fashionability, such that a scholarly project does something new and different to attract interest among the glut of publications. In fact, "interesting" is a complementary keyword to smart. One might praise a study of the cultural history of sex toys and the eighteenth-century novel not as sound or rigorous but as interesting and smart, because it makes a new and unusual connection. Rigor assumes the frame of scientific proof; smart assumes the frame of the market, in which one draws interest in a crowded field of competitors. Deeming something smart, to use Kant's framework, is a judgment of taste rather than a judgment of reason. Like most judgments of taste, it is finally a measure of the people who hold it or lack it.

"Smart" purports to offer a way to talk about quality in a sea of quantity. But it is often a narrow and transient quality. It aims not to build the blocks of knowledge nor cultivate the intellect of students, but to capture a brief bit of attention, like an advertisement. In this, it internalizes the ethos of the market for the university. As an attribution of quality of a person rather than a piece of work, it functions something like the old shibboleth, "quality of mind," which claimed to be a pure standard but frequently became a short-hand for membership in the old boys' network. It was the self-confirming taste of those who talked and thought in similar ways. It did not confirm merit on a level field but the moves and mannerisms of those already in the know.

"Smart," as a designation of mental ability, seems a natural term to distinguish the cerebral pursuits of higher education, but perhaps there are better words we might use. I would prefer the criticism I read to be useful and relevant, my colleagues responsible and unselfish, and my institution egalitarian and fair. Those words no doubt have their own trails of associations, as any savvy critic would point out, but they suggest cooperative values that are not always inculcated or rewarded in a field that extols being smart.

FIVE

Publicist Intellectuals

During the 1990s, there was a great deal of fanfare announcing a renaissance: Intellectuals were emerging from their jargon-insulated academic cloisters and taking to the streets, or at least to the magazine kiosks, made over as public intellectuals. Cultural critic Michael Bérubé offered a succinct formula for this alchemy in his book *Public Access: Literary Theory and American Cultural Politics* (1994), calling for literary and cultural critics to "bite-size" their work to reach larger audiences.

While it seems a virtue that academic critics cross over the public divide and occasionally grace the pages of glossy magazines like the *Atlantic* and the *New Yorker*, this publishing migration was not exactly as advertised. For one thing, it was not broadly democratic; the glossies, after all, reach only a limited, upscale slice of the public sphere. Granted, they offer a significant forum for discussion of social and cultural issues in the United States, but the fad for public access responded to changes in higher education as much as it indicated a new flourishing of civic conscience.

In my surmise, the top-billing of public intellectuals has been a response to the pressures facing higher education and the rewriting of its cultural "mission," in the face of massive funding cuts, downsizing, and the administrative touchstone phrase, "public accountability." As the dean of Arts and Sciences at the state university where I taught back in the 1990s urged us at a convocation: "[The question of funding] requires us to market the College to alumni and friends of the university [e.g., Glaxo/Burroughs Wellcome], and marketing means we have to help people develop a fuller understanding of the College, its composition, and its mission and scope and envision us more clearly."

This is very close to Bérubé's prescription for public access, but its goal is not by any means political relevance or social advocacy, or even to promote good old-fashioned humanistic values. Rather, it defines the mission of the university as beholden to corporate "friends" and their interests, and success as a function of advertising its utility to those interests. Which precisely fits the public zone of glossy magazines that people who sit on boards, send alumni checks, and send their brood to the hallowed halls of our universities might read. In this light, the makeover of public intellectuals formerly known as academics performs a kind of public relations function for client-conscious, budget-embattled universities.

Back in the 1970s, the rise of literary theory gave the humanities institutional weight. Theory was difficult and showed the specialized expertise required of its practitioners. It thus provided a professional rationale for the importance of literary and cultural studies, as well as the academic departments administering those studies. It shored their relative position within the university and helped them hold ground against the techno-rationalist social sciences, not to mention the industry- and military-subsidized hard sciences. Theory got rid of the touchy-feely aura of the humanities, refurbishing them with an aura of techno-expertise.

During the 1990s, that changed. The university has been called to justify its programs to the public at large, who "pay their salaries," or in the media channels that reach them. The revamped figure of the public intellectual offers up poster professors for public consumption, testifying that, yes, we too do important work and are not detached from the everyday world, so keep sending those tax dollars and tax-deductible contributions, and, most important, keep sending your kids and their college funds. Don't worry, we won't turn them into deconstructionists; they'll get to hear Cornel West, just like on TV.

It is a sour irony that the raising up the figure of the public intellectual has occurred at precisely the same time that the university workforce has been pared down, divided up into a bevy of part-time laborers without health or any other benefits. Whereas over 90 percent of academic-intellectuals had permanent positions in 1970, now only about one-third of those working in the intellectual vineyard are that fortunate, the remaining two-thirds holding temporary slots, frequently part-time—that is, if they have a job at all. This is obviously more cost-effective for universities, but one can only imagine the effect of this chronic and pervasive job insecurity on both nascent intellectuals and on the overall prospects for education.

In this brave new world of academe, the figure of the public intellectual might perversely foster a rationale for unfair labor practices, in effect blaming the victims for university downsizing: It's your fault, you haven't been out there hawking your wares to a popular audience, so you deserve what you get if you don't get a job, attain fame, or publish in *Harper's*.

For the fortunate few, this turn promotes a new career model, of academic stardom. In *Teachers, Writers, Celebrities*, the social critic Régis Debray traced the role of the French intellectual through the course of the twentieth century, the stress moving from teaching to writing for a larger public (think of Sartre) to becoming a celebrity. In the United States, the intellectual has gone from teacher to researcher to what I have called the "academostar."

The star model, offering name recognition and public appeal, suggests a kind of intellectual Horatio Alger story for those unemployed and underemployed to strive for, at the same time that actual institutional conditions make that dream all the more improbable. One could see the trend of academic-intellectual autobiographies, such as Henry Louis Gates's *Colored People* or Frank Lentricchia's *The Edge of Night*, as contemporary Alger stories, recasting humanities professors in terms of media success stories. The apotheosis of the public intellectual puts a glamorous face on the otherwise disintegrating situation of actual public access to education.

Unfortunately, the real story is that actual access to the accredited institutions of media, of publishing, and of academe is far from open and at best only allows limited forays from those outside the circuit of institutional privilege. The question of public access, then, is a question of reforming and opening those institutional channels, beyond simply one of recalibrating writing style to an upscale marketing group who might peruse the *New Yorker*, or chalking up sound-bites.

To start, we need a renewed and fortified vision of what public education should do, of who has access to the channels of education and culture, and of who has a franchise in the public sphere, whether or not the cameras are rolling. Rather than worry about packaging, we need to look at the contents inside the box.

SIX

The Ubiquity of Culture

If you are building a house, the first thing you do is probably not to plant flowers. You dig the basement, pour the foundation, frame the building, raise and shingle the roof, put up the siding, and so forth. Then, if you have time and money left, you might put in a flowerbed. The flowers might give you pleasure when you see them, but they are not usually considered essential to the house; they do not keep you dry in rain or warm in winter or fill your stomach.

The traditional idea of culture as high art conceives of culture as something like the flowerbed. While we might appreciate and value artifacts we deem beautiful, they are not essential to our primary physical needs. In a no-nonsense, colloquial view, culture is ornamental, secondary to if not a frivolous distraction from the real business of life. In classical aesthetics, culture is defined precisely by its uselessness and detachment from ordinary life. In psychology, Maslow's "pyramid of needs" places culture in the upper reaches of the pyramid, possible only after the broad base of material needs are taken care of, which are primary to psychological well-being. In the classical Marxist view, culture forms part of the superstructure, tertiary to the economic base, which determines human life. Accordingly, studies of culture, like literary or art criticism, have traditionally been considered refined pursuits, like gardening or horticulture, but not of primary importance to society, like politics, economics, or business.

Culture of course has another familiar sense: rather than the flowers of human experience, it encompasses a broad range of human experiences and products. Though abnegating its special status, this sense likewise plays off the agricultural root of culture, expanding the bed from a narrow plot to the various fields of human manufacture. Over the past few decades, this latter sense seems to have taken precedence in colloquial usage, in politics, and in criticism. We speak of proclivities within a society, such as "sports culture," "car culture," "hip-hop culture," or "mall culture." In political discourse, culture describes the tenor of society, such as "the culture of complaint," "the culture of civility," or "the culture of fear," and societies are defined by their cultures, such as the "culture of Islam," "the culture of democracy," or "the culture of imperialism," which generate their politics. In criticism and theory, culture, whether indicating race, class, nationality, ethnicity, gender, sexuality, abledness, locality, or taste, determines human identity, which in turn designates political interest. In short, "culture" has shifted from ornament to essence, from secondary effect to primary cause, and from a matter of disinterested taste to a matter of political interest. Consequently, pursuits that study culture, like literary or cultural criticism, have claimed greater political importance to society.

The reconception of culture does not dispel the idea of the house of society and the garden of culture, but reconfigures the process of construction. The question of a house presupposes the prior determination of culture, and a flowerbed is not an afterthought but part and parcel of that culture; one's culture determines whether one would own a plot of land and want a house rather than an apartment or a tent, and whether one would want a manicured lawn and attendant shrubbery. Culture draws the house plans before one pours any cement; it is the material that generates the world with such possible human activities and with businesses that produce cement, lumber, and potted plants.

Fifty years ago, Raymond Williams charged criticism to look at the conjunction of "culture and society." Now it seems that culture *is* society, interchangeable as a synonym for social interests, groups, and bases. Culture has shifted from a subsidiary (if special) role to primary ground, inverting the standard model of base and superstructure. Even a social theorist such as Pierre Bourdieu, who persistently foregrounded the significance of class, conceived of class less as a matter of material means than of taste, disposition, and other cultural cues. In the trademark phrase from his classic work *Distinction*, it is "cultural capital" that generates class position. Culture has become the base from which other realms of human activity—psychological, political, economic—follow.

The reign of culture has had its share of dissent. Marxists have attacked the gravitation toward cultural categories such as race, gender, or sexuality as a fracturing of a unified political program as well as a fall away from the economic ground of class, and liberals such as Richard Rorty have upbraided leftist intellectuals for their absorption in cultural politics at the expense of bread-and-butter issues such as health care and labor rights. From the other side of the aisle, traditionalists have bemoaned the turn toward culture as detracting from the special attributes of literature and art.

Both Francis Mulhern and Terry Eagleton, probably the most prominent inheritors of Williams's mantle, have weighed in on the dissenting side. In their books, Mulhern's *Culture/Metaculture* (2000) and Eagleton's *The Idea of Culture* (2000), they take the role of senior statesmen to check the overinflation of culture and offer some advice. The books are worth looking at because Mulhern and Eagleton are leading Left critics in Britain—Mulhern a *New Left Review* mainstay and main historian of modern British criticism, notably in *The Moment of 'Scrutiny'* (1979), and Eagleton the most well-known commentator on literary criticism and theory of his generation. In turn, the books tell us about the kind of critics that Mulhern and Eagleton are, Mulhern more a historian and Eagleton more a polemicist. The books are also worth looking at not because they propose new solutions, but because they exemplify the impasse of the debate. They both propose the limp idea that cultural studies needs more modesty. Instead, I think that it needs more political theory to sort out the crux of culture and society, and I propose that we look to Nancy Fraser's distinction between the politics of redistribution and of recognition. We need both.

Culture/Metaculture and *The Idea of Culture* overlap in broad outline. They are both short books that surmise the state of cultural studies, take to task its current misdirection, particularly its absorption in questions of subjectivity and identity, and argue for a restoration of its political legacy. But they are very different in manner and style, characteristic of their authors. Mulhern, in a brisk but assured survey, focuses on intellectual history, and his corrective is genealogical, attempting to supplant the British-centered genealogy with a broader, modern European one. Eagleton, in a ranging, topical examination, offers a kind of keyword study, and his corrective is more to disabuse the errors of various forms of culturalism (like multiculturalism) and contemporary theory (postmodernism, antifoundationalism, and relativism) than a reconstruction.

Each book represents the distinctive roles Mulhern and Eagleton have fashioned as critics. Mulhern takes the role of serious don, earnestly laying out intellectual currents, as one would expect from the author of *The Moment of 'Scrutiny'* or editor of *Contemporary Marxist Literary Criticism* (1992). Eagleton takes a more puckish role, eschewing a dispassionate stance and disabusing contemporary criticism, often with dismissive barbs and witty turns of phrase. In his early incarnations, like *Marxism and Literary Criticism* (1976), *Literary Theory: An Introduction* (1983), and *The Ideology of the Aesthetic* (1990), Eagleton marshaled lively (if opinionated) critical histories, but in his later incarnations, like *The Illusions of Postmodernism* (1996), he tends more toward the broadside.

Mulhern's argument turns on an unexpected reconstruction of the origins of cultural studies. He recasts its starting point from the Birmingham Centre for Contemporary Culture Studies, which is legendary for instituting Williams's arguments for the broad study of culture during the 1960s, to the longer and wider net of Kulturkritik. The first half of the book surveys a group of modernist European writers who criticized modern society, including Thomas Mann, José Ortega y Gasset, Sigmund Freud, Virginia Woolf, Orwell, T. S. Eliot, and F. R. Leavis. What these writers have in common, and what Mulhern recoups, is their critical stance toward modern life under capitalism. What they also have in common, but what Mulhern discards, is their elitist remove from common culture and politics.

Mulhern fuses this tradition with British cultural studies. This is unexpected because cultural studies typically casts itself in opposition to Kulturkritik, whereas Mulhern argues that they both participate in the same "metacultural" discursive formation. Kulturkritik privileges an elitist minority culture, that draws upon a high tradition and sets itself against popular culture; cultural studies retains the same coordinates but inverts Kulturkritik's values, privileging the popular and abnegating tradition, arguing not for a minority culture but for the worth of minority cultures. Both also claim the political authority of the cultural; the mistake is that they overestimate that authority. In Mulhern's narrative, Williams is a bridge figure, asserting the politics of culture but dispatching the paternalism of Kulturkritik.

The second half of *Culture/Metaculture* reprises the standard genealogy of British cultural studies, from Williams and Birmingham founder Richard Hoggart through Stuart Hall up to contemporary identity critics (mostly unnamed). Though Williams is cast as a foundational influence, Hall is the hero of the book, praised in particular for turning attention to Empire and for proposing a "non-reductionist theory of culture and social formations." Mulhern inventories Hall's achievements: his struggles in and against sociology; his assimilating structuralism to a revised Marxism; and his directing attention toward media in the 1970s, the politics of the welfare state in the 1980s, and ethnicity in the 1990s.

Despite these achievements, cultural studies has experienced a fall, drifting to banality, unreflective populism, and relativism. Mulhern's most vehement castigation is that "Politics is everywhere in Cultural Studies. The word appears on nearly every page," but without teeth, "predominantly phatic in accent." Cultural studies finally "subsumes the political under the cultural," where it again joins Kulturkritik, which likewise "reasoned politics out of moral existence, as a false pretender of authority." Thus, it only offers a "'magical solution' to the poverty of politics in bourgeois society." This is a severe diagnosis, but Mulhern's prescription is relatively mild. He argues that cultural studies suffers from immodesty in conferring excessive value on the political efficacy of cultural fields such as identity, an immodesty it "learnt willy-nilly from its authoritarian forebear, Kulturkritik," and recommends a dose of "modesty."

The strength of Mulhern's genealogical revision is to deepen the understanding of British cultural studies to modern European intellectual history and to discern its normally unnoticed ties to Kulturkritik. This is where Mulhern is most original and persuasive, demonstrating that cultural studies inherited rather than invented the problematic of culture, an insight usually forgotten in most histories, which start with Birmingham. A weakness of Mulhern's genealogy, however, is its partiality. It foregrounds only one family tree, of the European high modernist tradition, and that tree includes some distant relations while excluding some nearer cousins. For instance, it underplays Adorno and others from the Frankfurt School. It also gives an exemption to Hall, who could be seen as the pivotal figure for the turn away from Marxism to poststructuralism and the preoccupation with identity.

Further, Mulhern does not escape the metacultural problematic that he criticizes, since his history is almost entirely set within the realm of cultural discourse and its political intervention occurring there. It is not the kind of history that traces the material institutions of criticism, such as the changes in publishing, the position of men and women of letters, the massive growth of the university, and the migration of those from the non-European world during decolonization, all of which formed contemporary cultural studies during the post–World War II epoch. It is not the kind of institutional history that he marshals in *The Moment of 'Scrutiny'* about the interregnum between the great wars.

Mulhern does advert to institutional history, but declares that institutionalization "is among the darker themes of the collective autobiography" of cultural studies. Its henchman is academic professionalism; while "Kulturkritik was . . . amateur," cultural studies "has evolved into a profession" and "an organized academic pursuit, from the later 1960s onwards." This I find the most nettlesome argument of *Culture/Metaculture*. It contradicts Mulhern's account of the heroic origin of cultural studies in Raymond Williams and others, who were academics, and the initial formation of the Birmingham Centre, which was after all a moment of institutionalization. And it belies his taking Hall as a model figure from the 1970s to the 1990s. Overall, it is historically fuzzy in yoking institutionalization, which is by no means a contemporary phenomenon, with the post-1960s rise of identity politics.

Why does Mulhern, otherwise so careful, do this? He is drawn to two myths, that of the amateur man of letters or intellectual and that of a pre-institutional Eden. The myth of the amateur is a commonplace, but the amateur was neither free nor independent; rather, it was a category enabled by the surplus of capitalist accumulation, which granted leisure and privileged training to a small group to pursue activities like criticism. The elitism of Kulturkritik was consonant precisely with the class position of the "amateurs" who propounded it, and their elitism not only cultural but a disdain for democratic institutions. Surely this is nothing to be nostalgic about; rather than apologizing for being academic-professionals, I think it better to be gainfully employed in public institutions, without the disadvantages of a ruling class background.

Moreover, the era of the amateur does not represent a pre-institutional Eden, as any reader of George Gissing's *New Grub Street* will realize, but exhibits a different mode of institutionalization, in the modern period centered on journalism, publishing, and other literary institutions. The institution of the university, particularly under the welfare state, might easily be seen as a more rather than less democratic channel—perhaps of liberal rather than radical redistribution, but a redistribution nonetheless. It is doubtful that Raymond Williams or Terry Eagleton would have become prominent critics had they not been scholarship boys in the post–World War II university, and the opening of the profession of criticism to such critics could easily be seen as enjoining rather than impeding Left criticism. Rather than a draconian fall, one could instead view cultural studies' academic purchase as a victory in what was called during the 1960s a "struggle for institutions," which created the conditions to pursue the kind of work done by Hall and those at Birmingham, and presumably by Mulhern himself. This is not to hold up the largely academic location of contemporary criticism as an unalloyed good, but neither is it a dark theme.

———————

Eagleton's *The Idea of Culture* is less concerned with the genealogy or institutional history of cultural studies and more concerned with its present practices. Though he does touch on Kulturkritik (in fact citing Mulhern) and particularly on Eliot's and Leavis's notions of culture, his focus is on its current use, and his revision is not to reconstruct a better history but to redeem a better concept. His basic argument is fairly simple—that we should hold the idea of "culture as radical protest" over competing ideas, such as "culture as civility, culture as identity, and culture as commercialism"— and his recuperation relatively modest, returning to Raymond Williams's "notion of a common culture," based on socialist politics.

Eagleton's more complicated move is to recuperate what "common" means. While it represented a radical democratic impetus against high culture in Williams's formulation, in contemporary cultural theory the notion of a "common culture" has taken retrograde associations: it speaks for hegemonic culture, eclipsing other ethnicities, sexualities, and so on; it assumes an essential core; and it projects a universal human condition, which elides particularities of various social groups. Eagleton, with some nuance, negotiates a middle position between the extremities of dominant and minority, essential and different, and universal and particular. His synthesis is the commonality of our bodies ("A common culture can be fashioned only because our bodies are of broadly the same kind") and our "natural needs," which "are critical of political well-being." Lest this seem a blatant essentialism, he allows that, "of course human bodies differ, in their history, gender, ethnicity." But, he adds, "they do not differ in those capacities— language, labour, sexuality—which enable them to enter into potentially universal relationship with one another."

One could call this a pragmatic essentialism, similar to what the feminist critic Diana Fuss calls "essentially speaking," whereby one uses such concepts provisionally, acknowledging their limits, to achieve social goals. Eagleton spells this out in a 1990 interview: "I think that back in the seventies we used to suffer from a certain fetishism of method. . . . I would now want to say that, at the level of method, pluralism should reign, because what truly defeats eclecticism is not a consistency of method but a consistency of political goal." Correspondingly, in *The Idea of Culture* Eagleton argues that the pluralism of identities does not achieve radical political change, but "to establish genuine cultural pluralism [first] requires concerted socialist action." In other words, identity studies have it backward, and socialist politics are prior to identity politics.

While this argument for recuperating a common culture frames *The Idea of Culture*, the bulk of the book turns its energy toward disabusing various forms of contemporary criticism. That is, it is not a survey in the manner of *Literary Theory* or *The Ideology of the Aesthetic* or a reconstructive analysis like Mulhern's, but in large part an invective. Like Mulhern, Eagleton takes to task the overemphasis on culture, particularly on categories like identity, and its diluted sense of politics; he claims that, "Identity politics is one of the most uselessly amorphous of all political categories." Thus, he calls, again like Mulhern, for more modesty: "It has grown at the same time immodest and overweening. It is time, while acknowledging its significance, to put it back in its place." Unlike Mulhern, there is barely any consideration of the Birmingham project. Also unlike Mulhern, Eagleton names a number of villains, and his real target often seems a wide-ranging band of those who espouse postmodernism (a number of sentences begin with phrases like "for the postmodernist"), cosmopolitanism, relativism, and antifoundationalism rather than what ordinarily would be considered cultural studies. What most motivates him, it seems, is taking other critics down a peg.

While he claimed at one time that "deconstruction is the death drive at the level of theory" (in his 1981 book *Walter Benjamin*), now he seems to have reached a truce and absorbed some of its tenor (for instance, "cultures . . . are porous, fuzzy-edged, indeterminate"). He instead turns his guns toward pragmatists like Stanley Fish and Richard Rorty. Eagleton's strength has always been his unabashed, if sometimes unnuanced, polemical flair. The weakness is not only that such polemics cut with a broad sword, but that many of the critics he takes aim at have little to do with the study of culture. Fish, for instance, has addressed cultural studies only to dismiss it. In *Professional Correctness* Fish argues, like Mulhern and Eagleton, that contemporary critics wrongly conflate culture and politics, but unlike them, he finds the error to stem from Raymond Williams's original joining of literature and society. *Pace* Williams, Fish wants to restore literature as a specialized field; he does not deny history or politics, but argues that they belong to a different realm and literary critics should stick to literature. While Fish held considerable influence during the heyday of theory, he has become a sort of literary reactionary, and he has little influence on contemporary critics. Fish has been a favorite target of Eagleton's, but he has become an anachronistic enemy, like the Germans in movies, whom Eagleton reflexively invokes, almost with nostalgia for the battles of high theory and the time when the generation of theorists, like Fish and Eagleton, ruled the field.

Rorty presents a different case. Part of Rorty's criticism of philosophy was its focus on arid, technical issues, making itself irrelevant to political life. Indeed, much of his later writing dwelt on social issues, following the example of John Dewey, who was prominent in early twentieth-century educational reforms and democratic politics in the United States. Rorty himself castigated the American "cultural Left," as I mentioned, for its narrow academic address and its failing to take up basic social issues, like the minimum wage and universal healthcare. This might represent a unionist or liberal position on the model of the New Deal, but Eagleton collapses it to a difference between Right conservatism and Left radicalism. It is actually one between social democracy and Marxism. As I have suggested, Eagleton also broaches a pragmatist position in his eschewal of method for the sake of political goals. He is closer to Rorty than he acknowledges or, more to the point, productively sorts through.

In the midst of villains, the one unalloyed hero of *The Idea of Culture* is Raymond Williams. Eagleton obviously follows Williams's keyword model in examining "culture," and there is a certain poignancy to Eagleton's updating the project of his teacher. But it also reveals something of the way that Eagleton has fashioned himself as a critic and the particular bias of his work. He has followed the Williams of *Marxism and Literature* in his theoretical surveys, of *The Country and the City* in his literary criticism, and even of *The Border Country* in a novel and a few plays, but not of *Communication,*

Television: Technology and Cultural Form, or *Resources of Hope*. While Eagleton has never departed from a Marxist credo (as some in his generation have), he has remained largely in the domain of literature, with forays to the history of ideas, but avoided cultural studies, despite its carrying out a significant line of contemporary Marxist criticism. This is especially striking in comparison to Williams's other prize student, Stuart Hall, or for that matter Matthew Arnold or T. S. Eliot. It indicates an odd blindness in Eagleton's work, all the more striking given that he is probably the most deft and popular surveyor of criticism. There is a way in which Eagleton has always resided in the moment of literary theory—first coming to prominence with *Criticism and Ideology* (1976), stamping the field with his bestselling *Literary Theory*, and for the past decade targeting postmodernism in *The Illusions of Postmodernism* and *After Theory* (2004) as well as *The Idea of Culture*. His terrain of struggle has not been our common culture, but the texts and concepts of the history of criticism and their latter-day permutations.

There is a certain intractability to the debate over culture. Part of the problem stems from the term itself. "Culture" has become an impossibly capacious term that refers to a panoply of practices, products, and people. When Williams resuscitated the term in *Culture and Society*, he pitched it against its elitist and classed associations, in turn enabling the study of objects normally excluded from literary criticism. In a sense, that task has only succeeded too well, so now it encompasses seemingly everything. Like the air, culture is ubiquitous.

Eagleton and Mulhern respond to this dilemma, taking to task the expansion of the term and calling for the restoration of its more measured, former sense. But this tack represents a minor modification, and like most restorations, it is unlikely to change the minds of those who have allegiance to the new houses of identity. At best, it represents a weak solution to the dilemma, leaving the debate much the same.

Another problem is that "culture" is residually embedded in the framework of base and superstructure. The debate thus tends to demand an either/or choice, between the traditional Marxist view of the priority of the economic and the contemporary stress on culture as determining human experience. Part of its intractability is that this framework suggests a two-dimensional, spatial model, like a drawing of an iceberg, whereby the

Marxist holds that the economic constitutes 90 percent of the iceberg supporting the 10 percent cap of culture floating above, and the culturalist holds that culture comprises most of the ice. The relation of the two tends to be configured as a zero-sum equation, one having influence only at the deficit of the other, rather than operating on different planes, which would instead suggest "both/and."

A third problem is that many arguments about its politics remain in the field of literary or cultural criticism. Eagleton and Mulhern, despite disclaimers, reflect the paradox of criticizing culturalism culturally—Mulhern reconstructing the history of criticism, and Eagleton directing his polemic against the usual critical suspects. Despite their taking to task the paucity of politics in cultural studies, neither Eagleton nor Mulhern themselves bring political philosophy or political economy into the debate.

To my mind, the best solution to these dilemmas is Nancy Fraser's work on redistribution and recognition, first proposed in her influential 1995 *New Left Review* article, "From Redistribution to Recognition?" and expanded in her 2003 book (with Axel Honneth), *Redistribution or Recognition?* (Though Fraser's article appeared in *New Left Review* and drew considerable attention, including a 1999 volume of responses by Rorty, Judith Butler, Seyla Benhabib, and others, *Adding Insult to Injury*, neither Eagleton nor Mulhern cite it.) Fraser shifts the debate to the terrain of political philosophy and the question of social justice. This is fundamentally a pragmatist move: For Fraser, the interest is not to draw a true representation of reality and the correct ratio of economy and culture, but what best serves the goal of social justice. The enemy is subordination, and one might experience subordination both culturally, in the form of status, and economically, in the form of class.

Fraser distinguishes two lines of political philosophy, one aligning with Marxism and centering on class and economic distribution, the other with Max Weber and centering on status and cultural recognition. Fraser starts from the observation that inequality derives from injuries of status as well as of resources. Identity politics thus are not irrelevant in the struggle to redress inequality, but crucial to what Fraser elsewhere calls a "politics of needs." Needs are not just bodily, as researchers on childhood development tell us, but of consciousness.

Rather than one over the other, people suffer from both maldistribution and misrecognition, Fraser reasons:

Most such theorists assume a reductive economistic-cum-legalistic view of status, supposing that a just distribution of resources and rights is sufficient to preclude misrecognition. In fact, however, as we saw, not all misrecognition is a by-product of maldistribution, nor of maldistribution plus legal discrimination. Witness the case of the African-American Wall Street banker who cannot get a taxi to pick him up. To handle such cases, a theory of justice must reach beyond the distribution of rights and goods to examine institutionalized patterns of cultural value; it must ask whether such patterns impede parity of participation in social life.

Conversely,

not all maldistribution is a by-product of misrecognition. Witness the case of the skilled white male industrial worker who becomes unemployed due to a factory closing resulting from a speculative corporate merger. In that case, the injustice of maldistribution has little to do with misrecognition. It is rather a consequence of imperatives intrinsic to an order of specialized economic relations whose *raison d'être* is the accumulation of profits. To handle such cases, a theory of justice must reach beyond cultural value patterns to examine the structure of capitalism.

A well-known nettle in physics is how to explain the behavior of light: sometimes it behaves like particles that carom and ricochet, and sometimes it behaves like waves that oscillate in a more uniform motion. Fraser presents a kind of wave-particle theory of society, whereby social interaction sometimes behaves like the wave motion of culture, sometimes like the material particle of class. If one takes this dualist perspective, then one need not make a choice, and in fact the choice is a false one. As Fraser concludes, "redistribution and recognition do not correspond to two substantive societal domains, economy and culture. Rather, they constitute two analytical perspectives. . . . Unlike economism and culturalism, however, it avoids reducing either one of those categories to the other."

With Fraser, we should move past the debate over the correct ratio of culture, or the true apportionment of politics and culture. Rather, we should focus on what best serves the goal of justice and acts against injustice, whether it goes by the name of culture or class.

SEVEN

Credibility and Criticism: On Walter Benn Michaels

When I was growing up in the New York suburbs, there was an evangelist on every Sunday night named Reverend Ike. Reverend Ike's motto was, "Money is not the root of all evil; lack of money is the root of all evil." Walter Benn Michaels's message to those in literary and cultural studies for the past several years has been similar to that of Reverend Ike: It is not race or gender or sexuality or any of the other permutations of identity that are the root of inequality in our society; rather, it is class, which is not an identity but a matter of money. If you remedy the lack of money, then you would have no poor and inequality would disappear.

Michaels has thrived off being a contrarian and seems to derive a certain relish from it. He first made his name with the incendiary essay "Against Theory" (with Steven Knapp; 1982), attacking the presumptions of theorists that their statements would change practice. Since then, one of his main tacks has been to debunk the political presumptions of other critics. In his first book, *The Gold Standard and the Logic of Naturalism: American Literature at the Turn of the Century* (1987), he argues against the idea that authors like Theodore Dreiser subverted capitalism; rather, they were fully embedded in it. Since the mid-1990s he has been making arguments against the presumptions of identity politics, notably in his book *The Other America: Nativism, Modernism, and Pluralism* (1995) and a number of essays. Those were for academic audiences, but his 2006 trade book, *The Trouble with Diversity: How We Learned to Love Identity and Ignore Inequality*, published and heavily promoted by Metropolitan Books, puts the word out to a bigger congregation. Diversity isn't the solution; rather, it perpetuates racial categories, when we should want to get rid of them. Instead, Michaels throws his weight with the economic side of things, finding class to be the central issue.

I should be happy about this. In the airy heights of literary theory, I think we often pass over the bread-and-butter issues, and I have spent considerable time over the past several years researching and writing about the virtual indenture of young Americans under the weight of student debt and other effects of the privatized university. I also sponsored a good bit of left-leaning work, particularly on academic labor, for nearly two decades as editor of *the minnesota review*. And I have been a long-time member of the Socialist Party, the motto of which is "People Over Profits." I would like to see more attention to class and the injustices attendant upon it.

But I am not particularly encouraged by Michaels's jeremiad against the wayward identitarians. It seems to me that one cannot so easily brush away the massive problems and injustices attendant upon race or gender or sexuality; I think Nancy Fraser has sorted this issue out the most persuasively in showing that we need both a politics of redistribution and a politics of recognition. We need to remedy both economic inequality and status inequality; one does not solve the other, and money would not take away the injury of a denigrated status. People don't live, as the saying goes, by bread alone. But even if I were to agree with Michaels's argument, I am not encouraged, because I don't entirely trust Michaels's motives. It is a question of rhetoric, and it is surprising that someone as brilliant at argument as Michaels is so wrong about rhetoric.

The quintessential moment for me is in the conclusion of *The Trouble with Diversity*. The book was all over for a while, the subject of a "Book Event" by one of the main literary blogs, the Valve; featured at a special reception and book signing at the 2006 Modern Language Association Convention; and reviewed in most major papers. Since then, it has become one of the more recognizable positions in talk about politics and culture, and Michaels has not let up making the argument, so it is worth a close look. The conclusion begins with this personal statement, albeit couched in the third person:

> He makes $175,000 a year. But he wants more; one of his motives for writing this book was the cash advance. . . . Some readers will be tempted to see a discrepancy between these facts and the arguments against economic inequality made in the preceding chapters. But they should remember that those arguments are true (if they are true) even if Michaels's motives are bad, and they would be false (if they were false) even if his motives were good. Not to put too fine a point on it, the validity of the arguments does not depend on the virtue of the person making them. (191)

Oh, but it does. As any student of rhetoric can tell you, a key element of persuasion in social speech is ethos, or what we usually call character. In his *Rhetoric*, Aristotle distinguishes three elements of persuasion: the enthymemes, or arguments; the character of the speaker; and the disposition of the audience. Ethos matters because you are prone to judge the speech according to how you judge the speaker. And more consequentially, you are moved to do something about his or her argument, particularly if such an argument is what Aristotle called epideictic or deliberative, oriented toward change in the future, say in policy or law, as one assumes an argument about politics would be. If the goal of the argument is simply to win the point, then the argument is, well, only academic, and does nothing.

Enthymemes matter too, of course, but the terrain that Michaels surveys is not that of pure logic or reason. It is finally moral, based on premises about what a good society should or should not do. For instance, one could claim that inequality results from one's moral goodness or lack thereof, as determined by God. This is not an insupportable argument, and I dare say there are more than a few Americans who believe it, including some of my churchgoing relatives. It is not an argument about whether inequality exists but whether you think it is acceptable and whether something should be done about it, which is an ethical or political judgment.

Michaels is savvy enough to be aware of the question of ethos; hence his preemptive counterargument. But it is a bit of a liar's paradox—even if I am disingenuous, I might be right. He also tries to stave off questions of his credibility by putting the passage in the weird third person, as if to effect some distance and thereby confer credibility, like writing a job recommendation letter about oneself.

Virtue, or ethos, does matter. After reading *The Trouble with Diversity* as well as most of Michaels's other writing, one manifestly gets the sense that he likes to win arguments and to debunk others. Which is fine as far as it goes. It is the ethos of the academic gamesman—and he is a master at it, on the all-star team—that finds competitive glee in the practice. But it is finally an academic exercise, and you wouldn't follow him to any voter's booth, not to mention barricade. Michaels's target is what he often intones as "the academic left." This is a left that exists in the imagination of those who know of no other, more concrete left.

People do not do what you say they should do merely on the basis of the arguments. If they did, then no one would smoke, eat trans-fats, or drive too fast, since the arguments clearly tell them they should not. People do what you urge them to do more often if you do what you say, they are moved, and they emulate you. In the neglected second book of the *Rhetoric*, Aristotle distinguishes the emotions that a speaker might evoke. For Aristotle emotions are usually paired, indicating positive and negative reactions to events. One pair is envy and emulation: Aristotle notes that a good speaker prompts emulation, so that his audience wants to copy him, "to take steps to secure the good things" he has rather than to envy him and wish he did not have them.

Michaels is known for being an extraordinary teacher and lecturer. Having seen him give several talks, I can confirm the impression—he is dynamic, fully engaged, animated with argument. He provides a model of a teacher. But, by his own testimony, he is not a model about politics—and it does matter. To my knowledge—derived from his writing, interviewing him, and profiles such as one in the *New Yorker* in 1997—he is not active in any political parties, labor groups, or other practical political venues. So, I would put a challenge to him: Start signing on and doing things to remedy inequality. In this life, the root of evil is a matter of the way people act or fail to act.

The political critic Adolf Reed has a big blurb on the back of *The Trouble with Diversity*, so Michaels owes it to Reed to check out the Labor Party, which Reed has had a significant hand in organizing, particularly its campaign for "Free Higher Ed." It fits with Michaels's observations about universities finally reconfirming class hierarchies instead of alleviating them. Then I will start to believe him, and it might in fact temper the extremity of his arguments, giving them more credibility.

EIGHT

The Statistical Turn in Literary Criticism

Humanists usually take to math like cats to water. But lately literary critics have been embracing statistics and other quantitative measures.

One prominent example has been Franco Moretti. He is a leading critic of the novel, with books such as *Signs Taken for Wonders: Essays in the Sociology of Literary Forms* (1983) and *The Way of the World: The Bildungsroman in European Culture* (1987) on modernism, the bildungsroman, the epic, and other forms. But more recently he has been amassing statistics on novels, notably in his influential *Graphs, Maps, and Trees* (2007), as well as subsequent essays in *New Left Review*, that bring Big Data into novel criticism.

Moretti's recent work aims for the wide-angle rather than the close-up. Since the 1940s, a prime method in literary studies has been "close reading," offering interpretations that dissect the language, figures, and motifs of individual literary works. Even the theorists of the 1970s and 1980s, while making large claims about language or society, were often close readers. In contrast, Moretti calls for "distant reading." He argues that we typically talk about only a small sliver of the novels published, so we really do not have an accurate account of them. Instead, we should examine the mass of them to gain a fuller knowledge of their development.

The chapter, "Graphs," for example, conducts a huge survey of novels from several countries over 160 years, marking off the various genres that the novel has adopted in several graphs and charts. It demonstrates that genres coalesce in a fairly regular pattern and that they usually endure for only about twenty-five years. Moretti hypothesizes that this results from generations—not of authors, who might be productive over a long time, but of readers. In other words, as generations change, genres change, and "Graphs" provides a naturalistic explanation of literary evolution. As biology might tell you about the stages in the evolutionary development of cats, Moretti's approach tells you about those of the novel. In contrast to close reading, Moretti's approach does not tell you much about a particular novel other than that it is a "spy novel" or an "imperial romance," just as an evolutionary approach would not tell you about the particular cat in front of you other than that it is an Abyssinian or a bobcat.

Moretti's account is theoretical, but it represents a different way of doing literary theory from that of the 1970s and 1980s. Then a primary focus was the conceptual category of "narrative," and narrative theory was a thriving field, seeking the abstract structures that govern novels as one might seek the laws of physics that govern falling objects. Moretti's primary focus is the empirical category of the novel, and his approach is bottom-up rather than top-down, starting from the actual pool of books that were published, and from those drawing his surmises about their species, as one might do in biology. Moretti's goal is to give a fuller historical picture of the morphology of novels, and his project contributes to the rising field of "the history of the book" and the study of "print culture." This vein of criticism is less interested in interpreting individual works and more interested in understanding the culture that produced them, how they were distributed and read, and their audiences.

The heyday of literary theory exhibited what a number of commentators called "the linguistic turn": Critics treated society, culture, the psyche, and other phenomena like a language. In a sense, they extended the methods of literary criticism to look at other elements of culture, seeing society, for instance, as a set of signs to be understood through reading. Moretti's work suggests a "statistical turn," whereby critics treat literature as a body of empirical facts about which one gains knowledge through quantitative means.

The turn toward statistics was brought home to me when I attended a conference on anthologies at Trinity College in Hartford, Connecticut, in the spring of 2010. A good number of the talks drew on statistical profiles of anthologies or other collections of literature from various periods and national traditions. Several recounted building databases that anyone might draw on to do their own quantitative projects.

For instance, Ken Roemer, from the University of Texas at Arlington, and two trusty graduate assistants described how they built a database of

American literature anthologies. From the database they adduced what texts were reprinted and presumably most read during different periods. The point was not simply to compile an inventory but to find out whether it was true that the canon had been given over to Alice Walker and multi-culturalism. It was not, according to the data; in actuality, the canon has been relatively stable over the years.

Lynn Z. Bloom, Aetna Professor of English at the University of Connecticut, proved that there is an "essay canon," a phrase she coined in a 1999 *College English* article. Sorting through readers used in college writing classes, she (and her trusty assistants) tabulated how frequently particular writers appeared. (George Orwell, E. B. White, and Joan Didion topped the list.) The surprise of her research is that, just as there is a canon of poetry and of fiction, there is a canon of essays, even though they rarely receive critical attention. You don't see many close readings of Orwell's essays, but students still go through them regularly.

A panel, led by Tom Mole, a professor at McGill University and scholar of British Romantic literature, and including two of his graduate assistants, similarly took the statistical route and recounted building another database, this one focused on only one author, Lord Byron. The database tabulated all the reprints of Byron through the nineteenth century in various collections. At the click of a few keys, they could tell you which poems were most reprinted, which not, where, and when. The project put numbers to Byron's fame and could give you references to the particular poems that his fame rested on.

This project struck me especially because it was so specialized. I could readily see how statistics might be a good source of evidence to settle debates about the canon, but it suggested how quantitative means might be used in narrower fields—on any author, in any period. If you are a Thomas Pynchon scholar, you can get some assistants to start counting; if you are a Jane Austen scholar, you might look at the data on literacy or publishing in 1815, or the reprints since. While we might not be able to know the number of readers of Xenophon in classical Greece, we can ascertain the reprints of his writing in eighteenth-century England.

By my tabulation, 26 percent of the papers at the Trinity conference drew on some form of quantitative measure. The statistical turn might not supplant other kinds of literary criticism, but it represents a new stance. Rather than blanching at mathematical—or really social-scientific—methods, it assimilates them, producing a mode of research recognizable to those in other departments around the quad, not to mention those on grant committees. This has its upside and its downside. On the one hand, it adds to what we know about literature—in Moretti's case, giving us a fuller view of world literature that we otherwise would not have. On the other hand, it sidesteps the qualitative and gives less sense of the distinctiveness of literature. Many of the key elements that make a novel or poem special cannot be quantified, and broad categories do not help you understand the irreducible character of the cat.

This turn also takes a page from the sciences and social sciences in how it organizes research. It requires a team, in a kind of literary lab, rather than the lone critic at his library carrel or her coffeehouse, poring over a text. This again has an upside and downside. It calls for collaborative research, which is often praised but little done in the humanities. On the other hand, I suspect that it will be yet another way to make use of cheap, graduate student labor, or to create a subclass of literary lab workers, overseen by the professor-manager running the lab. Finally, I think that criticism still needs the lone voice, sometimes going against the grain to tell us what our culture means, rather than the compiler of data.

PART TWO

Profiles in Criticism

This section presents a series of profiles of contemporary critics ranging from the inventor of the first *Norton Anthology*, M. H. Abrams, to the revisionary queer theorist Judith "Jack" Halberstam. Profiles are a quintessential form of journalism, but they can offer a few distinct benefits over standard issue academic accounts. Most academic articles deal with a narrow issue or argument of a critic, whereas profiles aim to give a more synoptic sense of someone's work and career, of its arc and how they got there.

Moreover, these essays give a lived sense of what it is like to do criticism— why someone came to do the work they do, the places they have gone through, and the anomalous paths of careers. The central feature linking them is that they are drawn from extensive interviews I have conducted with over fifty critics, philosophers, and writers, so they present a critic's ideas in his or her own words, alongside my surmises. They also broach personal terrain, revealing people's backgrounds, politics, and motivations, that one usually does not find in an academic article.

Most of these profiles first appeared in the *Chronicle of Higher Education*, and the choices of subjects were governed by the editors there. Though a mélange—one could of course imagine many additional subjects, covering different fields—the pieces here do fill in some pieces of the puzzle of the history of criticism from the 1930s, when Abrams went to Oxford, studied with I. A. Richards, and learned about close reading, to the recent emergence of animal studies, in Donna Haraway's version, and present-day troubles in higher education in the United Kingdom, as recounted by Stefan Collini.

I should note that, while the bulk of essays focus on one person's work, the first and the last of them present composite pictures—the first about the fate of the latter generation of the "Yale school" of criticism, and the last about critics' attitudes toward their ungainly offspring, their books.

NINE

Prodigal Critics: Bloom, Fish, and Greenblatt

The rise of literary theory is often described in terms of an invasion. A commando team of French intellectuals landed on American shores in the late 1960s to infiltrate the leading universities and blow up literary studies. Twenty years later, after much ink and invective, French theory had conquered the field, supplanting the dominant mode of American criticism from the 1940s to the 1970s, the New Criticism.

That story has some truth, but it obscures as much as it reveals. The rise of theory was not just a foreign intrusion but developed from the inside. The New Criticism was dismantled less by French insurgents than by its own students, notably Harold Bloom, Stanley Fish, and Stephen Greenblatt. It was as much a family drama as a geopolitical one.

Bloom, Fish, and Greenblatt are odd bedfellows, representing very different theoretical approaches, Bloom a theory of poetic influence as Oedipal struggle, Fish a theory of interpretation that places meaning in readers rather than texts, and Greenblatt the "New Historicism." But all three were products of the New Critical world, centering on English rather than foreign languages and dealing with the most canonical of British authors in traditional periods. Moreover, all three underwent graduate training at Yale when Yale was the acknowledged center of New Criticism. They learned the New Criticism at the source, but their theories came to rebut each of its main tenets.

———————

Now the New Criticism seems crusty and conservative, the flat perspective of one's ancestors before we discovered the earth is round. But in midcentury the New Criticism revolutionized literary study. It infused life into the reading of literary works, opening them up for a rising generation of college students. It shed the dry, arcane focus of much of the scholarship of the previous generation. It also dispelled the touchy-feely impressionism of much teaching. Like a biologist with an enhanced microscope, the New Critic zeroed in on the specific features of a poem or a story. In turn, the New Criticism lent a scientific exactness and credibility to literary study.

The New Criticism started in the South in the 1930s, fostered by John Crowe Ransom at Vanderbilt, but by the early 1950s several leading practitioners, including Cleanth Brooks and Robert Penn Warren, Ransom's prize students, had migrated to New Haven. There they joined allies such as William K. Wimsatt Jr. and Austin Warren. They tended to offer close readings of texts more than large theoretical statements, but Wimsatt, in his book *The Verbal Icon* (1954), codified two of the main principles of the New Criticism.

The principles were more about what you should *not* do than what you should. The most famous was "the intentional fallacy," which rules out talking about the author; rather, one should talk only about the poem itself. An author's intentions are not reliable; rather, what matters is what is manifest in the poem. Next was "the affective fallacy" (the two fallacy essays Wimsatt wrote with the aesthetician Monroe C. Beardsley). It rules out talking about the audience, whose responses are not reliable either. They are subjective and thus fickle or idiosyncratic, so not a good way to find out about the inner workings of the poem either.

The New Critics also ruled out history and politics. They acknowledged their importance but parceled them out to their proper disciplines, to history or to the rising disciplines of sociology and political science. A literary critic should properly stick to the poetic qualities of a poem. Its historical qualities might have documentary value, but not literary value.

These prohibitions narrow the purview of criticism, but the New Critics were trying to distinguish its special role in contrast to the social sciences, which had barely existed in 1900 but rose to prominence after World War II. Eschewing chitchat and asserting a more precise knowledge, the New Criticism took some of the fuzziness away from the discipline of literature, giving it a stronger base in the research university.

By the 1960s the New Criticism had become commonplace—even Ransom remarked that much of it was "the merest exercises with words"— and was ripe for challenge. The rising generation obliged. Harold Bloom (Yale Ph.D., 1955) took on the keystone intentional fallacy, putting all the weight on the author and his psyche instead. In a series of books, notably

The Anxiety of Influence: A Theory of Poetry (1973; 2nd ed. 1997), he held that literary history was comprised of a series of Oedipal struggles, each important poet fighting against his precursors. A poem was not a verbal icon but a revenge plot.

Bloom himself expressed some Oedipal hostility about Yale. When asked in a 1985 interview about the atmosphere there during the 1950s, he didn't mince words, calling it a "nightmare," in part because of the idolizing of T. S. Eliot, who was a hero of the New Criticism. Bloom's version of theory was a homegrown reaction to Anglo-American formalism.

The next Yale student to bite the hand of the New Criticism was Stanley Fish (Ph.D., 1962). Fish countered the affective fallacy, arguing that all meaning resided in the experience of the reader. With less hostility and more flourish than Bloom, he one-upped the New Critics with "The Affective Fallacy Fallacy," a section of a 1970 essay that was reprinted as the first chapter of his major theoretical statement, *Is There a Text in This Class? The Authority of Interpretive Communities* (1980). There he further explained how the meaning of a poem derives from the interpretive community we inhabit, not some absolute object. Marxists find class; formalists find form.

In an interview I conducted in 2000, Fish remarked that "Wimsatt was like Kingsfield in *The Paper Chase*: he was fierce." (Fish also said it seemed like he was eight feet tall; Wimsatt was in fact nearly seven feet tall.) But Fish, learning the inside of formalism, turned it inside out, promoting a theory that drained meaning from a work and placed it in the audience.

If there is a family tree, the younger sibling is Stephen Greenblatt (Yale Ph.D., 1969), who made his mark inventing the New Historicism, which stresses "the embeddedness of cultural objects in the contingencies of history." Rather than a verbal icon, Greenblatt declares in the introduction to his influential *Shakespearean Negotiations* (1988), "There can be no autonomous artifacts."

Greenblatt noted in an interview I conducted in 2008 that, "The genius loci of Yale when I was there was William Wimsatt and he thought . . . you are interested in the object insofar as you can detach it from the surroundings. That is the way I was trained, and I'm a product of that. But at a certain moment this approach seemed intolerable or grossly distorted, and so I and other people began to do something else."

That something else varied and did sometimes tack toward French theory. Both Fish and Greenblatt talked in their interviews about encountering those on the Continental scene during the 1970s. And Yale of course was not the only nursery of theory (several prominent feminist critics attended Columbia, for instance). But the American New Criticism and its senators at Yale provided the ground from which a new generation of critics grew and departed.

––––––––––

Like most progeny, critics might rebel against their forebears but also bear their stamp. Despite their differences from the New Criticism, Bloom, Fish, and Greenblatt more quietly carry on some of its features. When I asked him about these links, Greenblatt said he had never thought much about it but confessed that parts of his method are "consonant with the kind of education I had at Yale," musing, "It often happens that the thing you are saying farewell to forever turns out to be the thing you are working slowly to arrive at."

One way they are similar is that they all pay allegiance to literature, and especially to poetry, as the New Critics did. None of them has veered toward the modern realm of the novel, not to mention the newer realm of cultural studies or popular culture, and all of them are known for their work on major literary figures, Bloom on the British Romantic poets, Fish on Milton, and Greenblatt on Shakespeare. They cover many of the same writers that Cleanth Brooks did in his 1947 book *The Well-Wrought Urn*.

Another way they are similar is that, though they draw theoretical surmises, they pay close attention to literature. While Wimsatt might have grumbled at the psychoanalytic language Bloom uses, he would recognize the attention to poems. Fish, though he shifts the site of meaning from the poem to the audience, does a close reading then of the poem in the audience; he remarked when I talked with him, "What heartens me through all of these changes is the commitment to close reading." Greenblatt is more a teller of stories, but still he uses the toolbox of contextual facts to illuminate a literary motif. As Cleanth Brooks examined the imagery of clothing and nakedness in *Macbeth*, Greenblatt examines the sliding portrayal of gender in Shakespeare's comedies.

A third way that they don't fall far from the tree is that they keep their distance from politics. In fact, Fish has a prohibition against it in his recent *Save the World on Your Own Time* (2008), where he holds that politics do not belong in criticism; only literary matters do. Bloom excoriates those critics who avow radical politics in criticism as the "school of resentment."

Greenblatt is less cranky and admits to liberal leanings, but he desists from the headier claims of theory, remarking to me, "I don't know if I ever, even in my most heady moments, believed that regime change would take place through literary criticism." Bloom's, Fish's, and Greenblatt's stance toward politics dispels another common story about the rise of theory. A corollary to the notion that it was a French invasion is that it represented 1960s counterculture, rendering the study of literature a "politics by other means."

This points to the fact that many of the key participants in the rise of theory were not 1960s radicals but of an earlier generation, what is called the "silent generation," born after the "greatest generation" who fought World War II but before the Baby Boomers. Bloom (born in 1930) and Fish (b. 1938) were children of the 1940s and 1950s, not the 1960s, and Greenblatt (b. 1943) was on the cusp, which perhaps explains his sympathy to history, although he too was more a child of the 1950s.

Attending university in the 1950s and early 1960s, they were among the first beneficiaries of the postwar expansion of higher education. Unlike graduate students in literature now, who often teach as much as tenured professors, they all sailed through on the raft of generous postwar funding, finishing in their mid-twenties and getting jobs right out, two of them in the rising University of California system.

Another feature of postwar higher education is that it opened the Ivy gates to a more diverse demographic. Bloom, Fish, and Greenblatt were not from the WASP elite but from Jewish families a generation or two from immigration. They got a boost from the meritocratic charge of the postwar university, and they entered a profession that was shedding its patrician adhesions. Theory, in other words, was cultivated in the rich loam of support for higher education, and the diversification of the demographic of its time. The new students, Bloom, Fish, and Greenblatt, learned the lessons of their teachers, and, like most good students, also superseded them.

TEN

A Life in Criticism: M. H. Abrams

M. H. Abrams is an iconic name in literary studies. It has appeared on nearly nine million copies of *The Norton Anthology of English Literature*, for which he served as general editor for nearly fifty years. In a detail that only scholars would know, it has also led the indexes of many a critical book. (In fact, one critic I know added a citation of Aarlef just to avoid that custom.) Besides the Norton, Abrams stamped the study of Romantic literature from the 1950s on. His book *The Mirror and the Lamp: Romantic Theory and the Critical Tradition* (1953), ranked twenty-fifth in the Modern Library's list of the one hundred most important nonfiction books of the twentieth century, and he was a prime participant in the debates over literary theory, especially deconstruction, during the 1970s and 1980s.

In the summer of 2007, I interviewed Abrams—Meyer Howard, but he goes by "Mike"—at his home in Ithaca, New York, up the road from Cornell University, where he has been a professor since 1945 and still goes to his office in Goldwin Smith Hall. Colleagues at Cornell had just held a ninety-fifth birthday celebration for him, and among the gifts was an inscribed copy of Thomas Pynchon's latest novel. Pynchon had been a student of Abrams's in the 1950s and sent it. Abrams has the book on the coffee table in his living room.

Abrams has been there for the major changes in literary study as well as in the modern research university. He started as an undergraduate at Harvard in 1930, as the country slid into the Great Depression. His father was a house painter, eventually opening a paint store, and Abrams was the first in his family to go to college. He had considered being a lawyer but decided to go into English because "there weren't jobs in any other profession, so I thought I might as well enjoy starving, instead of starving while doing something I didn't enjoy."

In a time of little air travel and no Internet, it was a smaller world. After his B.A., Abrams won a fellowship to study at Cambridge University in England, where his tutor was I. A. Richards, an important figure who first promulgated "practical criticism" and early cognitive theory. Through Richards he met W. B. Yeats, whom Richards "said had become a great poet even though he believed in fairies," and he got previews of T. S. Eliot's poems, since "Eliot would send some of his poems [to Richards] for comments before he published them," and Richards "would prop them on his mantelpiece."

Returning to Harvard in 1935, Abrams entered graduate school "in the days when, to get a Ph.D., you had to study Anglo-Saxon, Old Norse, Old French, and linguistics, on the notion that they served as a kind of hardcore scientific basis for literary study." (I will henceforth cease entertaining complaints from my graduate students about foreign-language requirements.) The academic study of literature was scholastic, oriented toward amassing recondite facts, obscure literary sources, and technical bibliographies.

That was changing through the efforts of people like Richards and their students, Abrams among them. Criticism (engaging directly with literary works through "close reading") rather than philology (accumulating historical details about them) was the new battle cry, and it drew Abrams and other "young bucks" of his cohort. "That was an exciting thing, I was a student, and students are always excited by what's new, not what's old," he remarked. The migration of literary critics from the public sphere into the university is often seen as a fall, but, as Edmund Wilson reflected in his 1943 essay "Thoughts on Being Bibliographed," the institutional pressures of journalism were no better and in many ways worse (Wilson remarked that they killed Poe), and academe provided a base for critics after the more plush 1920s. In turn, criticism enlivened the academic study of literature, especially teaching, for those of Abrams's generation and after.

Now the "New Criticism," the dominant method of close reading from the 1940s to 60s, seems narrow and constraining. But then it was a striking invention, and Abrams reminds us of its patent. Earlier critics like Coleridge or De Quincey had sometimes called attention to "a short passage," for instance "the knocking of the gate in *Macbeth*," but "there's no analysis applied to the whole of *Macbeth* until the New Critics." Abrams credits the New Critics with a focus on "verbal particulars" and "the construction of a poem" that "opened it up" for readers.

Although contemporary theorists might consign Abrams to the New Criticism, he actually gravitated more toward intellectual history. He had "qualms about [the New Critics'] shortcomings," especially their "careful avoidance of historical contextual matters as relevant to the understanding of a poem." *The Mirror and the Lamp*, which is still in print, and Abrams's major 1971 book *Natural Supernaturalism: Tradition and Revolution in Romantic Literature*, both look at the history and philosophy of the Romantic era in conjunction with the poetry.

Foregrounding that era, from the late eighteenth to the mid-nineteenth century, was part of a shift in literary studies. When Abrams started out, English centered on earlier periods, notably medieval and the Renaissance, and major figures like Spenser and Milton, and T. S. Eliot had dismissed the Romantic poets as inferior. Abrams helped turn the field toward the more modern sensibility of poets like Wordsworth and Shelley, who were more secular and concerned with problems of language and epistemology.

Another change Abrams experienced was demographic. Before mid-century, most faculties were WASP-laden. Abrams, born into a Jewish family, observes: "What broke the barriers was the Second World War, both because of Nazi persecution of the Jews for which many people felt they had to compensate, and because colleges were stripped of their faculties during the war. And then came the G.I. Bill, which flooded colleges and universities. . . . Colleges had to build faculties in a hurry and couldn't afford to be prejudiced the way they were used to, so they hired Jews and Catholics and Irish who had difficulty breaking into faculty ranks." Abrams benefited from a kind of affirmative action of his era—although it was still mostly "white bucks."

The Mirror and the Lamp had been Abrams's dissertation, and he reminds us of a different time of professional expectations, when the tenure gun was not quite so impatiently pressed to a junior professor's head. Abrams took "ten years of hard work revising the text," rewriting the first chapter "at least six times." It was worth it, since the chapter has been reprinted many times, probably because of its useful scheme distinguishing the types of criticism as mimetic, pragmatic, expressive, and objective. It encapsulated a tacit history of criticism building to the present: Classical critics, like

Aristotle, looked especially at how well art imitated reality; eighteenth-century critics like Samuel Johnson believed art should have a moral, pragmatic effect; Romantic critics thought art should express emotions; and contemporary critics took a more dispassionate, scientific perspective. The success of the book has surprised Abrams, and he thinks his later *Natural Supernaturalism* is, "just between you and me, a more important book."

Now Norton anthologies of literature are the standard, synonymous with the canon, but they began serendipitously, when somebody knocked on Abrams's office door in the late 1950s. It was the Norton president, who had heard that Abrams was teaching a survey course and suggested he "do an English literature anthology." Abrams thought, "Well sure, why not?" and basically expanded the course he was teaching. But instead of the usual "single editor or two trying to deal with everything from *Beowulf* to Thomas Hardy," one of Abrams's innovations was to gather a "group of seven editors" who were "experts in each field." Remarkably, they did not meet as a group until after the anthology came out—which, according to Abrams, was the secret to its efficient completion. He added that "none of us expected the success of the thing when it finally, after four or five years, hit the market."

Another innovation was that it "eliminated the snippet representations" in favor of complete works and incorporated introductions to each figure, "so that in the anthology you had the equivalent of a short history of English literature." And it was portable, printed on a normal rather than oversize double-column page and on onionskin paper to keep it light (Norton found a printer that also produced Bibles). For Abrams, the key "was not to force people to teach what you wanted them to teach, but give them the equivalent of a small library from which they could select what they would want to teach."

Perhaps the most remarkable thing about Abrams's career is that he has kept up for more than sixty years. Through the 1970s and 1980s he sorted through and questioned new schools of literary theory such as deconstruction and theorists like Stanley Fish and Jacques Derrida, in a well-known essay comparing Derrida's work to that of David Hume, the eighteenth-century British philosopher who radically questioned causality and the bases of knowledge (it is included in the 1989 collection of Abrams's writing, *Doing Things with Texts: Essays in Criticism and Critical Theory*). Abrams remarked, "I've been skeptical from the beginning of attempts to show that for hundreds of years people have missed the real point," his chief quarrel with the stance of much contemporary theory. While affable, he does not shy from debate, even with his former student, Harold Bloom, saying, "I enjoy a good intellectual fight, with somebody I disagree with, about what seem to be fundamental matters."

Given all that he has done, I assumed Abrams had the work habits of a machine. But he surprised me, confessing, "I've never been a very efficient worker, actually. But I work steadily. I used to go to the office seven days a week—to the despair of my wife—but not for a very long day. Three, four hours a day, but every day. It adds up, day after day after day after day." Though he handed off the editorship of the *Norton Anthology* to Stephen Greenblatt in 2005, he is still busy, exploring ecology and periodically updating his bestselling *Glossary of Literary Terms* (1957; 8th ed. 2004). When I asked how it feels to look back on all his work, he says, "I didn't expect the success of *The Mirror and the Lamp*, I didn't expect the success of the *Norton Anthology*, I didn't expect the success of the *Glossary*." But, he added, "I must confess, if I take down one of my essays now, it still seems to me good, and that I find a source of gratification."

ELEVEN

Bellwether: J. Hillis Miller

Careers seem to follow an inevitable logic. Looking back on a critic's career, we usually discern how the early work led to the later, and we connect the dots to explain how it developed and matured. But closer up, rarely are careers neat or straightforward. Like creative work, intellectual work tends to proceed in fits and starts, long plateaus sometimes sliding to a valley, sometimes interrupted by an unexpected turn, and intellectual careers are punctuated by shifts in style, method, or concern. Such turning points might testify to the lighting bolts of invention, but they also result from a strong dose of accident and circumstance. Careers are an alchemy of idiosyncrasy and institutions, personal predisposition and social movements, accidents and customary paths.

In the summer of 2008 I interviewed J. Hillis Miller, who has been a prominent literary critic for half a century, about the turning points of his career as well as the changes in criticism and the university that he has witnessed. Miller has had an exemplary career—attending graduate school at Harvard, holding appointments at Johns Hopkins, Yale, and University of California at Irvine, where he is University Professor emeritus, and publishing twenty-five books, including two recent volumes, on media and on Jacques Derrida. He is probably best known as the chief American promoter of deconstruction in literary studies. He did not start that way, though.

When he began graduate school in the late 1940s, English was staid and largely limited to studying British literature before the nineteenth century. As Miller reported, one prominent professor "would say quite openly that there's no such thing as American literature." Method tended toward the scholarly if not pedantic. Most literature professors did not do criticism—analyses of literary works—but accumulated arcane factual details. In the era before desktops, Miller recounted, "People used to make scholarly careers out of doing concordances . . . which meant that they sat there writing down entries on 3 × 5 cards. And people got big recognition doing that." This method informed pedagogy, too, and Miller told me about a course he took with "a famous Renaissance scholar, [who] spent the first three weeks of the graduate seminar dictating bibliography." At first he had planned on specializing in the Renaissance, but after that course Miller changed his mind.

Instead, he was drawn to critics who looked at "the actual texts of poems," like the American critic Kenneth Burke or the British critic William Empson. Why this turn? "One of the things I would have to stress is that it was accidental—but not quite," Miller recalled. "It was accidental that I opened that book [by Empson] because it was not on any of the syllabuses of any courses I had. But when I read it, I thought it was amazing. Here was somebody who tried to explain what was going on in the actual poems, which none of my teachers were doing."

To distinguish what you are doing from what your professors do is not unusual, but a new generation was filling academe. Though too young to have served in World War II (he was born in 1928), Miller was part of the wave that swept through universities in the period right after the war. Beginning graduate work in 1948, Miller whisked through in four years, finishing in 1952 to take part in the swelling of higher education, teaching those on the G.I. Bill and eventually their children.

Historians call that period the Golden Age of the university, and Miller offered a double perspective on it. His father, likewise J. Hillis Miller, was an academic, and in the 1940s his father became president of the University of Florida, which was "moving from 3,000 students to 15,000 to 20,0000, so he had a wonderful time—buildings to build, programs to establish, deans to appoint, faculty to hire, and lots of money." Miller concluded somewhat wistfully, "It's hard to imagine now."

A harsh turn of fate also affected Miller. On summer vacation after his first year in graduate school and staying in a remote part of Maine, he contracted polio, which disabled his right arm. However, if anything, this gave him more motivation. As he remarked in a 1987 interview, "It certainly had an effect on my life. My wife was a tremendous help. She prodded me in the direction I would have gone, which was an absolute determination to work hard. . . . It reinforced the feeling that, whatever you do, you ought to do it with your whole heart." That determination has been borne out in his shelf of books, more than two hundred articles, and a great deal of professional service over his career, including a term as president of the Modern Language Association in 1986.

After graduate school, Miller's work took a new route. His dissertation on the novels of Charles Dickens embraced "close reading," as did much other criticism of the time, rather than some arcane scholarly recovery. But, upon taking a position at Johns Hopkins in 1953, he encountered the new European trend of "consciousness criticism," which tried to capture the sensibility running through the entire body of work of a writer, gleaned from diaries, letters, and fragments as well as from novels and poems. Consciousness criticism was inspired by the Belgian critic, Georges Poulet, who was at Hopkins, although Miller first came upon Poulet's work fortuitously: "I was given [another professor's] office the first summer I was there, and there was a bookcase right beside the desk with a copy of the *Hudson Review* on it. I pulled it down and there was the first translation into English of Poulet's preface to *Studies in Human Time*, so I read it because I didn't have anything much to do during that hour, and I thought it was amazing. It was a conversion experience."

Embracing consciousness criticism, he entirely recast his manuscript on Dickens and went on to publish four books before he was forty, among them *The Disappearance of God: Five Nineteenth-Century Writers* (1963) and *Poets of Reality: Six Twentieth-Century Writers* (1965), both of which were reprinted in trade paperbacks. They examine the way that writers dealt with the modern predicament of the loss of faith—what happens after one concludes god is dead?—and stamped the understanding of Victorian and modern literature for a generation.

In the standard model of professional development, one's approach is shaped during graduate training, but Miller noted that, "My real education was Hopkins, much more than graduate school." One dimension of that continuing education was going to lunch with senior faculty: "We ate at the Hopkins faculty club, and it was all very friendly, but what they were doing, unostentatiously, was teaching me things about the profession." While largely positive, he admitted that some of the lessons "now I would think are problematic, like the sexist assumptions they took for granted. There were no women in the department."

By the time he was forty, Miller had already built a remarkable career, but he experienced a profound turn yet again when he encountered deconstruction and the work of Jacques Derrida. As he put it, "The discovery of Derrida was somewhat the same [as that of Poulet]. It happened by chance, I found it interesting in itself, and thirdly, I thought I could use it in my own work in English literature." Derrida "told me something that's right there before your eyes but that you hadn't seen," which is Miller's rule of thumb for a great critic.

He first came upon Derrida at the now-legendary 1966 conference at Johns Hopkins, "The Languages of Criticism and the Sciences of Man," which is often cited as the inauguration of "French theory" in the United States. Miller remembered the impact of Derrida's talk, which pointed out the contradictions to the presumably scientific basis of structuralism. Still, Miller was not aware of the change it augured, observing, "You may be present at something that in retrospect becomes a turning point, but you don't experience it like that at the time."

Miller told me a number of details of the conference that do not usually appear in the historical accounts. For instance, the legendary French psychoanalyst Jacques Lacan was angry that he had been upstaged by Derrida. There were also a number of comic moments, as when, during one of the question and answer periods, Lacan, who did not speak English very well, said, "Let him who agrees with me, rise up the finger." Another was when Lacan "was going to hold office hours the next day, and he said, 'If anyone wishes, they may come to my office at 11:00 tomorrow morning and mate with me.'" We tell history as a series of noteworthy events, but we remember its funky texture.

After Miller's turn to deconstruction, in 1972 he moved to Yale, where he joined Paul de Man, Derrida, Geoffrey Hartman, and Harold Bloom to form what was labeled the "Yale School" of criticism. Though Hartman and especially Bloom distanced themselves from it later, the five of them published the joint volume *Deconstruction and Criticism* (1979), announcing their new focus on the difficulties of language and the fissures in interpretation. In a subsequent series of essays and books, Miller explained deconstruction and the wave of theory breaking on American shores. Miller himself focused on "the linguistic moment," when literary works explicitly call attention to their own mode, for instance when a poem comments on language or poetry. Those moments raise philosophical questions, such as: What is the status of a statement about fiction when a fictive text is telling you? In other words, theory isn't outside poetry, but poetry invokes theoretical issues.

Though literary theory spurred a great deal of opposition—from advocates of the close reading that Miller had first embraced, among others—by 1986 Miller could announce, in the title of his MLA presidential address, "The Triumph of Theory." That same year Miller moved once again, to the University of California at Irvine, which became a grand junction for literary theorists. Since then he has taken the position of a kind of senior literary statesman, commenting on the ethics of criticism and the state of the humanities in the corporate university, as well as giving talks in China, South America, and elsewhere over the globe.

He has also continued his engagement with the thought of Derrida, especially Derrida's later considerations of new media. I interviewed Miller in his house on Deer Isle, in Maine, where he has a study in a second-floor room that angles out like a ship's prow toward a small inlet, with windows overlooking a garden and the water, and he is obviously still on the job. His desk, built underneath the prow of windows, was filled with neatly stacked piles of books, manuscripts, and paper. He was pondering Derrida's idea that media is not just a vehicle but "changes what can be said." That idea again showed him something he hadn't seen, about the way that language itself inflects the possibilities of thought.

TWELVE

The Political Theory License: Michael Walzer

Michael Walzer asks big political questions in plainspoken ways. For instance, he begins his recent book, *In God's Shadow: Politics in the Hebrew Bible* (2012), asking of the Bible's various books: "How is political society conceived? How should political power be used? . . . When is it right to go to war? What are the obligations of ordinary citizens or subjects?"

Walzer has been asking these kinds of questions, about war, justice, community, and what it means to be an intellectual, for nearly sixty years, in books such as *Just and Unjust Wars* (1977; 4th ed. 2006), which has sold over 150,000 copies. He has also been questioning our actual politics, within the United States as well as without, in Vietnam, Israel, Iraq, and other parts of the globe, in the occasional op-ed piece in the *New York Times* and in books such as *Getting Out: Historical Perspectives on Leaving Iraq* (2009, coedited with N. Mills). Before there was a term "public intellectual," he readily commuted from positions as a professor at Princeton, Harvard, and the Institute for Advanced Studies, where he is now emeritus, to more public climes, regularly writing for *Dissent* magazine, which he coedited for many years, and *The New Republic*, where he is a contributing editor.

One premise of Walzer's thinking is that "criticism follows from connection," as he writes in *A Company of Critics: Social Criticism and Political Commitment in the Twentieth Century* (1988; rev. ed. 2002). That goes against the usual view that an intellectual surveys politics from an Archimedean height; in the book, Walzer reasons that creates a "thin" attachment and, "if he were a stranger, really disinterested, it is hard to see why he would involve himself in their affairs." In November 2011, I interviewed Walzer, and he elaborated with a metaphor: "The critic is in the cave and is committed to the well-being of the other people who are there with him."

This idea of connection leads Walzer to emphasize the ways in which people shape their values in communities, whether national, religious, or ideological. This view is sometimes called "communitarianism." While the standard theory of liberalism, for instance of John Locke or Walzer's onetime colleague at Harvard, John Rawls, stresses the rights of individuals, Walzer focuses instead on the ways that rights are formed in the context of a group or community. As suggested by the title of another of his books, *Spheres of Justice: A Defense of Pluralism and Equality* (1983), he does not have a one-size-fits-all theory of justice but finds that it is adjudicated in its particular contexts.

In some ways, Walzer is an inheritor of the New York intellectuals, a group that was prominent in the 1940s through the 1970s and commented on politics and culture. Walzer was a student of one of the leading members of that group, Irving Howe, who was a lifelong socialist as well as a literary and cultural critic, and who cofounded *Dissent* magazine in 1954. However, Walzer became a New York intellectual in Waltham, Massachusetts.

After growing up in Jewish communities in New York and Johnstown, Pennsylvania, where his family had a small jewelry store, Walzer went to Brandeis University, in Waltham, in 1953, when the university was just five years old. There he took courses with Howe and another New Yorker, the sociologist Lewis Coser, although he took most of his courses in history. Walzer took only a sophomore survey of literature with Howe, but it made an impression. In our interview he recalled, "I came home at winter break and told my parents that I wanted to be an intellectual when I grew up. They asked, as many parents have in similar situations, 'How do you make a living?' I said, 'By becoming a professor, I guess.'"

With Howe and Coser, he read the major European intellectuals of the time, like Albert Camus, George Orwell, and Ignacio Silone, who would later fill the roster of *A Company of Critics*. He also got invited to the launch party of *Dissent* and soon started writing for it. After graduating, he recounted, "My effort to imitate Irving Howe led me to write three pieces of literary criticism," including one on the British play *Look Back in Anger*. But "after that I decided that there were other things I did better."

One of them was politics, and for graduate school he went to the government department at Harvard because it afforded him a "political theory license." Political science, he observed, "was a very open field at the time— that was before the rational choice people got to it. You could write history,

you could write biography, you could do political theory." He was interested in the history of revolutions, but chose the Puritan rather than the
French instance for his dissertation. He self-effacingly told me, "my French
was not good enough, so I had to fall back on my English," but it also
augured his persistent concern with the ways that religion runs through
political life. It became his first book, *Revolution of the Saints: A Study in the
Origins of Radical Politics* (1965).

The G.I. Bill is legendary for its effect on American higher education,
yet the postwar boom may have had a greater impact not on those born in
the teens or 1920s who served in World War II, but on the subsequent generation, those born in the 1930s, like Walzer. The political theory license
was abetted by the fact that "the academic world was in this expansive
phase," Walzer acknowledged, and at Harvard he studied politics with
others of his generation, including Gabriel Kolko, who became a foreign
policy expert, the historians Stephan and Abigail Thernstrom, and Martin
Peretz, who became the editor of *The New Republic*. "But," he told me,
"I don't think I could have survived as a graduate student without *Dissent*."

He had already written several pieces for it, and in early 1960, after
reports of the first sit-ins in the South, "Irving Howe called me and asked
me to go down there for *Dissent*. I was reading Puritan sermons and writing
my dissertation, but I dropped that and just went." However, it was not as
distant as one would expect because "I found myself listening to Baptist
sermons on Exodus. So I had to come back and tell my ex-Trotskyist colleagues at *Dissent* that this was not a revolt of the workers and peasants; this
was a heavily religiously inflected movement."

I asked him whether he felt a split personality when moving between
academic and political worlds, but he replied, "I found it fairly easy because
of the political theory license." He went on to muse, "Purely academic work
never entirely appealed to me. I always used to think that had I been in
Europe where there was a social democratic party, I might have ended up as
the editor of the party journal, the 'theoretical journal' as it was called, of
the German or French or British socialists. I don't think I would have
become an academic. But in the United States, that career wasn't available."

Another advantage of the political theory license is that you could deal
with politics in teaching. As he explained, "Political theorists have a license
to do something that other academics don't have: to defend a political position in the classroom and in the learned journals." So he could give a course,

for instance, on socialism and "let students know I had views." He is careful to add, "I presented opposing views in their strongest versions, which I didn't have to do at a political meeting."

Walzer was active in the civil rights movement in the early 1960s, but as the decade wore on he became more active around the Vietnam War. He commented, "the early moment in the civil rights movement was a moment of a very close black and Jewish collaboration. Later on, there were breaks in that collaboration and tensions. With the rise of Black Nationalism, whites in general were invited to step aside, and we did." After teaching at Princeton for several years, he moved back to Harvard, and he immersed himself in campaigns against the war in Cambridge.

His speaking and organizing about Vietnam prompted him to think about political obligations, resulting in *Obligations: Essays on Disobedience, War, and Citizenship* (1970) and *Political Action* (1971), and about war, resulting in *Just and Unjust Wars*. He recounted how he came to the latter: "I was running around the country talking against the war and using a language of 'unjust war,' 'intervention,' 'noncombatant immunity,' 'shielding civilians.' Where was this coming from? I was drawing on an intellectual tradition I didn't know much about, so I began to read Catholic just war theory, and the book is really a secularization of Catholic just-war doctrine."

Just-war theory uses a moral framework to establish fair principles to enter war, conduct it, and rebuild after it. For example, Walzer argues that there is an obligation of governments to identify combatants and thus not kill indiscriminately. This sounds reasonable, but it is not as clear as one might think. A realist might say that modern warfare makes it impossible to discriminate among combatants, or that collateral damage is inevitable, or that civilians participate in their government's policies. Walzer's work stresses the moral imperatives of politics, and his distinctions about war have had some influence. While most would not consider the recent President Bush an exemplar of philosophical probity, his administration went to great lengths to define those it held as prisoners "enemy combatants." This is because it was responding to just war theory. Whether it did so in good faith or cynically is a different question.

From Harvard, in 1980 Walzer was appointed to a professorship at the iconic Institute for Advanced Studies, where he is now emeritus. Throughout, he has continued to work with *Dissent*, for over fifty years on its board and for half that time serving as coeditor. At seventy-seven, he still keeps a full schedule; when I interviewed him, he had just come from giving a talk at the CUNY Graduate Center, and he was on his way to an evening meeting of *Dissent*'s staff. For several years, he shared editorial duties with Michael Kazin, son of the New York intellectual Alfred Kazin and a well-known historian himself, although Walzer finally retired from the editorial mantle in 2013. (I have occasionally contributed to *Dissent* over the past decade and been happy to work with Walzer.)

Throughout his career, Walzer has been in dialogue with other political theorists, like Rawls or Robert Nozick, with whom he once taught a course on socialism versus capitalism. But I was struck by how his theoretical stance, eschewing universal or transhistorical measures and stressing plurality and the particular, has affinities with literary and cultural theorists that I am more familiar with, for instance the French philosopher Jacques Derrida and the American pragmatist Richard Rorty. They are of the same generation, born in the 1930s, and they pit themselves against transcendental reference points and master narratives or truths, instead stressing the centrality of interpretation and historical contingency.

Walzer confirmed my impression, saying, "I was writing against the Marxist school of critical theory, who believe that, if you are to function politically at all, you need to have a big world-historical theory. I do not believe that; I have come to believe that it is useful to have pieces of a theory, but big meta-theories more often produce arrogance and authoritarianism in the movement or in the state. The moral understandings of the critic are more important in shaping and giving power to the criticism than the grand theory."

This view prompts his own politics: "The politics I'm closest to is a kind of liberal socialism. But my version of social democracy is one that tries to take into account the need that people have for community, which social democrats often ignored because they were focused so much on the state and what it has to do."

Among the various communities that Walzer belongs to, perhaps his deepest personal connection is with the American Jewish community. He also travels regularly to Israel, and he defends its right to self-determination. In *Just and Unjust Wars*, he deems Israel's role in the 1967 Six Day War a fitting one and a good victory. Still, he is critical of current policy. He commented that when he and his wife, the literary scholar and former provost of the New School, Judith Walzer, first visited Israel in 1957, "it was a much smaller country, I should say," and the 1967 "victory opened the way for Israeli right-wingers and religious Messianists to adopt an expansionist politics that I have been critical of since Day 1, since the first settlement."

In keeping with his view that "what most people need is a state of their own," he believes that there should be a Palestinian state, although he remarks this is not disinterested: "There is a sense in which Israel needs a Palestinian state right now more than the Palestinians do, because Israel won't be a Jewish state unless it is a smaller state."

One of Walzer's first articles in *Dissent* was a criticism of the French in Algeria, and when I pressed him that a critic now might see Israel's relation to the Palestinians similarly, he retorted, "Yes, but no one who criticized French policy in Algeria called the existence of France into question," and added that there is too often a hostility on the part of the European Left toward Israel.

Inside Israeli politics, he believes that "Israel needs a separation of synagogue and state." That has motivated much of his recent scholarly work, such as the two-volume collection he has coedited, *The Jewish Political Tradition* (2000/2003), and *In God's Shadow* (2012). As he put it to me, he wants to "deny the orthodox a monopoly on the tradition. This tradition has to be accessible and criticizable by everybody. In the hands of the orthodox, it can produce a very nasty politics. We have to get a grip on the tradition and start a process something like the Reformation of Catholic Christianity."

Of *In God's Shadow*, he says, "I'm a trespasser in this field. Since biblical scholarship is a field of such erudition, with people who know six ancient languages, I have been very hesitant," pondering it for twenty years. "But now I figure that I am getting too old to wait any longer." He announces his goal as simply "to figure out what the biblical writers thought about politics."

THIRTEEN

The Critic as Wanderer: Terry Eagleton

Literary critics might be divided into two types: settlers and wanderers. The settlers stay put, dwelling on a set of texts or issues. Their work, through the course of their careers, puts stakes in a specific intellectual turf. The wanderers are more restless, starting with one approach or field but leaving it behind for the next foray. Their work takes the shape of serial engagements, moving their stakes to new camps. The difference is not between knowing one thing like a hedgehog and knowing many things like a fox, in Isaiah Berlin's dichotomy. That is effectively the difference between being an expert and being a generalist, and both the settler and the wanderer might demonstrate expertise. Rather, it is a different use of knowledge and expertise. It also might reflect a stance toward climate and circumstance: the wanderer is drawn by climatic changes, whereas the settler hunkers down and watches them pass.

Stanley Fish, for instance, might seem a protean critic, commenting on public as well as academic issues, but he has actually "hawked the same wares," as he once put it in an interview I conducted, returning to certain issues of interpretation as well as to the texts of John Milton over the course of his career. J. Hillis Miller, on the other hand, has morphed over a long career from a traditional commentator on Dickens and nineteenth-century British literature to phenomenological readings of modernist poets and novelists, then shifted again to become the primary American proponent of deconstruction, and more recently has taken on the role of defender of the humanities, ethics, and the future of literary studies.

While the difference between the two types might seem a conscious choice, it is probably more an expression of disposition. Settlers gravitate toward consistency and stability, looking for different facets of the same terrain, whereas wanderers are pulled toward the new and the next, finding the facets that motivate them in different terrain. It is perhaps a relation to time: Settlers are drawn to Parmenidean sameness, wanderers to the Heraclitean flux.

Terry Eagleton has been a quintessential wanderer. Eagleton is probably the best-known literary critic in Britain and the most frequently read expositor of literary theory in the world. His greatest influence in the United States has been through his deft surveys, variously on poststructuralist theory, Marxist criticism, the history of the public sphere, aesthetics, ideology, and postmodernism. His 1983 book *Literary Theory: An Introduction*, which made readable and even entertaining the new currents in theory and which has been reprinted nearly twenty times, was a text that almost every literature student thumbed through during the 1980s and 1990s, and it still holds a spot in the otherwise sparse criticism sections of the local Barnes & Noble. His public position in Britain is such that Prince Charles once deemed him "that dreadful Terry Eagleton." Not every literary theorist has received such notice.

In June 2006 there was a conference at the University of Manchester, where Eagleton was John Edward Taylor Professor of English Literature, in honor of Eagleton and taking stock of his prodigious work and career. I attended the conference—I was on a panel that questioned him, and I am responsible for his selection in *The Norton Anthology of Theory and Criticism*—looking for a handle to encapsulate his career, but instead found a kaleidoscope of themes, topics, and fields. The speakers at the conference remarked on his interest in Irish literature; his focus on aesthetic theory; his use of humor; his early engagement with French Marxism; his engagement with feminism; his forays in fiction and drama; his slide from theory to journalism; his path as a scholarship boy; his debunking of high culture; his criticism of postmodernism; and his playfulness. His work encompasses a carnival of themes.

Eagleton's wandering is not idiosyncratic, though, but presents a microcosm of the changes in criticism over the past forty years. Like Zelig or Forrest Gump, Eagleton seems to have been there at all the crucial moments. He began precociously during the 1960s, publishing three books in his twenties as a rising figure on the British New Left, particularly on the Catholic Left. Then he embraced French structuralist theory, bringing the dense theoretical edifice and idiom of the Marxist philosopher Louis

Althusser to Britain in *Criticism and Ideology* (1976), his one book not in plain language. After that, he became the primary expositor and popularizer of theory, in *Marxism and Literary Criticism* (1976), *Literary Theory* (1983), *The Function of Criticism* (1984), *The Ideology of the Aesthetic* (1990), and *Ideology: An Introduction* (1991). In his downtime, he also published a novel and several plays, notably *Saint Oscar* (1989), on Oscar Wilde, which was made into a film starring Stephen Rea. The play brilliantly channels Wilde's epigrammatic style, even though it only uses one actual quote from Wilde.

Through the 1990s he departed from his synoptic overviews to diagnose the fate of theory, and his diagnosis was not good. In *The Illusions of Postmodernism* (1997) and *The Idea of Culture* (2000) he excoriated the relativism and vacuity of identity politics, and in *After Theory* (2003) he recommended a return to Aristotle's view of ethics and to study of religion. He became an almost curmudgeonly gadfly, not as a radical reborn as a neoconservative but as an old radical bemoaning the misguidedness of the young.

One way to characterize Eagleton's later career is that, rather than a theorist, he took the more traditional position of man of letters, with books on Irish literature, the English novel, and tragedy, as well as his assessments of theory, and he has been a dauntingly prolific reviewer (many collected in *Figures of Dissent* [2000]). Eagleton's path might have something to do with the difference between the British and American scenes, the former still resisting academic professionalism and valuing the amateur, the latter adopting a more professionalized, academic bearing. (At the conference, most of the British critics simply talked, the virtue of which can be spontaneity and engagement with the audience, the deficit randomness and little scholarly anchoring, whereas the Americans read papers, the virtue of which can be a more thought-through argument, the deficit an arcane immersion.) The difference probably derives from the more permeable wall between academic and public in Britain, where Eagleton has written regularly for major newspapers like *The Guardian* and monthlies like the *London Review of Books*. There is still a prominent public sphere for literary criticism in Britain, whereas in the United States, despite the bruiting of the public intellectual, there is a wide chasm between the rarefied heights of the *New Yorker* and the small magazine.

Perhaps the most distinctive trait of Eagleton's work is his style. Rather than high academic ponderousness, it employs deft synopses and punchy polemics. Eagleton is a master of the one-liner, sometimes to encapsulate a difficult theory ("deconstruction is the death drive on the level of theory") and often to issue a devastating putdown ("Stanley Fish is the Donald Trump of American academia, a brash, noisy entrepreneur of the intellect"). In "The Politics of Style," an essay on Fredric Jameson, the leading Marxist critic in the United States, Eagleton observes that Jameson appropriates a wide range of philosophical thought, recombining them in a dense dialectical process. Eagleton likewise has a talent for covering a remarkable range, but he digests ideas in a centrifugal process, spinning out the husks from the kernels. Consequently, reading Jameson can be like reading Hegel or Adorno, whereas reading Eagleton is more like reading Anthony Lane, the virtuoso film reviewer for the *New Yorker*. You read their reviews to come upon cheeky lines as well as crisp summaries, and there have not been many jokes in the corpus of contemporary theory.

In "Why I Write," George Orwell distinguishes four primary motivations of a writer: ego, aesthetic appreciation, to record history, and politics. Orwell notes that any writer's motivations fluctuate and mix, but that he eventually chose to write for politics. Eagleton has obviously been motivated by socialist politics, consistently avowing them throughout his career. However, in his remarkably unrevealing memoir, *The Gatekeeper* (2001), he suggests a curious addition to Orwell's list: obsessiveness, almost to the degree of addiction. He confesses that he is almost embarrassed when he talks to colleagues who have difficulty writing: "Instead of finding myself unable to write books, I find myself unable to stop," and he muses that, "Perhaps there is somewhere in the world an Authors Anonymous, where the overproductive can gather discreetly in small supportive groups, able to declare without shame that they have just binged on a theoretical treatise or knocked off four essays in a row."

While one could see settlers as compulsively focused and wanderers as addicted to motion, the strange habit of writing is probably a disposition common to any successful literary critic or other scholar. It might arise from ambition and no doubt has an element of ego, but it is probably finally the habit, even on weekends or on sunny summer days, of unrelentingly putting words on paper or screen. There are better and worse ways to make use of one's habits, and the goal of a more just and equitable society seems like a good one.

FOURTEEN

From Cyborgs to Animals: Donna Haraway

If each decade has its symbolic creature, the 1980s was the Age of the Cyborg. The cyborg invaded our cultural imagination in the now-iconic film *The Terminator* (1984), William Gibson's novel *Neuromancer* (1984), and Donna J. Haraway's essay "A Cyborg Manifesto" (1985). The cyborg seemed to encapsulate advances in technology and biology, as PCs, artificial hearts, and other handy gadgets became widespread and permeated our lives. They were no longer alien to us but part of us.

Published in *Socialist Review* and mobilizing a wide range of theoretical references, Haraway's essay was an unlikely candidate to capture the zeitgeist. But it struck a chord, characterizing one aspect of postmodernism, of the world changing from nature to simulation and things to information. The essay became a touchstone in the heyday of literary theory, reprinted in a slew of anthologies and cited copiously. It also drew audiences outside academe, among them science fiction fans and writers, performance artists, and those who might peruse *Wired*.

In 2009 I interviewed Haraway at her home in Santa Cruz, California, to glean her reflections on "A Cyborg Manifesto" twenty-five years later, as well as to find out about her work since. About the manifesto she commented, "People read it like a Rorschach," sometimes seeing it as a celebration of technology, sometimes a fierce criticism. Like the cyborg, it was both, and not quite either.

The essay was motivated, as Haraway described it in our conversation, by "a kind of kneejerk, anti-technology, anti-science position in the left broadly, and in the feminist left in particular." Against a popular line of feminism that saw women as closer to nature than men, she recoded them as cyborgs. Haraway was trying to create a new myth: like Linda Hamilton in the second *Terminator* (1991), women could be pumped up, too, not by shedding technology but by using it. However, the essay was at the same time a criticism of "informatics," or the way that new technologies of communication work at the behest of capitalism and U.S. militarism.

The cyborg suggests a futuristic world, of silicon and software, so it might come as a surprise to those who know only the early essay that Haraway's work over the past decade has moved to the earthier world of animals. With *The Companion Species Manifesto: Dogs, People, and Significant Otherness* (2003) and *When Species Meet* (2008), she has become an influential figure in the developing field of animal studies. If her first manifesto stamped the Age of the Cyborg, her recent books mark the Age of the Animal.

Haraway's key idea is that animals are "companion species." This seems less provocative than the concept of cyborg, but it has some teeth: It rebuts the traditional Western view that man rightly has "dominion over the fish of the sea, and over the fowl of the air, and over the cattle" (Genesis 1:26). Haraway sees it the other way around: We are not kings in a great chain of being, but, in her parlance, we are all critters. This idea has a good deal of consequence in how we relate to and what we do with animals.

Though animals seem a long way from cyborgs, Haraway sees them as "in the same litter." "I think in ecologies [that] are always at least tri-part: humans, critters other than humans, and technologies," she explained, "In the cyborg work I foregrounded the technological dimensions of that triad, and in the current work I'm foregrounding the other organisms in the triad." Much of her writing examines concepts that we ordinarily think of as opposed, like organisms and machines or humans and animals, and shows how they interweave.

Deconstructing opposed categories is a familiar move in poststructuralist theory, but unlike that of most postmodern theorists, Haraway's work is grounded in science. She has a Ph.D. in biology from Yale, which she attended during the early 1970s on a National Defense Education Act fellowship. "I had an Irish-Catholic girl's brain and I became a national resource with Sputnik," she wryly remarked. "I wasn't a national resource before, then I was." She first trained to be an experimental biologist, but she admitted that, "I was never a good lab scientist. I killed most of my organisms through appalling errors; I moved too fast; I didn't have the patience;

I didn't have good hands." She also realized that she "was interested in biology as a deep cultural and historical phenomenon, and not fundamentally committed to doing it."

Leaving the lab, Haraway began her career teaching the history of science, which fed her research exploring the culture of biology and biologists. In the 1970s, she published important essays in the feminist journal *Signs* and elsewhere about the ways that science produces "situated knowledge" rather than objective knowledge, and her major study, *Primate Visions: Gender, Race, and Nature in the World of Modern Science* (1989), details the ways that primatologists project their gender, racial, and social views on the world of apes.

Haraway's training gives her a perspective different from many who do cultural studies of science. She is not an antagonist but avowed when we talked that "I love science. My Ph.D. is in biology—that means I've spent a lot of time in labs, with other organisms, and I know a lot of people who do science." While teaching at Johns Hopkins and elsewhere in the late 1970s, she also learned a lot about literary and critical theory, which was coming to the fore at the time. Unfortunately, though, she observed that the commerce between the two was usually lopsided: "I learned a whole lot more about semiotics and psychoanalysis than folks learned about biology. It was never quite symmetrical."

In popular discourse, it is often remarked that contemporary thinkers are "secular humanists." But actually, one perspective that theorists and scientists share is antihumanism, against "the notion that the proper study of mankind is man," as Haraway put it. "I've never been humanist; we live in a huge nonhuman world," and she shares with many biologists the sense "that the most fabulous thing about the world are the other critters." In her recent work, Haraway debunks what she calls "human exceptionalism."

Besides her formidable studies of biology, a personal circumstance prompted Haraway's recent work: getting a dog, Cayenne. As Haraway mused, "You know, what we do becomes what we write. Most of us start whatever we do from biographical accidents," and hers started a decade ago when she got "this puppy youngster who's just a dynamo, an amazingly talented athlete and who's taking training seriously, and I'm interested in doing sports at a serious level with a member of another species." They participate in agility competitions in California and environs.

An Australian shepherd, Cayenne is geared more toward tasks than other dogs. When I went to Haraway's house, Cayenne was more standoffish than most dogs; she didn't bother to nose at me, but lay at a distance from where we were talking. However, she revved up when Haraway did a few minutes of a complicated drill with her in the back yard.

Her experience with Cayenne has led Haraway to think more about the philosophical question of "how might an ethics and politics committed to the flourishing of significant otherness be learned from taking dog-human relationships seriously," as she writes in *The Companion Species Manifesto*. It has also led her to the cultural history of animals. "When you take things seriously and track them," she elaborated when we talked, "you track somebody like Cayenne into the history of eugenics, into the history of breed clubs, Nazi animal rights legislation . . . and the history of herding dogs and the post–gold rush transformation of California ranching ecologies," among other strands.

When I asked about the danger of indulgence in the turn toward autobiography, she clarified that "it's personal in a very impersonal sense too," insofar as "some weird biographical thing can turn out to be a world-historical phenomenon," like the question of animals, agriculture, and ecology now. She added, "Cheap food has been an imperial strategy since before Rome. Animals are at the heart of what's going on in the world today. So I think of animal studies as smack dab in the middle of things in the same way that" scientific research was during the Vietnam War, when she was a student and worked with a group called Science for the People.

A good deal of work in animal studies might be divided on the axis of theory and activism. Haraway, as she does with other dichotomies, tries to work between both poles. The theory side often dwells on concepts such as the nonhuman and draws on canonical figures in French theory, Jacques Derrida and Gilles Deleuze. While Haraway has affinities with this side, she also has reservations. When we spoke, she allowed that "Derrida did some wonderful stuff, but he doesn't start animal studies." And she quipped that, "Big name theorists lend a shiny cachet . . . that some people run with that makes me vaguely nauseous." Instead, her litmus test is if one is a "committed, on-the-ground animal person." She still considers herself a theorist, but said that her recent writing "is doing theory more in the vernacular," using stories, emails, and other informal elements.

Haraway has a more fraught relation to the activist side of animal studies, which focuses on animal rights and sometimes compares the killing of animals to a holocaust. She advocates the "flourishing of other animals" and criticizes "the animal-industrial complex," but she still eats meat and maintains, as she put it, a "continuing affirmation of the goodness of doing lab experiments with other organisms up to and including killing."

Similar to her argument about the cyborg, that the human does not represent some idyllic state before machines, she holds that we should not consider animals as inhabiting some idyllic state without humans. In her words, rather than seeing "domestic arrangements between human beings and other animals as always the imposition of human domination . . . the history of co-domestication is a multi-species phenomenon. It's not that we domesticated them and turned them into instruments for our ends, but these are co-evolutions of ourselves and other organisms we live with."

To deal with current agriculture and animals, she favors pragmatic measures, such as the organic farming in "central California agriculture scenes that I think deserve a future, like the pasture-raised chicken scene or the Churro sheep world." About research, she proposed: "You minimize laboratory animal experimentation, you minimize suffering, you substitute, you develop systems that don't require whole animals." Still, she was unabashed in adding, "That said, the engagement of human beings and technologies and other organisms in the projects of knowing I believe to be good, and I don't mean just because they cure diseases. I think curiosity is a precious and fragile and not very nice virtue." She retains her belief in the efficacy of science.

A tad bit defensively, Haraway carries the animal rights argument to its logical extreme, claiming that it would make modern agricultural animals either "museum specimens" or extinct, both of which she finds unacceptable. Still, she confesses that, "It's impossible to work off the fantasy that animals are for human use. I'm not comfortable, and I don't think we should be."

FIFTEEN

Intellectuals and Politics: Stefan Collini

We typically speak as if we choose our politics, but oftentimes politics chooses us. We might tick off a D or an R registering for an election, or we might declare in our academic work our position "as a Marxist" or "as a feminist" or "as a free marketer." But sometimes a situation confronts us, and our politics take shape in ways we might not have expected or predicted.

During the past few years, the British intellectual historian and critic Stefan Collini has been drawn into the thick of controversies over higher education in England. In 2010, the new Conservative-led government, headed by David Cameron, pushed through policies to replace public funding for postsecondary education with high fees, spurring student protests, alarm from faculty, and praise from conservative pundits. At the time, Collini wrote widely circulated pieces for the *London Review of Books* (*LRB*) and *The Guardian* criticizing the shortsightedness of those moves. With them and his subsequent trade book, *What Are Universities For?* (2012), he has become a major voice for the opposition, defending the need for public support of universities.

In England, as in many other European countries, higher education had traditionally been publicly financed, with minimal or no tuition fees, and it was, as Collini explained in an interview I conducted with him in January 2013, "a more centralized and uniform system than is in the United States." Even elite universities like Cambridge and Oxford are essentially public institutions and open to all through national examinations. Unlike the case in the United States, fees are regulated by government. "There were no fees until 1998, and very limited fees from 2006 onwards, but universities were still largely paid for out of public sources," Collini explained.

That quickly changed, however, after the election of 2010. Before the election, a committee, chaired by Lord Browne, the former chief executive of BP, had been commissioned with bipartisan support to propose reforms. Its main recommendation was to remove the cap on university tuition and allow institutions to assess their own rates. The new government largely accepted the Browne Report's recommendations, and the cap for fees jumped from £3000 to £9000, or from about $4,700 to $14,100—not extraordinary to American eyes, but a fundamental change to the British. Collini proceeded to dissect the problems with the plan, one being that it was an unusual if not shoddy process. Such committees customarily issue a policy paper that is then debated, but, Collini recounted, "the Browne committee and the future conservative government had exchanged views, shall we say," and simply put the policy in place. In other words, "the government had, without real public discussion, removed a large part of the public funding of the universities."

Another problem is that it's unclear whether the new system saves money. In fact, it might cost more. In Collini's analysis, the Browne Report was patently ideological, "fundamentally to make universities more responsive to so-called 'market forces.'" A further irony is that, though Conservatives had claimed the new policies would introduce price competition, almost all universities have raised their fees to the maximum, £9000.

Besides his criticisms, Collini has unapologetically defended the cultural and intellectual role of universities. As he remarked, "we shouldn't underestimate how much members of the general public outside universities expect intellectual matters to be what universities ought to explore." He added, even "people from the business world with whom I've spoken don't want the justification of the university to be given entirely in terms of the percentage points of the GDP"; rather, they "value the capacity to analyze and present a case, cultural awareness, the ability to write—all those things that are better formed by doing traditional academic subjects than the more narrowly vocational ones."

Collini's *LRB* essays went viral, circulated not only in England but also around the world, as other countries deal with similar pressures. Collini himself has mixed feelings about the response, remarking, "I can't say this has been an altogether enjoyable experience. It's a very rough-and-tumble world, in which accuracy in reporting play a small part and partisan affinities play a large part." Yet, he has also been encouraged and even moved, for instance when, after he gave a talk at a literary festival, "a man came up and asked me to sign copies of my book for his sons. He said, 'You give them hope.'"

While he himself was surprised at being catapulted into the political sphere, Collini's scholarly work has often focused on intellectuals and politics, illuminating figures such as John Stuart Mill, Matthew Arnold, T. S. Eliot, and Raymond Williams in books including *Public Moralists: Political Thought and Intellectual Life in Britain 1850–1930* (1991) and *Absent Minds: Intellectuals in Britain* (2006). Over the past two decades, he has also built a formidable body of work as an essayist and reviewer for the *LRB*, the *Times Literary Supplement* (*TLS*), *The Guardian*, and *The Nation*. He has become a leading literary and cultural critic in England.

Collini brings the tools of history to the field of critical writing. In this, he diverges from many of his generation—those born in the 1940s and receiving their doctorates in the 1970s—who embraced literary theory, and he explains a writer's views in the context of his or her time. For example, he begins his introduction to the Canto edition of C. P. Snow's "Two Cultures," an iconic essay about the division between the sciences and the humanities, with the story of Snow's 1959 lecture on the topic at Cambridge University, elaborating how Snow was responding to the scene there, particularly to the Cambridge critic F. R. Leavis and his advocacy of the primacy of literature, as well as to larger concerns in British culture, such as worries about the fracturing of knowledge that arose during the Romantic period and debates about literary education, notably between Thomas Huxley and Arnold, during the Victorian era. We usually take Snow to be talking simply about the contemporary research university, but Collini reconstructs the full intellectual network.

Though Collini turns to the more empirical ground of history over theory, he shares with critics of his generation a sensitivity to the difficulties of interpretation. As he emphasized in our conversation, "Once you start to unearth the history a bit more, what you see starts to become more variegated. The transmission of ideas is uneven and might have loops, bumps, gaps, intermissions or resumptions." It also usually differs from commonplace views, and Collini works to demythologize them. *Absent Minds*, for instance, counters "the feeling that, in the United States as in Britain, true intellectuals are to be found in some other culture, very often thought to be in France," as Collini put it to me. In fact, England has had a distinctive tradition of intellectuals, including modern philosophers like A. J. Ayer and writers like George Orwell, although what unifies the tradition might be questioning the very concept of the intellectual.

Edmund Wilson is frequently intoned in the United States as an exemplar of the public intellectual. In his influential 1987 book, *The Last Intellectuals*, Russell Jacoby claims that public intellectuals have waned with the rise of the suburbs and expansion of higher education, and independent figures like Wilson have gone extinct. Collini provides a different perspective in an essay in his book, *Common Reading: Critics, Historians, Publics* (2008), which starts with the sentence, "Edmund Wilson is an object of fantasy." He proceeds to show how Wilson was an old-fashioned man of letters even in his own time and had quirky, not always public interests. Moreover, he was out of fashion by midcentury, when much of his writing had gone out of print. He gained a second life only after publishers like Jason Epstein, who founded Anchor paperbacks in the 1950s, reprinted his earlier work. This suggests that the public intellectual is as much a product of the efforts of publishing as the aims of the critic.

I asked Collini his view of "the last intellectuals" argument, and he replied, "I am not a doomsayer who believes that there was a Golden Age or that intellectuals have come to an end." He added the corrective that most previous critics like T. S. Eliot were hardly public or popular; "at the time, it would have looked more like writing for minority audiences who were deeply unpopular." In fact, "the success that we think we find in earlier intellectuals is often a retroactive creation."

One could see Collini himself as a public intellectual, but when I mentioned that, he demurred: "I ought to start by saying that I am an academic and a scholar, and my life has been shaped by working in the university." He also observed, "I don't think we should kid ourselves that writing for the *TLS* or *LRB* is writing for some fictional 'general public.' It's a nonspecialized but still extremely sophisticated readership."

Perhaps the better distinction is the crossover critic. Many of the people we call public intellectuals are academics who occasionally cross over to more public arenas. Their skill is inhabiting both spheres, drawing from the well of the scholarly while talking in more commodious ways. It is tempting to see the public side as more genuine and less mannered, but Edmund Wilson himself, in "Thoughts on Being Bibliographed," offered the caveat that commercial magazines expect "fashions of the month or week and foster mechanical writing, rejecting original thinking "as the machines that make motor parts reject outsizes." Contrary to its maligned reputation, an academic location has the benefit of mitigating most venal pressures, as well as providing a knowledge base.

Another distinctive element that Collini brings to his writing is an ironic wit that makes us see a topic in a fresh light. For instance, he begins an essay: "25 June 2003 saw the centenary of the birth of the failed Hertfordshire grocer E. A. Blair." From that, he describes George Orwell's years as a small storeowner and dispels some of the myth about Orwell—he had a decent but modest reputation in his own time, and only much later became an icon emblazoned on T-shirts.

Collini's humor also came through in one of his rebuttals to the Browne Report in *The Guardian*. In parody, he reversed the current pecking order, saying that the government was defunding science and technology to "recognize that arts, humanities, and social sciences are essential to society's well-being." He also reasoned that, based on a consumer model, we should not need to subsidize fields such as science and technology; rather, it is only right that curricula be based on "the will of 18-year-olds" who might not want to study them. American criticism could use a little more of this kind of humor.

If one were to connect the dots, one might see Collini's career as a steady progress, as he has constructed a picture of British thought and criticism from the nineteenth century to the twentieth and moved from young scholar to Cambridge don who comments in the *TLS*. But Collini doesn't see it quite that way, offering, "Somebody reviewing *Absent Minds* said that it's clear, going all the way back to *Liberalism and Sociology* [his first book, appearing in 1979], that Collini had a master narrative of the rise of liberalism in mind. I don't recognize that in those books, but I'd also have to say, autobiographically, Collini had no very clear idea in his mind, certainly not any kind of 'master narrative.'"

He ventured that "an element of counter-suggestibility in my makeup" has informed his work. While many historians were talking about "history from below," he dealt with major figures, and while a number of British historians of his generation espoused Marxism, he kept his distance from "imposed group positions." Perhaps most strikingly, he moved away from the discipline of history, migrating to literature.

After Ph.D. work at Cambridge in the early 1970s, he wrote on and taught the history of social science at the University of Sussex, producing *Liberalism and Sociology: L. T. Hobhouse and Political Argument in England 1880–1914* as well as several other jointly written works. But he grew restless, finding that, "in many ways, my own strongest affinities and attractions were not to social and political thought but to literary and cultural criticism," and he moved to Cambridge in 1986 to take a position in the English department, where he has been since, rising from lecturer to professor.

A pivotal moment was writing *Matthew Arnold: A Critical Portrait* (1988; rev. ed. 2008) for Oxford University Press's "Past Masters" series, which marked his shift to literature as well as to a more crossover style. The series has a set format and provides accessible overviews, and "That meant that I had to write in a slightly less ploddingly scholarly manner than I had. I didn't have to write a footnote for everything I said and pin together quotations from sources. So it was liberating stylistically." Around that time he also started writing regularly for venues like *TLS*, and Collini stresses "a concern with engaging the reader, which a great many academic writers don't show much sign of."

Doing literary journalism, though, does not reflect a conversion, of the kind many American critics professed during the 1990s, when they renounced theory and embraced more personal or accessible writing. It is more of a symbiosis, and Collini remains rooted in history, for instance in his current research, which involves digging through the archives of Penguin Books to discern how their paperbacks shaped intellectual life in England after World War II.

The political climate in England also prompted a turn. Though he had protested the Vietnam War at one point, he recollected that "in my twenties I spent more of my time trying to understand late Victorian Britain than I did trying to understand my own contemporary political situation." However, "my own sense of political identity has grown since the 1980s," and "one of the things that sharpened it was the advent of Thatcherism." With the softened edges of memory, Thatcher has come to be a revered figure, but in her time she enjoined a good deal of controversy, as she worked to dismantle the welfare state. Her policies were responsible for some of the first cuts of public services, including higher education.

Collini himself had benefited from the postwar expansion of the welfare state. He grew up in the southern suburbs of London, "but I was not in a genteel family—both my parents struggled to a fairly fragile, lower middle-class level of prosperity," he told me. However, he did well on exams and "was a beneficiary of the very selective public education system in Britain at that time," going to Cambridge on scholarship.

He noted in our conversation that it was a historically unique situation: "I'm lucky in my generation; if I had been born fifteen or twenty years earlier, from my social background, I certainly wouldn't have had most of the opportunities that I have had." Similarly, he also acknowledged that, given the cuts enacted in the Thatcher (and Reagan) era, "if I'd been born fifteen or twenty years later, certainly in Britain, I think the road would have been much rockier in the lack of jobs and declining working conditions in universities."

This awareness motivates his current criticism of higher education policy in Britain. It is a truism that the personal is the political, but the political also arises from witnessing how such policies affect those around us, and those who come after us.

SIXTEEN

The Editor as Broker: Gordon Hutner

Editors work behind the scenes. They set up the show but rarely get to take the bow. They fill a variety of roles that make writing possible—like a producer, they might put together the funding and build the institutional structures; like a director, they might make the choices that shape the show; like an agent, they might promote particular authors; like a script doctor, they might improve the text; and like a stagehand, they might do the grunt work on the sets on which the actors play.

Yet, if you look at accounts of contemporary criticism, you rarely find their names. Though contemporary scholars have looked at "history from below," those of us in literary studies still tend to see criticism in terms of marquee figures rather than the range of people who work in the field. But a critic is not self-made.

Gordon Hutner has been one of the most influential editors of his generation, founding and editing the journal *American Literary History* (*ALH*), which has stamped the direction of work in the field since 1989. As it approached its twenty-fifth anniversary, I interviewed Hutner in June 2012 to ask about *ALH*, as well as about his own scholarship on twentieth- and twenty-first-century American fiction.

Editing is "the lifeblood of the profession," Hutner had noted in an essay on academic publishing. Against the top-down view of academic work, he also pointed out that tasks like putting out new editions, compiling anthologies, and editing journals, among other things, "matter to members of the professoriate as much as, if not more than, writing thesis-length books," which are otherwise the standard of measure. In our interview, I asked Hutner how he would define the role of the editor in a nutshell, and he replied, "a broker, who tries to bring forward and promote what she or he thinks of as the best examples of the most important new scholarship and criticism." The editor's aim is not to advocate one tendency or standpoint, but to seek essays that "depart from prevailing wisdom." They might cover "a new area that's worth tracking or offer a grand crystallization" of an established topic, and they should look outward, opening "a subfield up to readers outside the subfield."

That particularly applies to *ALH*, which is responsible for a broad field, and under Hutner's eye it has provided a forum for the main critical initiatives of the past two decades, such as the New Historicism, which turned from a focus on form to the social and cultural context of American literature, and it has pointed to new critical directions, such as queer theory and ecocriticism, and new topics, including print culture and globalization. The journal has also captured a wide-angle view of American literature, from Columbus and the diversity of the Americas to "Twenty-first Century Fiction." (Although only a part-time Americanist, I should say that I have published two essays in *ALH*.)

One of its strengths is that *ALH* has drafted several generations of critics, and Hutner takes pride in the number of graduate students or early assistant professors he has ushered into print. As he affirmed, "It's been one of the happier happenstances that so many people who turned out to have pretty darn good careers published either first or early on in *ALH*. And it still happens."

Hutner started *American Literary History* in an inhospitable time. A great number of literary journals were founded in the 1960s, and a wave of journals focusing on literary theory were founded in the 1970s, but by the 1980s funds were scarce and journals plentiful. Still, Hutner, then an assistant professor at the University of Wisconsin, was convinced that there was a need because the standard bearer in the field, *American Literature*, "was not seizing the opportunities in front of it and was too hidebound." "The field seemed to me wide open," he told me.

A new generation was taking the helm, with New Historicists like Walter Benn Michaels reorienting our understanding of the political effect of late nineteenth-century American fiction, feminist critics like Jane Tompkins recovering a rich history of sentimental writers, and African Americanists like Kenneth Warren revising our understanding of realism's relation to racism. While this generation arose from the ferment of literary theory, *American Literature*, founded in 1929, was publishing staid articles about

"Thoreau's Moon Mythology," "Henry James's Rewriting of Minny Temple's Letters," and "Horizontal and Vertical Movement in Robert Frost's *Mountain Interval*," to cite three examples from 1986.

A year abroad provided a catalyst. Hutner spent 1985–86 in Belgium on a Fulbright. "When you're there, you're responsible for summarizing what's happening in American literary studies," rather than just one's specialty, he recounted. At the same time, "being away for a year, I was able to look with some detachment at what was going on," and thus when he came back he had a plan in mind for a journal that would, "above all, publish things that were fresh."

Returning to Wisconsin, "I tried to talk my colleagues into forming a collective," Hutner recalled, "but people were reluctant to give up their own scholarly agendas, though everyone was willing to support me." Serendipitously, a friend told him that Oxford University Press was looking to acquire journals. Oxford took what Hutner called "a modest financial chance on it," though he demurred when I asked him the amount: "Let's just say that I would have been better off teaching summer school if I was looking for remuneration."

Hutner had a head start because, while he was in graduate school at the University of Virginia during the late 1970s and early 1980s, he had worked for six years as an editorial assistant on *New Literary History* (*NLH*), a preeminent theory journal. There he absorbed the lessons of Ralph Cohen, who had founded *NLH* in 1969 and would edit it for forty years. Cohen was not, in Hutner's words, "trying to forward a particular agenda," but wanted "people to see what else is going on," and he was especially good at showcasing a wide tableau of methods, from Marxism and feminism to medievalism and Prague semiotics. The experience, Hutner reported, "solidified my temperamental disinclination against monism."

The key difference from *NLH* is probably the position of theory. A major function of *NLH* was to introduce international developments of theory, whereas *ALH*, appearing after the foment of theory and centered on a literary field, has provided a forum more for the reinvigorated literary history of recent generations. As Hutner averred, "there is a lot of literary history still to write."

Hutner himself has been rewriting the history of American fiction, notably in his book, *What America Read: Taste, Class, and the Novel, 1920–1960* (2009), which covers not only modernists like Faulkner but a great many other writers, like Joseph Hergesheimer and James Branch Cabell, who were considered among the best writers of the 1920s and 1930s but have since been forgotten, largely because they represent middle-class taste, Hutner surmised. "We were writing literary history from an extremely limited, partial shelf, based on very, very few books," and the resulting "history that looks at five novels spread out over fifty years seems contrived."

In some respects, Hutner's approach aligns with a new critical movement to study the large mass of novels produced. Most notably, Franco Moretti, a founder of the Stanford Literary Lab, has drawn on quantitative and other means to account for three centuries of novels published around the globe. For *What America Read*, Hutner adopted a hybrid method, surveying more than fifty books per decade but also giving short readings of some of them.

That approach is probably less controversial than difficult to emulate, since it takes a great deal of labor to filter an inventory of several hundred novels. Hutner reported that it took him more than a decade to research *What America Read*, his second book. He observed that that would not be possible for a junior professor doing a first book; first books are typically based on readings to demonstrate a basic interpretive skill considered fundamental to professional criticism. But real innovation often occurs with second books, when one is freed from such pressures and can make "a new step or explore a new direction," Hutner reflected.

More recently, Hutner has extended his research to "twenty-first century fiction." To do *What America Read*, he combed through magazines and newspapers for reviews; for his new project, he found there is a less coherent review culture, so instead he is looking at winners of the main literary prizes, like the Pulitzer or National Book Award. He has ascertained a list of 125 novels, such as Richard Russo's *Empire Falls* (2001) and Jennifer Egan's *A Visit from the Goon Squad* (2010), that seem to form the main body of works of the period thus far.

His approach again gives us a fuller sense of literary history than the one that we usually purvey in academe. "The novels about which contemporary scholars fall all over themselves didn't win any major prizes," Hutner quipped, and we too rarely talk about books such as Anne Tyler's *The Accidental Tourist* (1985), which won a National Book Critics Circle award and was a finalist for the Pulitzer. In a recent exchange in *ALH*, he argued even more pointedly: "literary academe has failed miserably, almost completely, in the one extramural mission entrusted to it that it might have been able to sustain: the creation of a book-reading, book-buying public. Instead, academe disdained the assignment." Still, Hutner finds hope in critics taking a renewed public role: "Scrutinizing the writing of our day, we might even have something to say to the populace—not to mention our students—about the books of their time instead of leaving it to Oprah, for then we would be producing readers, not just consumers."

It is inevitable that changes in media come up in talking about publishing, and Hutner sees its virtues as well as problems. He conjectured that projects like special issues are less viable: "With the Internet, people don't read the whole issue so they don't see how they build some kind of narrative, but just click on the one that seems most interesting to them." On the other hand, he thinks that new media might revitalize reviewing. For *ALH*, he has long featured "essay reviews" to cover new and significant directions in the field. But he calls for "an online magazine that reviews all our books." Otherwise, "The sad truth is that as a profession we don't do a good job brokering the new scholarship."

Even after twenty-four years, he has not slowed in his brokering. It is still "my job to scour conferences and the like looking for people who are doing things that are a little bit different, and keeping the journal supple in that way." When I asked how much longer he thought he'd do the journal, he acknowledged that, "My study of journals suggests that most of them have a trajectory of around thirty years"—with exceptions like *NLH*. He welcomes new journals, saying "it's time for somebody else to get started and surpass us." But, he added, "we will not go quietly."

SEVENTEEN

Gaga Feminism: Judith "Jack" Halberstam

Masculinity has a bad reputation. It is not entirely undeserved, and the strength of feminist criticism, especially as it arose in the 1970s and 1980s, was pointing out the masculine bias of our society and its cultural artifacts, such as literature. So it was something of a surprise when, in the late 1990s, Judith "Jack" Halberstam resuscitated masculinity. It was not the usual idea of masculinity, however: It was what she termed, in the title of her 1998 book, "female masculinity." It turned to an aspect of gender that had been largely ignored in both feminism and queer studies, and Halberstam represents a second generation of queer theory, underscoring the transitive nature of gender, or "transgender."

In January 2011, escaping the bustle of the annual Modern Language Association convention in Los Angeles, I interviewed Halberstam to ask how she came to do this kind of work. Part of her motivation was familiar to most scholars: She wanted to correct customary thinking in the field. "There was a gaping hole in feminism. One subject for whom feminism has always had a hard time speaking is the masculine woman," she recounted. It "fell out of the universalizing category that feminism assumed." Moreover, talk about masculinity did not usually "extend beyond the boundaries of maleness." Even after the advent of queer theory in the early 1990s, according to Halberstam, the masculine woman was considered "abhorrent and pathological," a "real taboo" among feminists and a figure that "grossed out and threatened" most men.

Halberstam is not an unconditional proponent of masculinity—she noted that "it can be a bit toxic" and excoriated the "laddish culture" of the middle part of England, where she grew up—but she pointed out that it makes sense that women would want to adopt masculinity: "In a male-dominated society, masculinity has a lot of value, and a lot of the really fun activities get allocated to men. That's where the action is, so I think it's a lot easier to explain girls' and women's attraction to masculinity than it is to explain male attraction to femininity in a culture that devalues femininity."

Another element of her motivation was personal. As she writes in *Female Masculinity*, "For a large part of my life, I have been stigmatized by a masculinity that marked me as ambiguous and illegible. Like many other tomboys, I was mistaken for a boy throughout my childhood, and like many other tomboy adolescents, I was forced into some semblance of femininity for my teenage years." She seeks to remedy this and "make masculinity safe for women and girls."

Even in her adult life, Halberstam sometimes faces that stigma, and in *Female Masculinity* she tells a story about going into a women's room at the Minneapolis airport when two guards banged on her stall door. (They retreated when they heard her voice, which is almost fluty at points, with a soft British accent.) With this anecdote, she encapsulates the issue of gender as "the bathroom problem." Though we consider ourselves to have made progress about gender and sexuality, there are still only two public categories to which one can belong. Halberstam's work aims to remedy "the bathroom problem," so that we might recognize not only men and women but also the various genders that people actually have.

A fundamental insight of feminism was that gender is not the result of nature, indelible and given; rather, it is the result of culture and history. Although this seems like an old saw now, it was a discovery that shook the world, both inside and outside academe.

If the era from the late 1960s through the 1970s saw "the rise of gender," in the words of one history of feminist criticism, the 1990s saw, in the title of Judith Butler's landmark book, "gender trouble." Black, postcolonial, and gay and lesbian scholars, among others, criticized the limitations of feminism, charging it with speaking largely for white, middle class, heterosexual women. Butler's insight was to understand gender as a performance. Whether gender was constructed or natural, it implied a given content; a performance suggested a temporal act. Butler's prime example was the drag queen, who emphasized the way in which gender was posed and the way it deconstructed.

The deconstruction of gender precipitated a shift from feminism and gay and lesbian studies to queer studies. The category of gender seemed inadequate, issuing identities, whether straight or gay; the category of sexuality became more central through the 1990s, indicating practices and suggesting the instability of identities. A heterosexual person, after all, might perform queer acts, and queer theory influenced several fields in this period. Queer became a new way to see culture.

Halberstam works in queer theory, focusing, for instance, on drag king culture and the way in which it complicates notions of gender and sex. But she also returns to gender, asserting in her contribution to *Keywords for American Cultural Studies* that "we are not quite ready to do away with gender" because "socially sedimented categories are hard to erase, and efforts to do so often have more toxic effects than the decision to inhabit them." She also diverges from much queer theory in her style, which is refreshingly direct, and her archive, which encompasses popular films and cartoons like *The Fabulous Mr. Fox* as well as literary works like Radclyffe Hall's 1934 *Well of Loneliness*.

In our interview, Halberstam acknowledged Butler's work, which she said displaced "the confessional feminist politics I was surrounded by" in graduate school at the University of Minnesota in the late 1980s and "opened up a lot of doors intellectually." But she also made a point of saying that *Gender Trouble* was not the only book to complicate womanhood, and in particular she praised Esther Newton's *Mother Camp: Female Impersonators in America*, a 1972 ethnography of drag queens. Halberstam held up Newton as a model, commenting that her "work on queer issues didn't do her any favors in her career. She spent her whole career at SUNY–Purchase and never had grad students, yet she minted people like me and countless others in the profession, in an act of completely selfless generosity. I think, in the contemporary scene of academia, that's a dying art. People are driven by their own concerns and their own careers." She added, "I learned from Esther not to write things just to get a certain kind of critical acclaim, but to stick to projects you think are important and then to turn around and try to hold the door open for other people."

Like many people in her (and my) academic generation, who received graduate training in literature in the late 1980s and got their first jobs in the early 1990s, Halberstam is versed in postmodern theory, but she also seeks to reach a wider public audience. (I have called this the "posttheory genera-tion," arising in the wake of high theory and pinched by shrinking jobs, as well as the culture wars.) As she put it, "A lot of academia is about talking to each other, but I always like to have another kind of audience as well. I think we have to work in both directions," academic and public. She recognizes the value of "doing the difficult work of turning commonsensical ideas into something unfamiliar," but "there's something snotty and elitist about the idea that bringing something forward in an accessible way is less valuable."

In our interview, Halberstam criticized the sometimes self-involved stance of academic work, remarking, "I'm often at talks where people seem oblivious whether you're awake or not. They're just in their own little world, and that version of academia doesn't appeal to me." She offered this quick ethnographic analysis: "Academia is full of people who were the nerdy kids in class, who did all of their homework and aced all their exams," retorting, "Well, that's not me. I'm not worried about always being the smartest person in the room." In fact, she first came to the United States because she had failed her qualifying exams in Britain, and her father, a math professor, had just moved to the University of Illinois at Urbana–Champaign, so she enrolled there for a year, eventually transferring to the University of California at Berkeley for her undergraduate degree, which she finished in 1985.

In *The Queer Art of Failure* (2011), Halberstam calls her approach "low theory." She draws the phrase from a founder of cultural studies, Stuart Hall, who rebuts a prominent line of Marxist thinking that describes social structures at a high level of theoretical abstraction and eschews individual phenomena as empiricism. Hall, according to Halberstam, "says you can't shoot too low if you're a committed intellectual." Rather, we should be engaged with people on the ground, and a major element of Halberstam's work has been looking at subcultures like drag kings in a book she collabo-rated on with the photographer Del LaGrace Volcano, *The Drag King Book* (1999), as well as in a collection of her essays, *In a Queer Time and Place: Transgender Bodies, Subcultural Lives* (2005).

Another dimension of low theory is discussing films like *Chicken Run* or *Dude, Where's My Car?* She calls this her "silly archive," and remarks about humor that "I wish I could read more of it in academia." It is not frivolous, because "the smile that you sometimes bring up is both humor and recogni-tion, and humor can be quite good at bringing up that kind of recognition."

There is a downside to low theory and accessibility. Halberstam has been criticized for what some say are simplistic pronouncements, but she hasn't been put off. "I've developed a reputation for speaking my mind or being too blunt. It's a way to make enemies in the profession," she said, "but if you're not making enemies, you're trying too hard to please."

Halberstam's bluntness stirred up a controversy that reached the pages of *Harper's Magazine* in the fall of 2010. In an article called "American Electra," Susan Faludi, reporting on the state of feminism, found a divisive struggle between generations of women that she termed "ritual matricide." One piece of evidence was a conference she attended at the New School at which Halberstam also spoke, and she used Halberstam as a prime example of the flaws of "theoretical and consumer-saturated academic feminism," because Halberstam held that "pop stars are where the inspiration for feminism is going to come from," in Faludi's rendering.

Halberstam filled out the story. After hearing complaints about younger feminists, she tried to connect with the largely undergraduate audience, many of whom were not familiar with older versions of feminism, so "I said, 'Well, here's a fresh breeze with Lady Gaga.' That gets turned into 'Lady Gaga feminism' and parodied in her article as me saying, 'Forget about real life politics, just listen to Lady Gaga, have a little pleasure, and relax.'" In contrast, Halberstam's point was that the performer has progressive sexual politics and often uses her platform to advocate for gay and transsexual rights.

The problem, for Halberstam, is not simply that Faludi missed those nuances, but that she resorted "to beating a dead horse, suggesting that feminism is driven by mother/daughter tensions and that the daughters haven't taken the lessons of their mothers seriously." Instead, Halberstam observed that "Mother/daughter relationships, because we live in a male-dominated society, are notoriously conflictual, laden with negativity, and never have been a good model for feminism. You only have to see *Black Swan* to see the toxicity of that bond. There are a lot of tensions built into mother/daughter dynamics particular to coming of age in societies that are built around demands on femininity that are impossible to meet. The mother becomes the place where those demands are vocalized, so the daughter has to hate her. So my point was, let's get rid of this old chestnut of the mother/daughter relation!"

Halberstam responded to Faludi's argument on a blog to which she regularly contributes, bullybloggers, and is now finishing a book for Beacon Press called *Gaga Feminism: Sex, Gender, and the End of Normal*. It meets Faludi's charge head on, using Lady Gaga as a mascot for new sex and gender models in the information age. Finally, though, rather than anger, Halberstam expresses disappointment about the affair, recognizing that "Faludi has written two very good books—*Backlash* was excellent, *Stiffed* was excellent—so I was super excited that she was going to be at that conference. But she didn't do herself any favors in that piece."

There is a classic essay of feminist theory called "The Sex Which Is Not One." Halberstam's insight is that gender is not one, nor two, but multiple. She herself, though given the name Judith, also goes by the nickname "Jack." It is a litmus test of what you think about gender if you call Halberstam her or him.

EIGHTEEN

Book Angst

Scholarly books seem planned, rational enterprises, but they are often ad hoc productions, arising accidentally and not always going according to design. They also induce mixed reactions from their authors, and how their authors feel about them might diverge widely from how those books are received. An author might favor his first book over his next twenty, or the offbeat one that got little notice.

The analogy to children is inescapable, memorably expressed in early American literature by Anne Bradstreet in "The Author to Her Book" (1678), her reflections on her first published, which begins "Thou ill-form'd offspring of my feeble brain," and goes on to talk about how it is a ragged, "rambling brat" whose "Visage was so irksome in my sight," though she relents, saying "Yet being mine own, at length affection would/Thy blemishes amend, if so I could."

In a long-standing series of interviews I have conducted with literary and cultural critics, it would sometimes surprise me when a critic would remark that her favorite book was not the one everyone would associate with her name, but one that received much less attention. Or he wondered about the book he did not write. Or she told the strange path a book traveled to come into being.

For instance, when I talked to M. H. Abrams, a luminary in literary studies, he made sure to say that his book *The Mirror and the Lamp: Romantic Theory and the Critical Tradition* (1953) was not his best. Which was a surprise, since it was a standard citation for fifty years and had been voted 23 in the Top 100 nonfiction books of the twentieth century, no small achievement for an academic book with copious footnotes from a university press. But he coyly remarked, "Just between you and me, *Natural Supernaturalism:*

Tradition and Revolution in Romantic Literature (1973) is a more important book." He had no idea that *The Mirror and the Lamp*, which stemmed from his dissertation, would have such success, although he did add that he rewrote it several times to get it right.

Sometimes reception can be less kind, seemingly missing the point. The feminist critic Nancy K. Miller is well known for her work on autobiographical criticism, stamping the trend in her 1991 Routledge book, *Getting Personal: Feminist Occasions and Other Autobiographical Acts*. But she thought that her subsequent *Bequest and Betrayal: Memoirs of a Parent's Death* (1996) was really her best book. It combines scholarship on autobiography and writing about her own life and is fuller and more sustained than *Getting Personal*, but it seemed to fall between the cracks, between those who read academic criticism and those who look for heartfelt memoir, rather than drawing both. She recalled, "I would give the book to friends who weren't academics and they'd say, 'I have to confess, I only read the [autobiographical] parts in italics.' I thought, 'Oh god, I worked so hard to get the italic parts to work with the critical parts.'" But, she surmised, "everybody has one book that they've done that they feel never really caught on or has been misunderstood, but it was their favorite."

Sometimes, as with children or lovers, a first book takes on added significance. J. Hillis Miller has had an illustrious career, publishing over thirty books and acting as the chief American proponent of deconstruction, but when I talked with him he hesitated for a moment about his first book, *Charles Dickens: The World of His Novels* (1958). I had remarked that I was impressed with how it gave an overview of Dickens's career, a much different approach from his later deconstructive interpretations that focus on the ways in which texts do not cohere. He paused and murmured that his wife in fact thought it was his best, and that he wondered if it was true.

Another thread in the interviews is how books come about by luck as much as pluck. Walter Benn Michaels's first book, *The Gold Standard and the Logic of Naturalism* (1988), is often taken to lead a generation of "New Americanist" interpretations of American literature. But Michaels reported that the book came together entirely by accident. He had already achieved tenure at Berkeley on the basis of several articles (oh, bygone days), so he was not in the usual rush for a book, and most of his publications were about theory. But he had written several essays on American literature, he was teaching it, and his colleague, Stephen Greenblatt, who was editing a book series on the "New Historicism," encouraged him to put together his essays for it. At first, Michaels recounted, "I said no; I had no interest in a book," but Greenblatt persisted, and "I had just started seeing some photography that I really admired by Jim Welling, and I thought if the press would give me a thousand dollars to commission a cover, I would write Welling to see if he would do it. I thought that it would be very cool to have a book with a cover that was a piece of art. So they did, and he did, and I did."

Hindsight can have a bite as well, and sometimes people wonder about the books they didn't write. When I interviewed Jonathan Culler, a leading expositor of French theory and author of the bestselling *Literary Theory: A Very Short Introduction* (1997), I commented that I thought his essay "Literary Criticism and the American University," which opens his book *Framing the Sign: Criticism and Its Institutions* (1988), was the best short account of the institutional history of criticism. He looked toward the ceiling and mused, "Perhaps it was a vein I should have pursued." I replied that he still might.

Judith "Jack" Halberstam, who is an influential figure in queer theory, provided a sobering thought about our book-based culture in the humanities. She talked about the ephemerality of academic work and how we often have a false idea that we write for the ages when we actually write for a few years, if that. Still, looking back on her signature book, *Female Masculinity* (1998), she granted, "I'm happy that it has endured," although she added that time sometimes dulls the effect of a book, observing that, "some people now see it as pointing out the obvious, when it wasn't like that in the '90s." She also recalled working over her first book, *Skin Shows: Gothic Horror and the Technology of Monsters* (1995), and thought the work was worth it: "It's a book I remain fond of. There are essays I've written where I think, 'maybe I should have held onto that a bit longer,' but I don't think it's a terrible book."

Sometimes there is a kind of book karma. That is, writers correct the mistakes of their last book in their next. Wayne Koestenbaum, a well-known figure in queer theory as well as a poet and art critic, told me this story about his first book, *Double Talk: The Erotics of Male Literary Collaboration* (1989): "When it arrived at my apartment and I opened it and saw the cover, I thought, 'This is so great, I wish it were a novel.' I wanted the same cover but different contents." (The cover has a photograph by George Platt Lynes depicting a nude male with a baby carried in his thigh.) So he proceeded to write different kinds of critical books, from *The Queen's Throat: Opera, Homosexuality, and the Mystery of Desire* (1993) through *Andy Warhol* (2001) up to his recent *Humiliation* (2011). The first version of *The Queen's Throat* was "twice as long and had footnotes," but he dropped the notes and "cut out all the transitions [and] rewrote the whole book as fragments, adding the personal stuff." He decided that he would not be bound by academic conventions because "I wanted to write a book that I could be really happy with and that would make me feel whole as a human being. That sounds corny, but it's true." When I asked whether that required a privileged position to do, he responded with what I find good advice: "The basic privilege to write about what you want, in the style you choose, is anyone's privilege. The doing of it may not be easy, but the amount of compromises that writers and academics unnecessarily make in the name of prudence is another matter altogether."

PART THREE

The Predicament of the University

If you work in a college or university or if you just read the newspapers, you cannot escape the impression that higher education is going to hell in a handbasket. In other sections I talk about the influence of the American university on criticism and critics—how it has enabled and limited their work, how it has shaped criticism, and how it has made it "academic"—but in this section I focus directly on higher education, on its current troubles and also on our cultural imagination of it in fiction and film.

When I was in graduate school, I thought that the university was a boring topic, like talking about a sports arena rather than the sports that went on inside. I have become much more aware of the university as I have worked in it, of how it is perhaps the central social institution of our time, and how it is a place of work as well as a place of the humanistic ideal of learning. Over the past few decades, as the university has been subject to corporatization, it seems that its humanistic bearing has slipped away. No longer is it a prime institution of the welfare state, providing a public service to the citizenry for a minimal fee, but it has become a prime institution of the neoliberal state, a pay-as-you-go consumer enterprise. Neoliberalism seems like a distant abstraction, but practices like the casualization of professorial labor and the enlistment of students into debt are neoliberalism in action.

The first two essays present my analyses of student debt. Initially appearing in *Dissent* magazine in 2006 and 2008, they stem from my experiences, taking on student debt in the privatized 1980s, when I was in graduate school, and not paying it off until 2008, after working as a professor for nearly twenty years. But my case is not the worst of it—it makes my humanistic and social democratic hairs bristle to see my students and those coming after me bound by debt, with little choice. It hardly represents the best hope of the university, nor of our democratic possibilities.

The next two essays, "The Academic Devolution" and "The Neoliberal Bias," flesh out the turn toward neoliberalism, and the subsequent essays sketch the way that the shifts in higher education have made their way into our cultural imagination. I talk about the trend of novels and films that feature the depressing conditions of academic labor, and in the final essay I present one solution, albeit with a touch of satire.

My focus is largely on the humanities and liberal arts, but many of the policies and practices I examine affect all of campus. Student debt is unfortunately a cloud that covers at least two generations of Americans, and counting.

NINETEEN

The Pedagogy of Debt

I wrote the first version of this essay in the summer of 2005 and retain its original opening because it recounts my personal experience of student debt. Even though I have since paid the debt off—after twenty years and only the week before I turned 50—I thought it worthwhile to include because it's the only place where I tell my own story, and also to lend some longitudinal perspective. Particularly after the Occupy movement, it sometimes seems as if the problem of student debt arose after the financial crisis of 2007–2008. Not true—its precipitous rise began in the 1980s and has cast its shadow over a great many collegians along the way.

Otherwise, I have updated the statistics where possible and made various revisions. As an epilogue, I still do not own a house—my down payment went to the immaterial property of my daughter's education and my own—but I have been able to travel overseas since then. My daughter left independent film to take a job at the Museum of Natural History, which is more secure and has better benefits.

I am a statistic. I am one of more than 35,000,000 Americans on the rolls of student debt. Every month I write out a check for $660 to Sallie Mae. I simply abbreviate the entry in my checkbook as SM. It hurts.

At forty-six and fifteen years out of grad school, I still owe around $9,000 from my guaranteed student loans (GSLs)—I could not afford to pay them at first, so I took the maximum four years of forbearance and began paying them in 1994. Now I also owe PLUS loans for my daughter's undergraduate education, making a combined total of $34,000, for a payment of $660 a month for the next ten years. Besides that, my daughter, who graduated in 2002, herself owes about $25,000.

Confession, memoir, and autobiography have been common in literary criticism over the past decade, but despite all the various kinds of self-exposure people make, from sleeping with one's professors to secretly devouring romances, this is not the kind of thing people usually talk about. Contrary to reputation, it is not sex that is the great forbidden; people talk about sex all the time. Rather, the forbidden is to talk about money. In the quintessentially middle-class precincts of academe, people don't descend to speak of breadbasket issues like salary and debt. It's crass, like clipping coupons. And it's shameful, reflecting your failing—you must have done something wrong, or you're not good enough to make more money.

But I think we need to talk about student debt, especially now, because it has increased so precipitously. We need to talk about it if we care about higher education, as well as about the rising majority that is subject to it. Especially if you're a professor, we need to talk about it because it affects so many of those in the classroom seats in front of us. It is in fact the new paradigm of college funding. Consequently student debt is, or will soon be, the new paradigm of early to middle adult life. Gone are the days when the state university was as cheap as a laptop and considered a right, like secondary education. Now higher education is, like most social services, a largely privatized venture, and loans are the chief way that a majority of individuals pay for it.

Debt is not just a check every month but colors the day-to-day experience of my life, whether I live in a smaller or larger apartment, whether I can buy a house (not yet), whether I can travel to Europe (not since I was an undergraduate), or whether I can eat out (too often, considering the debt). My bill to the company store has almost ended, but it is just beginning for most of my students, and they owe far more than I did.

Debt surely tones the experience of my daughter's life. She has a job in film in New York, but it only pays about $20,000 a year. As a single parent, I am proud to subject my friends to videos where you can see her name in the credits, but, as anyone familiar with New York real estate knows, her take-home barely pays half the rent for a small apartment. The owners of the film company tell her that she is paid partly in credits, and I console her that it's better than grad school (same pay but more interesting). But it determines the texture of her life, whether she can have a slice of pizza, a pack of Ramen, or a proper meal for dinner, and how long she can wait before she goes to the doctor when a sore throat feels like strep.

To be sure, my particular circumstances are anomalous compared to most of my colleagues, who have children at a later age and might have two incomes. Still, I was relatively lucky in the great academic job lottery, and as a full professor I make a decent salary, $25,000 above the mean for American families of four. Hailing from the working classes, I've made it, attaining the gold of a professional perch. But this is the American dream?

Over the past decade, there has been an avalanche of criticism of the "corporatization" of the university. Most of it focuses on the impact of corporate protocols on research, the reconfiguration of the relative power of administration and faculty, and the casualization of academic labor, but little of it has addressed student debt. Because more than half the students attending university receive, along with their B.A. or B.S. degrees, a sizeable loan payment book, we need to deal with student debt.

———

The average undergraduate federal student loan debt for a graduating senior in 2012, one can extrapolate from current data, will be $27,840 (figures come from the NCES, or National Center of Education Statistics of the U.S. Department of Education, and there is lag of a few years in their tabulation). It was a relatively modest $2,000 in 1982 ($4,650 in 2012 dollars), but began its phenomenal ascent during the Reagan years, when unsecured loans were deregulated, to reach $9,200 in 1992 (about $14,500 adjusted to 2012 dollars) and $18,900 in 2002 ($24,050 in 2012), and two out of three American students have it. If one adds personal charge card debt, which averaged $4,100 in 2008, those two-thirds receive not only a diploma but also a payment book for about $32,000. Also consider that many students have significantly more than the median—in 2008, 25 percent of federal borrowers had over $30,000 in student loans and 14 percent over $40,000 (these 2008 figures come from the 2010 National Postsecondary Student Aid Study from NCES). On top of that, many students take private loans in addition to federal ones, and they have ballooned since 1996, when 1 percent took them, to 14 percent in 2008, and which total over $17 billon in 2008, a disturbingly large portion *in addition to* the $68.6 billion for federal loans that year. Moreover, also consider that the mountain of debt does not stop with a bachelor's degree but, for over 60 percent of those continuing their educations, adds about $25,000 for those with a master's, $52,000 for doctorates, and $80,000 for professional degrees in 2008. Last, bear in mind that this does not include the debt that parents take on to send their children to college, whether through programs such as federal PLUS loans or through home refinancing and other personal loans.

Federal student loans are a relatively new invention. The GSL program began only in 1965, a branch of Lyndon B. Johnson's "Great Society" programs intended to provide supplemental aid to students who otherwise could not attend college or would have had to work excessively while in school. In its first dozen years, the amounts borrowed were comparatively small, in large part because college was comparatively inexpensive, especially at public universities. From 1965 to 1978, the program was a modest one, issuing about $12 billion *in total*, or less than $1 billion a year. By the early 1990s, the program grew immodestly, jumping to $20 billion a year, through the first decade of the new century rose to over $70 billion a year, accounting for the majority of "aid" that the federal government provides, surpassing all grants and scholarships.

Part of the reason that debt has increased so much and so quickly is that tuition and fees have increased at three times the rate of inflation. Tuition and fees have gone up from an average of $924 in 1976, when I first went to college, to roughly $10,600 in 2012. The average encompasses all institutions, from community colleges to Ivies. At private schools, the average jumped from $3,051 to about $28,000 in the same period. In 1976, the tuition and fees at Ivies were about $4,000; now they are nearer $45,000. The more salient figure, tuition, fees, room, and board (though not including other expenses, like books or travel to and from home), has climbed from $3,101 in 1980 to $6,562 in 1990, $10,820 in 2000, and $18,497 in 2010. If food had increased at the same rate from its 1980 prices, ordinary eggs would now be about $6.00 a dozen and butter about $12.00 a pound.

This has put a disproportionate burden on students and their families— hence loans. The median household income for a family of four was about $24,300 in 1980, $41,400 in 1990, $54,200 in 2000, and $61,000 in 2010. Alongside the debt that students take on, there are few statistics on how much parents pay and how they pay it. It has become common for parents to finance college through home equity loans, refinancing, and other personal loans. While it is difficult to measure these separately, paying for college no doubt forms part of the accelerating indebtedness of average American families.

There used to be a quaint saying, "I'm working my way through college." Now it would be impossible to work your way through college unless you have superhuman powers. According to one set of statistics, during the 1960s, a student could work fifteen hours a week at minimum wage during school and forty during the summer and pay his or her public university education; at an Ivy League or kindred private school, the figure would have risen to about twenty hours a week during school. Not ideal, but possible. Now, one would have to work *fifty-two hours a week all year long*, even during school; at an Ivy League college you would have to work *136 hours* a week all year (there are 168 hours in a week). Thus the need for loans as a supplement, even if a student is working and parents have saved. In addition to the steep rise in debt, many students are working long hours during school—according to one survey, students at public institutions average twenty-five hours a week. You don't need a Ph.D. to realize that neither cultivates good educational conditions.

The reason tuition has increased so precipitously is more complicated. Sometimes politicians blame it on the inefficiency of academe, but most universities, especially state universities, have undergone budget cuts and enacted cost-saving measures for the past twenty years. Tuition has increased in large part because states fund a far smaller percentage of tuition costs. In 1980, states funded nearly half of their universities' costs; in 2000, they contributed only 32 percent, and it is less than 25 percent now. Universities have turned to a number of alternative sources to replace the lost funds, such as "technology transfers" and other "partnerships" with businesses, and seemingly endless campaigns for donations, but the steadiest way, one that is replenished each fall like the harvest, is through tuition.

Although state legislators might flatter themselves on their belt-tightening, this is a shell game that slides the cost from the public tax roll to individual students and their parents. This represents *a shift in the idea of higher education from a public entitlement to a private service.* After World War II, policymakers like James Bryant Conant, the president of Harvard and a major influence, held that the university should be a meritocratic institution, bringing in not just the well off but the best and the brightest to build America. To that end, the designers of the postwar university kept tuitions low, opening the gates to record numbers of students, particularly from classes previously excluded. I have called this "the welfare state university" because it instantiated the policies and ethos of the postwar, liberal welfare state.

Now the paradigm for university funding is no longer a public entitlement primarily offset by the state but a privatized service, whereby each citizen has to pay a substantial portion of his or her own way. I call this the "post–welfare state university" because it carries out the policies and ethos of the neoconservative dismantling of the welfare state, from the "Reagan Revolution" through the Clinton "reform" of welfare up to the present draining of social services. (Bill Readings, in his influential *University in Ruins*, called it "the University of Excellence," unmoored from traditional rationales such as national culture, but I think it more historically accurate to name it "the post–welfare state university.") The principle is that citizens should pay more directly for public services, and public services should be administered less through the state and more through private enterprises. The state's role is not to provide an alternative realm apart from the market but to grease the wheels of the market, subsidizing citizens to participate in it and businesses to provide social services. Loans carry out the logic of the post–welfare state because they reconfigure college funding not as an entitlement or grant but as self-payment (as with welfare, fostering "personal responsibility"), and not as a state service but a privatized service, administered by megabanks such as Citibank, as well as Sallie Mae and Nellie Mae, the original federal nonprofit lenders that became independent for-profits in the 1990s. The state encourages participation in the market of higher education by subsidizing interest, like a startup business loan, but eschews dependence, as it leaves the principal to each citizen. You have to depend on your own bootstraps.

This also represents a *shift in the idea of higher education from a social good to an individual good*. In the postwar years, higher education was conceived as a massive national mobilization, in part as a carryover from the war years and ethos of solidarity, in part as a legacy of the New Deal, and in part as a response to the Cold War. It adopted a modified socialism, like a vaccine assimilating a weaker strain of communism in order to immunize against it. Although it maintained a liberal belief in the sanctity of the individual, its unifying aim was for the social good, to produce the engineers, scientists, and even humanists who would strengthen the country. Now higher education is conceived almost entirely as a good for individuals, to get a better job and higher lifetime earnings. Those who attend university are construed as atomized individuals making a personal choice in the marketplace of education to maximize their economic potential. This is presumably a good for the social whole, all the atoms adding up to a more prosperous economy, but it is based on the conception of society as a market driven by individual competition rather than social cooperation, and it defines the social good as that which fosters a profitable market. Loans are a personal investment in one's market potential rather than a public investment in one's social potential; like a business, each individual is a store of human capital, and higher education provides value added.

This represents another *shift in the idea of higher education, from youthful exemption to market conscription, which is finally a shift in our vision of the future and particularly in the social hope for our young.* The traditional idea of education is based on social hope, providing an exemption from work and expense for the younger members of society so that they can explore their interests, develop their talents, and receive useful training, as well as become versed in citizenship—all in the belief that society will benefit in the future. Society pays it forward. This obviously applies to elementary and secondary education (although, given the voucher movement, it is no longer assured there either), and it was extended to the university, particularly in the postwar era. The reasoning melds citizenship ideals and utilitarian purpose. The classical idea of the American university propounded by Thomas Jefferson holds that democratic participation requires education in democratic principles, so it is an obligation of a democracy to provide that education. (The argument relates to the concept of holding a franchise: just as you should not have to pay a poll tax to vote, you should not have to pay to become a properly educated citizen capable of participating in democracy.) The utilitarian idea, propounded by Charles Eliot Norton in the late nineteenth century and Conant in the mid-twentieth, holds that society should provide the advanced training necessary in an industrially and technologically sophisticated world. The welfare state university promulgated both ideal and utilitarian goals, providing inexpensive tuition and generous aid while massively expanding its facilities to welcome a widening segment of the populace. It offered its exemption not to abet the leisure of a new aristocracy (Conant's aim was to dislodge what he saw as the entrenched aristocracy of Harvard); it presupposed the long-term social benefit of such an exemption, and indeed the G.I. Bill issued a return of 7:1 for every dollar invested, a rate of return that would make any stockbroker turn green. It also created the conditions for a strong civic culture. (It is an irony that conservatives bemoan the passing of civic culture at the same time that they extol the market that has replaced civic with market culture.) The new paradigm of funding views the young not as a special group to be exempted or protected from the market, but as already fair game in the market. It extracts more work—like workfare instead of welfare—from students, both in the hours they clock while in school as well as in loans, which are finally a deferred form of work. Debt puts a sizeable tariff on social hope.

Loans to provide emergency or minor supplemental aid are not necessarily a bad arrangement. But as a major and mandatory source of current funding (most colleges, in their financial aid calculations, stipulate a sizeable portion in loans), they are excessive if not draconian. Moreover, over the past three decades, they have been more an entitlement for banking than for students. Since the federal government insures the loans, banks bear no risk, and in fact make extraordinary fees from late payments or delinquent loans. Even by the standards of the most doctrinaire market believer, this is skewed capitalism. The premise of money lending and investment, say for a home mortgage, is that interest is assessed and earned in proportion to risk. As a result of these policies, the banks have profited continuously, with Sallie Mae, the largest lender, reaping phenomenal amounts (in many years between 30 and 50 percent).

There is no similar safety net for students. Even if you are in bankruptcy and are absolved of all credit card and other loans, the one debt you cannot discharge is student loans. As I show in the next chapter, the current loan system has an uncomfortable resonance with colonial indenture. We are only now starting to see the effects of the student loan system, but it clearly runs in the opposite direction of the G.I. Bill, leaving many in distress, or simply, according to statistics, keeping those from less privileged classes, particularly of color, from going to college.

Debt is not just a mode of financing but also a mode of pedagogy. We tend to think of it as a necessary evil attached to higher education, but extraneous to the aims of higher education. What if instead we were to see it as central to people's actual experience of college? What do we teach students when we usher them into the post–welfare state university and its mantle of debt?

There are a host of standard, sometimes contradictory, rationales for higher education. On the more idealistic end of the spectrum, the traditional rationale is that we give students a broad grounding in humanistic knowledge—in the Arnoldian credo "the best that has been known and thought." A corollary is that they explore liberally across the band of disciplines (hence "liberal education," in a nonpolitical sense). A related rationale is that the university is a place where students can conduct self-exploration;

while this sometimes seems to abet the "me culture" as opposed to the more stern idea of accumulating knowledge, it actually has its roots in Socrates' dictum to know oneself, and in many ways it expresses Cardinal Newman's primary idea in *The Idea of a University*. These rationales hold the university apart from the normal transactions of the world.

In the middle of the spectrum, another traditional rationale holds that higher education promotes national culture: we teach the profundity of American or, more generally, Western culture. A more progressive rationale might reject the nationalism of that aim and posit instead that higher education should teach a more expansive and inclusive world culture, but it still maintains the principle of liberal learning. Both rationales maintain an idealistic strain—educating citizens—but see the university as attached to the world rather than as a refuge from it. At the most worldly end of the spectrum, a common rationale holds that higher education provides professional skills and training. This utilitarian purpose opposes Newman's classic idea, but it shares the fundamental premise that higher education exists to provide students with an exemption to gain a head start before entering adult life. Almost every college and university in the United States announces these goals in their mission statements, stitching together idealistic, civic, and utilitarian purposes in a sometimes clashing but otherwise conjoined quilt.

The lessons of student debt diverge from these traditional rationales. First, *student debt teaches that higher education is a consumer service*. It is a pay-as-you-go transaction, like any other consumer enterprise, and students are not special but consumers subject to the business franchises attached to education. All the entities making up the present university multiplex reinforce this lesson, from the Starbucks kiosk in the library and the Burger King counter in the dining hall, to the Barnes & Noble running the bookstore and the pseudo–Gold's Gym running the rec center, as well as the convenient cash machines and myriad online portals that smooth the financial flow of it all. We might tell students that the foremost purpose of higher education is self-searching or liberal learning, but their experience tells them differently.

Second, *student debt teaches career choices*. If you are in the two-thirds who have it, it teaches that it would be a poor choice to wait tables while writing a novel, or to become an elementary school teacher at $24,000, or to join the Peace Corps. It rules out culture industries such as publishing or theatre or art galleries that pay notoriously little, or nonprofits like community radio or a women's shelter. The more rational choice is to work for a big corporation or go to law school. Nellie Mae, one of the major lenders, discounted the effect of loans on such choices in a 2003 study, reporting that "only 17% of borrowers said student loans had a significant impact on their career plans." It concluded, "The effect of student loans on career plans remains small." This is a dubious conclusion: 17 percent on a survey is not negligible. The survey is also skewed because it assessed students' responses at time of graduation, before they actually had to pay the loans, get jobs, and pay bills, or simply when they saw things optimistically. Finally, it is fundamentally flawed because it assumes that students decide on career plans tabula rasa. Most likely students have already recognized the situation they face and adapted their career plans accordingly. The best evidence for this is the warp in majors toward business. Many bemoan the fact that the liberal arts have faded, in real terms, whereas business majors have nearly tripled, from about 8 percent before World War II to 22 percent now. This is not because students have become more venal or no longer care about poetry or philosophy; rather, they have learned the lesson of the world in front of them and chosen according to its, and their, constraints.

Third, *student debt teaches a worldview*. In *Born to Buy*, the sociologist Juliet Schor shows how advertising indoctrinates children into the market. Student loans continue that lesson, in fact directly conscripting college students. Debt teaches that the primary ordering principle of the world is the capitalist market, and that the market is natural, inevitable, and implacable. There is no realm of human life outside the market; ideas, knowledge, and even sex (which is a significant part of the social education of students) simply form submarkets. Debt teaches that democracy is a market, whereby freedom is constituted as an ability to make choices from all the shelves. And the market is a good thing because it prompts better products through competition rather than leisured reflection or cooperation, and it is fair because, like a casino, the rules are clear and anyone, black, green, or white, can lay their chips down. It is unfortunate if you don't have many chips to put down, but the house will spot you some, and having chips is a matter of the luck of the social draw. There is an impermeability to the idea of the market: You can fault social arrangements, but who do you fault for luck?

Fourth, *student debt teaches civic lessons.* It teaches that the state's role is to augment commerce, abetting consuming, which spurs producing; its role is not to interfere with the market, except to support and protect it. Debt teaches that the social contract is an obligation to the institutions of capital, which in turn give you all of the products on the shelves. It also teaches the relation of public and private. Each citizen is a private subscriber to public services, and should pay his or her own way; social entitlements such as welfare promote laziness rather than the proper competitive spirit. Debt is the civic version of tough love.

Fifth, *student debt teaches the worth of a person.* The worth of a person is measured not according to a humanistic conception of character, cultivation of intellect and taste, or knowledge of the liberal arts, but according to one's financial potential. Education provides value added to the individual so serviced, in a simple equation: you are how much you can make, minus how much you owe. Debt teaches that the disparities of wealth are an issue of the individual, rather than society; debt is your free choice.

Last, *student debt teaches a sensibility or feeling.* It inculcates what Barbara Ehrenreich calls "the fear of falling," which she defines as the quintessential attitude of members of the professional/middle class who attain their standing through educational credentials rather than wealth. It inducts students into the realm of stress, worry, and pressure, reinforced with each monthly payment for the next fifteen years, and possibly more.

———————————

If you believe in the social hope of the young, the present system of student debt is wrong. And if you look at the productivity statistics of the college-educated World War II generation, it is counterproductive. We should therefore advocate the abolition of student debt. Despite Nellie Mae's bruiting the high rate of satisfaction, a number of universities, including Princeton and UNC–Chapel Hill, have recognized the untenable prospect of student debt and now stipulate aid without loans. This is a step in the right direction. It should be the official policy of every university to forgo loans, except on an emergency basis. And it should be the policy of the federal government to convert all funds to direct aid, such as Pell Grants, or even better, to free tuition.

Free tuition is the one long-term solution that goes to the heart of the problem. Adolph Reed, as part of a campaign of the Labor Party for "Free Higher Ed," has made the seemingly utopian but actually practicable proposal of free tuition for all qualified college students. He reasons that, if education is a social good, then we should support it; that it had great benefit, financial as well as civic, under the G.I. Bill; and that, given current spending on loan programs, it is not out of reach. By most estimates, free tuition at public institutions would cost only a little more than how much is thrown to the student loan program—and Reed points out that it would only be a small portion of the military budget. In fact, it would save money, cutting out the current federal student loan bureaucracy and the subsidies to banking. The brilliance of this proposal is that it applies to anyone, rich or poor, so that it realizes the principle of equal opportunity.

Free Higher Ed gets to the root of the problem, but another proposal I have suggested is for loan abatements or forgiveness to help those already stuck under the weight of debt, taking inspiration from European models of national service, and throwbacks such as the Works Progress Administration. Such a program would call for a set term of, say, two or three years of service in exchange for a fair if modest salary, and forgiveness of a significant portion of education loans per year in service. AmeriCorps makes a feint in this direction, but offers relatively small amounts for the work required, and there are several existing programs that we might look to instead. One is the very successful North Carolina Teaching Fellows Program for undergraduates. It carries a full scholarship as well as other "enrichments" designed to recruit exceptional but less wealthy high school students to go into teaching. It requires that students teach in less privileged school districts, often rural or sometimes inner city, for a term of three or four years after graduation. On the postgraduate level, there are similar programs designed to bring doctors to rural or impoverished areas that lack them, that subsidize part of medical school training in exchange for a term of service. We should build a system of "National Teaching Fellows" who would teach and consult in areas that have particular need.

Such a program would have obvious benefits for students, giving them a way to shed the draconian weight of debt, as well as giving them experience and, more intangibly, a positive sense of public service. As a side effect, at its best it would foster a sense of solidarity, as the national service of the World War II generation did for soldiers from varied walks of life, or as required national service does in some European countries. The program would put academic expertise to a wider public use, reaching those in remote or impoverished areas. Just as law-and-order political candidates promise more police on the streets, we should be calling on and pressuring political candidates for more teachers in our classrooms and thus smaller class sizes, from preschool to university.

These proposals might seem far-fetched, but programs like Social Security, the WPA, the G.I. Bill, or the Peace Corps, also seemed far-fetched a few years before they were enacted. There is a maxim, attributed to Dostoyevsky, that you can judge the state of a civilization from its prisons. You can also judge the state of a civilization from its schools—or more generally, from how it treats its young as they enter their franchise in adult life. Encumbering our young with mortgages on their futures augurs a return of debtors' prisons. Student debt impedes a full franchise in American life, so any American should be against it.

TWENTY

Student Debt and the Spirit of Indenture

When we think of the founding of the early colonies, we usually think of the journey to freedom, in particular of the Puritans fleeing religious persecution to settle the Massachusetts Bay Colony. But it was not so for a majority of the first Europeans who emigrated to these shores. "Between one-half and two-thirds of all white immigrants to the British colonies arrived under indenture," according to the economic historian David W. Galenson, totaling 300,000 to 400,000 people. Indenture was not an isolated practice but a dominant aspect of labor and life in early America.

Rather than Plymouth, Jamestown was a more typical example of colonial settlement, founded in 1607 as a mercantile venture under the auspices of the Virginia Company, a prototype of "joint-stock" corporations and venture capitalism. The first colonists fared badly because, coming primarily from gentry, they had little practical skill at farming and were ravaged by starvation and disease. In 1620, the Virginia Company shifted to a policy of indentured servitude to draw labor fit to work the tobacco colonies. Indenture had been a common practice in England, but its terms were relatively short, typically a year, and closely regulated by law. The innovation of the Virginia Company was to extend the practice of indenture to America, but at a much higher obligation, of four to seven years, because of the added cost of transit, and also because of the added cost of the brokerage system that arose around it. In England, contracts of indenture were directly between the landowner and servant, whereas now merchants or brokers in England's ports signed prospective workers, then sold the contracts to shippers or to colonial landowners upon the servants' arrival in America, who in turn could resell the contracts.

By about 1660, planters "increasingly found African slaves a less expen-sive source of labor," as Galenson puts it. An economically minded historian like Galenson argues that the system of indenture was rational, free, and fair—one had a free choice to enter into the arrangement, some of those indentured eventually prospered, and it was only rational that the terms be high because of the cost of transit—but most other historians, from Edmund S. Morgan to Marcus Rediker, agree that indentured servitude was an exploitive system of labor, in many instances a form of bondage nearing slavery, its close cousin, and regard it as a disreputable aspect of American history. For the bound, it resulted in long hours of hard work, oftentimes abuse, terms sometimes extended by fiat of the landowner, little regulation or legal recourse for laborers, and the onerous physical circumstances of the new world, in which two-thirds died before fulfilling their terms.

College student loan debt has revived the spirit of indenture for a size-able proportion of contemporary Americans. It is not a minor threshold that young people entering adult society and work, or those returning to college seeking enhanced credentials, might easily pass through. Rather, because of its unprecedented and escalating amounts, it is a major con-straint that looms over the lives of those so contracted, binding individuals for a significant part of their future work lives. Although it has more varied application, less direct effects, and less severe conditions than colonial indenture did—amounts vary and some might have family help, some attain better incomes after college, and it does not bind one to a particular job on the frontier—student debt permeates everyday experience with concern over the monthly chit and encumbers job and life choices. It also takes a page from indenture in the extensive brokerage system it has bred, from which more than three thousand banks take profit. At core, student debt is a labor issue, as colonial indenture was, subsisting on the desire of those less privileged to gain better opportunities and enforcing a control on their future labor. One of the goals of the planners of the modern US university system after World War II was to displace what they saw as an aristocracy that had become entrenched at elite schools; instead they promoted equal opportunity in order to build America through its best talent. The rising tide of student debt reinforces rather than dissolves the discriminations of class, counteracting the meritocracy and creating a new underclass. Finally, I believe that the current system of college debt violates the spirit of American freedom in leading those less privileged to bind their futures.

In "The Pedagogy of Debt," I detail the basic facts and figures of student loan debt, pointing out how it rewrites the social contract from a public entitlement to education to a privatized service and how it teaches lessons not listed in most textbooks. Here, I take a close look at the analogy to indenture. "Indenture" is sometimes used as a metaphor for debt, but only a vague one, whereas I will show how it corresponds, in many actual practices as well as in legal and political principle, with its colonial forebear. While it might not be as direct or extreme, it represents a turn in American politics to permit such a constraint on those attempting to gain a franchise in the adult or work world, and thus should be changed.

Indentured servitude seems a strange and distant historical practice, like burning witches, that we have progressed far beyond. But there are a number of ways that college student loan debt revises some of its ethos and features for the twenty-first century:

PREVALENCE. Student loan debt is now a prevalent mode of financing higher education, applying to two-thirds of those who attend. If upward of 70 percent of Americans attend college at some point, it applies to half the rising population. Like indenture through the seventeenth century, it has become a common experience of those settling the new technological world of twenty-first-century America, where we are continually told that we need college degrees to compete globally.

AMOUNTS. Student debt has morphed from relatively small amounts to substantial ones, loosely paralleling the large debt entailed by colonial transport. The average federal loan debt of a graduating senior in 2010 was $25,250 (from the US Department of Education's National Center for Education Statistics; there is a lag in the tabulation of the statistics of two to three years). Also consider that, as happens with averages, many people have significantly more than the median—25 percent of federal borrowers had more than $30,000 in undergraduate loans, and 14 percent had more than $40,000, according to the 2008 National Postsecondary Student Aid Study (the Department of Education issues the study every four years, and that of the class of 2012 is due in 2014). Added to federal loans are charge cards, estimated at $4,100 per graduating student in 2008, and private loans, which have skyrocketed since 1996, when 1 percent of students took them, to 14 percent in 2008, and which have risen in total to $17.1 billion, a disturbingly large portion *in addition to* the $68.6 billion for federal loans.

Further, more than 60 percent of those continuing their educations have graduate debt, which more than doubled in the past decade, to a 2008 median of about $25,000 for those with masters, $52,000 for doctorates, and $80,000 for professional degrees. Remember, that is on top of undergraduate debt.

LENGTH OF TERM. Student debt is a long-term commitment—for standard Stafford, guaranteed federal loans amortized over fifteen years. With consolidation or refinancing, the term frequently extends to thirty years— in other words, for many returning students or graduate students, until retirement age. It is not a brief, transitory bond, say, of a year, as it was for those indentured in England, or of early student debtors who might have owed $2,000 in 1982. Though not as concentrated as colonial indenture, student debt looms longer over a student debtor's future.

TRANSPORT TO WORK. Student indebtedness is premised on the idea of transport to a job—the figurative transport over the higher seas of education to attain the shores of credentials deemed necessary for a middle class job. The cost of transport is borne by the laborer, so an individual has to pay for the opportunity to work. Some businesses alleviate debt as a recruiting benefit, but unfortunately they are still relatively few. (Conjoined with debt we should also consider the precipitous rise in student work hours—over twenty hours per week for students at public universities, which tends to lower grades and impede graduation rates. Servitude, for many current students, begins on ship.)

PERSONAL CONTRACTS. "Indenture" designates a practice of making contracts before signatures were common (they were torn, the tear analogous to the unique shape of a person's bite, and each party held half, so they could be verified by their match); student debt reinstitutes a system of contracts that bind a rising majority of Americans. Like indenture, the debt is secured not by property, as most loans such as those for cars or houses are, but by the person, obligating his or her future labor. Student loan debt "financializes" the person, in the phrase of Randy Martin, who diagnoses this strategy as a central one of contemporary venture capital, displacing risk to individuals rather than employers or society. It was also a strategy of colonial indenture.

LIMITED RECOURSE. Contracts for federal student loans stipulate severe penalties and are virtually unbreakable, forgiven not in bankruptcy but only in death, and enforced by severe measures, such as garnishee and other legal sanctions, with little recourse. (In one recent case, the social security payment to a person on disability was garnisheed.) In England, indenture was regulated by law and servants had recourse in court; one of the pernicious aspects of colonial indenture was that there was little recourse in the new colonies.

CLASS. Student debt applies to those with less family wealth, like indenture drawing off the working classes. That this would be a practice in Britain before modern democracy and where classes were rigidly divided is not entirely surprising; however, it is particularly disturbing in the United States, where we ostensibly eschew the determining force of class. The one-third without student debt face much different futures and are far more likely to pursue graduate and professional degrees (for instance, three-quarters of those receiving doctorates in 2004 had no undergraduate debt, and, according to a 2002 Nellie Mae survey, 40 percent of those not pursuing graduate school attributed their choice to debt). Student debt is digging a class moat in present-day America.

YOUTH. Student debt incorporates primarily younger people, as indenture did. One of the more troubling aspects of student debt is that often it is not an isolated hurdle but the first step down a slope of debt and difficulties. Tamara Draut, in her exposé *Strapped: Why America's 20- and 30-Somethings Can't Get Ahead* (2005), shows how it inaugurates a series of strained conditions, compounded by shrinking job prospects, escalating charge card debt, and historically higher housing payments, whether rent or mortgage, resulting in lessened chances for having a family and establishing a secure and comfortable life. The American Dream, and specifically the post–World War II dream of equal opportunity opened by higher education, has been curtailed for many of the rising generation.

BROKERS. Student debt fuels a financial services system that trades in and profits from contracts of indebted individuals, like the Liverpool merchants, sea captains, and planters trading in contracts of indenture. The lender pays the fare to the college, and thereafter the contracts are circulated among Sallie Mae, Nellie Mae, Citigroup, and more than three thousand other banks. (Even with recent shifts to direct federal lending, banks still service the loans.) This system makes a futures market of people and garners immense profit from them.

STATE POLICY. The British crown gave authority to the Virginia Company; the US government authorizes current lending enterprises, and, even more lucratively for banks, underwrites their risk in guaranteeing the loans (the Virginia Company received no such largesse and went bankrupt). In the past few years, federal aid has funneled more to loans rather than any other form of aid (about 60 percent of all federal aid, whereas grants account for less than 40 percent).

My point in adducing this bill of particulars is not to claim an exact historical correspondence between indentured servitude and student indebtedness. But it is not just a fanciful analogy, either. It is disturbing that it has any resonance at all, and that we permit, through policy and practice, the conscription of those seeking the opportunity of education, especially the young, into a significant bond on their future labor and life. While indenture was more direct and severe, it was the product of a rigidly classed, semifeudal world, before modern democracies; student debt is more flexible, varied in application, and amorphous in effects, a product of the postmodern world, but it revives the spirit of indenture in promulgating class privilege and class subservience. Fundamentally, it represents a shift in basic political principle, turning away from the democratic impetus of modern American society. The 1947 Report of the President's Commission on Education, which ushered in the vast expansion of our colleges and universities, emphasized (in bold italics) that "free and universal access to education must be a major goal in American education." Otherwise, the commission warned, "If the ladder of educational opportunity rises high at the doors of some youth and scarcely rises at the doors of others, while at the same time formal education is made a prerequisite to occupational and social advance, then education may become the means, not of eliminating race and class distinctions, but of deepening them." Their goal was not only an abstract one of equality, but also to strengthen the United States, and by all accounts American society prospered. Current student debt, in encumbering so many of the rising generation of citizens, has built a roadblock to the American ideal, and in the long term it weakens America, wasting the resource of those impeded from pursuing degrees who otherwise would make excellent doctors or professors or engineers, as well as creating a culture of debt and constraint.

The counterarguments for the rightness of student loan debt are similar to the counterarguments for the benefits of indenture. One holds that it is a question of supply and demand—a lot of people want higher education, thus driving up the price. This doesn't hold water, because the demand for higher education in the years following World War II through 1970 was proportionately the highest of any time, as student enrollments doubled and tripled, but the supply was cheap and largely state funded. The difference between then and now is that higher education was much more substantially funded through public sources, both state and federal; now the expense has been privatized, transferred to students and their families.

Of indenture, Galenson argues that "long terms did not imply exploitation" because they were only fitting for the high cost of transport; that more productive servants, or those placed in undesirable areas, could lessen their terms; and that some servants went on to prosper. For Galenson, it is a rational market system; he does not mention its less rational results, such as the high rate of death, the many cases of abuse, the draconian extension of contracts by unethical planters, or simply what term would be an appropriate maximum for any person in a free society to be bound, even if they agreed to the bondage. He also ignores the underlying political question: Is it appropriate that people, especially those entering the adult world, might take on such a long-term commitment of constraint? Can people make a rational choice for a term they might not realistically imagine? Even if one doesn't question the principle of indenture, what is an appropriate cap for its amounts and term? In the case of student debt, although it might be a legal choice, it is doubtful whether it is always a rational choice for those who have no knowledge of adult life. One of the more haunting responses to the 2002 Nellie Mae survey was that 54 percent said that they would have borrowed less if they had to do it again, up from 31 percent ten years before. One can only imagine that this informed judgment has climbed as debt continues to rise.

Some economists justify student loan debt in terms similar to Galenson's. Because college graduates have made, according to some statistics, $1,000,000 more over the course of their careers than those who have not gone to college, one prominent argument holds that it is rational and right that they take on debt to start their careers. However, while many graduates make statistically high salaries, the problem is that results vary a great deal: some accrue debt but don't graduate; some graduate but, with degrees in the humanities or education, are unlikely to make a high salary; more and more students have difficulty finding a professional or high-paying job; and the rates have been declining, so a college degree is no longer the guaranteed ticket to wealth that it once was. An economic balance sheet also ignores the fundamental question of the ethics of requiring debt of those who desire higher education and the fairness of its distribution to those less privileged.

———————————

Only in the past few years has there been much attention to the problem of student loan debt, but most of the solutions thus far, such as direct lending or interest rate reductions, are stopgaps that do not affect the structure and basic terms of the system. The system needs wholesale change. As I discuss in "The Pedagogy of Debt," I think that the best solution is "Free Higher Ed," put forth by the Labor Party. It proposes that the federal government pay tuition for all qualified students at public universities, which would cost $50–70 billion a year, not negligible but a small portion of the military budget. It would actually jettison a substantial layer of current bureaucracy— of the branches of the federal loan program, of the vast banking octopus servicing student loans, and of college financial aid offices—thereby saving a great deal of current spending. For those who believe in the social good of higher education, free tuition should be the goal, and it is not impracticable.

One influential reform has been "Income Contingent Loans," which adjust the rate of payment according to salary. The invention of educational policy expert Bruce Chapman, they were first adopted in Australia in 1989, and have been used in England for two decades. They represent a pragmatic compromise, not abolishing debt but providing relief for those with the most debt and least resources. One of the most pernicious aspects of the current structure of student loan debt in the United States is that it puts a particular burden on those who have lower incomes, especially at the beginning of their careers. For instance, an elementary school teacher with a salary of $23,900 (the 2005 median) who has a debt of $40,000 for four years at a private college would have to pay about 15 percent or more of her salary before taxes. After taxes it might be closer to 25 percent, which would make ordinary living expenses difficult. A chief virtue of Income Contingent Loans is that they stipulate a minimum threshold below which one does not have to pay—around $25,000 in Britain—and they have other safeguards for debtors, for instance capping the required payment, in Australia at 8 percent and in the United Kingdom at 6 percent of salary. The model of Income Contingent Loans has been adapted in the United States in "Income-Based Repayment" programs, which provide some relief, but the

US system has a labyrinthine set of criteria for eligibility (if you've missed one payment, you are permanently out), unlike those in other countries, for which everyone is eligible and that are an automatic part of the tax system. We need a simplified, standardized, low-interest, uniform plan.

While we should continue to press for reforms, we should keep in mind that, in principle, our current system reinstitutes a form of indenture for many, so we should aim for its abolition. We should also keep in mind that the problem is not the result of a financial crisis, but the result of policy, of the deregulation of unsecured personal loans beginning in the 1980s, as well as the defunding of higher education. It is a bad policy, corrupting the goals of higher education, producing inequality and overtaxing our potential for the sake of short-term, private gain. But, since it is a policy, we can change it.

TWENTY-ONE

The Academic Devolution

In 1968, Christopher Jencks and David Riesman published a book called *The Academic Revolution*. It tells the success story of American higher education, from small, sectarian colleges to the major universities of the postwar era. Its revolution is not that of students but the professionalization of faculty and the new stress on research. By 1968 Jencks and Riesman observe that, for the first time in American history, professors were more preoccupied with research than teaching, with their discipline than their campus, and with graduate education than undergraduate. Stressing "the rise to power of the academic professions," Jencks and Riesman might well have called their book "The Rise of the Professors."

The revolution didn't happen by accident. It was planned during the Second World War, as those in Franklin Roosevelt's administration worried about the postwar years and invented the G.I. Bill, among other things, to stave off a return to economic depression, as well as to build America through "the endless frontier" of science, as adviser Vannevar Bush called it. It was promoted by the Report of the President's Commission on Education, or "Truman Commission," in 1947, which called for massive public investment in higher education to provide opportunity for Americans across class and race lines. It was incited by Sputnik and the subsequent creation, in 1958, of the National Defense Education Act. Like the federal highway system, which was brokered for the sake of national defense, the United States developed a national system of affordable higher education and university-based research.

Published by Doubleday, *The Academic Revolution* was something of a public event. There was a large audience for updates on the state of American higher education, and it was met with a wave of histories, position statements, and reports, such as a forty-book series from the Carnegie Commission on Higher Education, that adduced all manner of demographic and other data about the spread of higher education to a majority of Americans. The burgeoning university was a measure of the postwar boom, like the great American car companies that put rubber on the pavement of the new highways.

Forty years later, the revolution seems distant history, and a reaction has set in. From a time of expansive federal and state funding, accounting for upward of 60 percent of university budgets and resulting in unprecedented support for research across the disciplines, low tuition for students, and plentiful jobs for faculty, we have experienced a prolonged period of cutbacks, with federal and state support reduced to 30 percent, resulting in the rise of commercially directed research, skyrocketing tuitions (by a factor of ten in thirty years, more than three times the rate of inflation), and the shrinkage of permanent faculty positions.

Sometimes it seems as if the reaction was inevitable, but, like the revolution, it did not happen by accident. It expresses the policies of neoliberalism, repealing the policies of the New Deal and the Great Society and shifting the university from being a public entitlement like high school to more of a pay-as-you-go, privatized service. It was primed with legislation such as the Bayh-Dole Act of 1980, which allowed universities to hold patents, resulting in their directly adopting corporate strategies and commercial goals for research. It was paved with a shift in federal aid from grants to loans, by 2010 tipping the scale at $80 billion annually in student loans compared to $50 billion in grants, and with the privatization of Sallie Mae, from a federal nonprofit founded in 1965 under the Higher Education Act to, beginning in 1996, a private enterprise. This led to an astronomical increase in student debt, from about $2,000 per graduate in 1982 to about $23,000 twenty-five years later. The reaction was also forged with the managerial policies of contemporary corporate capitalism, resulting in a steady decline of full-time, tenure-stream faculty jobs, so that now the predominant position of faculty is casual—part-time, temporary, nontenurable, and low-paid—and nearing the academic version of day laborer. In my field, English, the current statistic is that 32 percent of faculty members have tenure-line jobs, meaning that more than two-thirds do not. Formerly a representative figure of the postwar meritocracy—one who demonstrates merit in school, regardless of background, and succeeds to a secure, professional, middle class career—the professor is now an embattled creature.

It took some time for the commentary to catch up to the reality. Through the 1980s and 1990s commentary was drawn to the smoke and fireworks of the political correctness debates, but since the mid-1990s there has been a growing wave of reports on the distressed condition of higher education. A main line examines the "corporate university" and its dangers, in both academic studies, such as Sheila Slaughter and Larry Leslie's *Academic Capitalism: Politics, Policies, and the Entrepreneurial University* (1997), and public reports, such as Jennifer Washburn's *University, Inc.: The Corporate Corruption of Higher Education* (2005). Only recently has there been attention to student debt, with exposés such as Alan Collinge's *The Student Loan Scam: The Most Oppressive Debt in U. S. History* (2009), as well as my essays, "Debt Education" (2006) and "Student Debt and the Spirit of Indenture" (2008), originally published in *Dissent* and reprinted in this volume. In addition, a persistent strand, probably more prominent inside academe and less known to a wide public, has focused on faculty. Two recent books, Frank Donoghue's *The Last Professors: The Corporate University and the Fate of the Humanities* (2008) and Marc Bousquet's *How the University Works: Higher Education and the Low-Wage Nation* (2008), provide the best general accounts of what has happened to faculty, particularly in the humanities. Together they make a sobering sequel, exactly forty years after, to *The Academic Revolution*.

If *The Academic Revolution* celebrated the heyday of professorial power, *The Last Professors* sings, as its title suggests, its elegy. Its basic thesis is that professorial positions, especially in the traditional core of the humanities, are an endangered species and henceforth will exist only in the most elite refuges. In his best and most depressing chapter, "Competing in Academia," Donoghue synthesizes the statistics of those who survive the sluiceway from graduate school to tenure-stream job. Not only do a minority of those with PhDs get permanent positions, but Donoghue shows that the real ratio is in fact much more severe, nearer to 1 in 10. He traces the extraordinarily high rate of attrition of those in graduate school, which is much greater, for instance, than those in law or medical school. This is compounded by those who finish but are stuck in the purgatory of "postdocs" or part-time, "adjunct" positions. Donoghue's account and other statistics make clear that the claim that faculty is populated by tenured radicals is a myth: It is actually populated by overworked and underpaid adjuncts or graduate students. Instead of being exemplary figures of the postwar meritocracy, the current generation of faculty more likely represents the job-traumatized.

The news in the rest of the book is no more encouraging. Donoghue looks at other cornerstones of academic life, such as tenure and publishing. He shows how tenure and its presumed protections of academic freedom have effectively been curtailed, given the paucity of tenure-stream jobs, and he comments on the state of academic publishing, which has adopted blatant market protocols, resulting in the drying up of the traditional research monograph, even though academic presses presumably exist to support them. He also reports on the rise of for-profits, like the University of Phoenix, that teach vocational subjects and do not confer tenure, and sees them as a key rather than peripheral segment of the future of higher education. In turn, disciplines like English will go the way of the classics, except at top-ranked schools. Although they will retain the humanities, they, too, have been corrupted, in Donoghue's diagnosis, by the race for prestige and "prestige envy," driven by annual rankings such as those in *U.S. News and World Report*.

The strength of *The Last Professors* is that it puts all of these features of the academic landscape in a composite picture, one that reads like a well-paced trade book rather than a belabored academic tome, and I expect it will be eye-opening for those unfamiliar with what has been happening to higher education. It does not present firsthand reporting, but Donoghue provides a short, deft synthesis. The weakness of the book is that, despite its alarming diagnoses, it offers no prescription or course of treatment, and it is finally a deeply fatalistic book. The only suggestion that Donoghue makes is a resigned one, in the last paragraph, that we study institutional history. This is a decent idea, but it takes the perspective of a stoic philosopher, accepting the vicissitudes of life, good or bad, with a dispassionate stance of reflection and without trying to do anything about them. Donoghue's dispassion makes *The Last Professors* a seemingly balanced account, but it is devoid of a sense of politics.

Stanley Fish is a presiding spirit of the book, noted in the acknowledgments and discussed in the first chapter, and Fish wrote a fulsome post on his *New York Times* blog in January 2009 about it, concluding, "After reading Donoghue's book, I feel that I have timed it just right, for it seems that I have had a career that would not have been available to me had I entered the world 50 years later. Just lucky, I guess." (Would one say this if democracy verged on extinction?) Donoghue seems to have taken to heart Fish's pronouncements that literary criticism and politics are separate spheres and that critics should do their jobs of interpreting literary works and leave politics to those in political science.

One lesson of the history of the American university is that it is not an ivory tower but resides at the heart of American politics, forged through the continual negotiation and sometimes outright struggle between public and private, civic and business, and egalitarian and elitist interests. Over the past thirty years, the latter interests have come out on top, but the story is still being written. This sense of struggle does not register in Donoghue's history. To wit, in his first chapter he debunks the rhetoric of crisis that seems to permeate talk about higher education, noting how business-minded commentators in the early 1900s called for more vocationalism. Donoghue's point is that such tensions have always been there, little has changed, and there is no crisis. It does seem as if cries of crisis arrive with annoying regularity each season, but sometimes they are worth heeding and call for struggle. The other part of the history that Donoghue does not mention is that those early twentieth-century businessmen did not get their way, and the university followed a different direction at midcentury.

Another lesson that I hope my opening paragraphs make clear is that the modern American university is the product of policy. The results of policy are not entirely predictable nor indelible—the G.I. Bill, for instance, was designed as a small program but became transformative, and student loans were designed as minor, supplemental aid under the Great Society but became oppressive—but Donoghue presents a university in which change just happens and follows an inevitable path. (Here he shows the influence of Fish's version of pragmatism.) One policy, for example, that Donoghue does not seem to be aware of regards the status of for-profit universities to receive federal student loans. Before 1996, there were much stricter regulations on for-profits and they did not receive nearly the same portion of loans. However, after heavy lobbying, the for-profits engineered a change in law, and they now account for nearly a quarter of federal student loans. For-profits have become a major growth industry on the back of federal policy. Though it would be a long battle pitting the evangelists of the market against those who believe in public institutions, one can imagine that the policy might be changed for the better.

Marc Bousquet's *How the University Works*, like *The Last Professors*, diagnoses the troubles of higher education, especially the pinched conditions of faculty in the humanities, but Bousquet finds those conditions cause for opposition, taking, as his title suggests, the perspective of labor. Bousquet first made his mark with an essay, "The Waste Product of Graduate Education," that appeared in *Social Text* in 2002 and forms part of the introduction and last chapter of this book. It trenchantly debunks the standard view that graduate school is a kind of apprenticeship whose travails one endures for the deferred rewards of a lifelong professional career. Bousquet rebuts this thinking with a surprising but logical interpretation of the statistics, pointing out that if a majority of people don't get jobs, then it's not really an apprenticeship; instead, the majority of new PhDs become the waste of the system: They can no longer stay on as "graduate teaching assistants" and, even though they are experienced teachers, they are expelled. The system perpetuates itself by bringing in "new meat," a new round of cheap teaching labor, rather than giving those it has trained full-fledged professorial jobs. Work in the contemporary university is not particularly humane.

The lack of jobs is typically attributed to "the market," with the supply of teachers exceeding the demand. Bousquet attacks the mindless invocation of the market to explain away what is in fact a labor policy. Considering the increasing number of undergraduates, he points out that current demand is actually quite high, but many full-time jobs have been converted to casual, contingent ones. Professors are not becoming extinct but more thoroughly exploited, or, as he puts it, "We are not 'overproducing teachers'; we are underproducing jobs."

From the situation of graduate students, Bousquet widened his scope to consider what keeps the system going, and a good part of the book examines the role of administration, the one growth area of high-paying jobs over the past twenty years. He shows how tenure-line faculty in English—the lucky minority remaining who have full-time jobs—have more and more been reconfigured as middle managers rather than teachers or researchers. They run writing programs and oversee the graduate students or adjuncts who staff high-enrollment courses like composition. (Both Bousquet and Donoghue are English professors, and their analyses gravitate toward their home terrain, but they do have wider relevance, since English typically is one of the largest departments with the largest number of student hours at any university.) Bousquet also looks at upper administration, which has expanded and prospered precisely as it has downsized faculty. The innovation of current administration is to "informationalize" teaching labor, that is, to marshal it with the speed of a keystroke, so it can be delivered flexibly and "just in time." Adjuncts, for instance, might be hired a week before term or let go a day after, and are much more flexible than pesky tenured professors. The revolution this time is a managerial revolution.

One other component of this revolution is the stunning rise in undergraduate work hours. In his best and most haunting chapter, "Students Are Already Workers," Bousquet exposes with the brio of a muckraker the sheer number of hours many students work, as well as the poor conditions of their work. Now students at state universities work an average of twenty-five hours a week (at private universities, students instead garner more debt, which after all is deferred labor), and Bousquet, taking a page from Barbara Ehrenreich's *Nickel and Dimed*, presents students' stories of their experiences. The rise in student work has a rippling set of consequences, such as poorer grades, lengthening time to graduation, high dropout rates, and intensified stress. For a majority of students, the experience of higher education is not one of intellectual exploration and growth, but extended, underpaid labor and duress.

For Bousquet, labor stitches together the experience of students, faculty, and administrators in the university. Though this might seem a basic insight, there is considerable resistance toward seeing academe in terms of labor. Plumbers are laborers, whereas students are, well, students, professors are autonomous professionals, and the university is a kind of collegial club rather than a factory. This entrenched attitude impedes those of us in academe from recognizing our actual position and doing anything about it. It induces blithe indifference from many tenured faculty or, from those less blithe, fatalism. In response, Bousquet's prescription is a simple, old-fashioned one: organize. This is easier to say than to do, but Bousquet's analysis of graduate education arose from his time, while a graduate student in the mid-1990s, in the union at the City University of New York and in the Graduate Student Caucus of the Modern Language Association, including two years as its president, so it is not an abstract suggestion. Bousquet's surmise is that the movement for equitable labor and conditions in the university will come from adjuncts and students rather than from permanent faculty, and he takes as a model an adjunct union in Chicago that has negotiated relatively fair terms of contract.

One problem with the focus on labor is that it is most directed to an intra-academic audience, to those on the shop floor, and in some ways *How the University Works* is caught between being an intra-academic call to arms and a public exposé. It is hard to garner public sympathy for professors, or for labor, on the terms of labor; rather, the ground of appeal is what professors provide and what needs they serve. Faculty is not really used to thinking this way; we are accustomed to thinking of ourselves as independent researchers who teach, whereas the public understanding of faculty is primarily that we are teachers. It is not what the public should do for us; it is what we do for them. Bousquet answers this with the pithy statement, "Cheap teaching is not a victimless crime." This is a case that those of us in higher education have to make more strongly to enjoy and deserve the support of those outside our local.

This also suggests the uncomfortable recognition that the "Academic Revolution" might have had its excesses, insofar as it gravitated toward professorial self-interest. The rationale is of course that professors should have autonomy to do their research—academic freedom—but it also detaches professors from direct public accountability. We need to reevaluate the apportionment of our work, and of the prestige it garners, between research and teaching. To embrace the recognition that we are labor likely means that we would also have to recognize ourselves more forthrightly as teachers.

In the chapter on student work, Bousquet reaches out to a broader audience. The chapter continues the thematic concern for labor, but in manner and mode, it sticks out like a *Nation* article in contrast to the more academic tenor of the bulk of the book. Although it makes the book slightly lopsided, it also suggests an important direction that research should go. We need more reports of students' experiences of higher education, which violate any decent sense of education, to spur policies that remedy them.

As in most reactions, those who attained power during the revolution have been led to the chopping block. The sharp swing in power has enhanced the attraction of an apocalyptic view. Despite its criticism of crisis narratives, *The Last Professors* leans toward an apocalyptic view, projecting a "last man." The labor perspective of *How the University Works*, while it might deglamorize some of the burnish of professors, brings the crisis to earth, showing that we can do something about it. Institutions, after all, are made by people. Though they sometimes seem like monoliths subject to their own implacable logic, they can be made in better and worse ways.

TWENTY-TWO

The Neoliberal Bias of Higher Education

At least since the culture wars first flared in the late 1980s and early 1990s, we've been hearing about the "liberal bias" of professors. In books and op-eds by conservative pundits such as Roger Kimball, Dinesh D'Souza, and George Will (who asserted in 1991 that Lynne Cheney, then director of the National Endowment for the Humanities, had a more important job than her husband, then secretary of defense), we heard the charges again and again: the radicals of the sixties had ascended to positions of influence and power in our universities and were trying to indoctrinate our children with leftist social and cultural ideas.

At the same time, American higher education *was* changing radically, but not in the way that conservatives like Kimball, D'Souza, and Will worried about. Over the past four decades, universities have undergone pronounced changes in funding and orientation, turning toward progressively higher tuitions and other private sources as public support shrank, toward commercialization of research and other aspects of the academic multiplex, and toward more corporate-style management. Whatever the bearing of academic discourse, these changes reflect what we might call "the neoliberal bias," dispensing with the liberal policies of the post–World War II years, when higher education flourished under the auspices of strong state and federal support. The neoliberal mantra holds that the best inducement to human activity is competition, so public services should be privatized and on a market basis; accordingly, higher education has morphed to "the corporate university," "academic capitalism," or, as I have dubbed it, "the post–welfare state university."

Think of college student loan debt. Particularly after Occupy, it seems as if student debt is a new problem prompted by the financial crisis of 2007–2008.

But it actually arose as a deliberate implementation of neoliberal policy in the 1980s. Before then, under the auspices of the post–World War II welfare state, culminating in Johnson's Great Society, university tuitions were low, largely subsidized by public sources, and student loan amounts relatively small. In 1982, the average federal student loan debt for a graduating senior was about $2,000—not negligible, but a modest amount for four years (about $4,650 adjusted to 2012 dollars). By 1992, the average jumped to $9,000 ($14,500 in 2012 dollars), in 2002 to $19,000 ($24,050), and in 2012, by my estimate, to about $28,000. (That does not include private loans, which have risen exponentially over the last decade.) This ascent resulted from the deregulation of loans begun in the Reagan era alongside the defunding of public entitlements. Rather than the cost of college carried by the state—by our collective payment—it has been privatized, the cost borne by each individual. It has also created lucrative new financial markets, with high profits for Sallie Mae and other student loan holders. (Sallie Mae had been a governmental body but was privatized through the late 1990s, reaping high profits since.) The precipitous rise in college student loan debt is neoliberalism in action.

Other elements of the neoliberal bias in higher education include the push for research to bring in corporate funds or lead directly to commercial patents, the morphing of administration to a CEO class detached rather than arising from faculty, the casualization of a majority of faculty in part-time, adjunct, or contingent positions, and the pressure on students, working long hours as well as taking loans to pay tuition. Given these changes, there is a strange disconnect between the rhetoric about liberal professors and the material reality of higher education.

In the recent book, *Why Are Professors Liberal and Why Do Conservatives Care?* (2013), the sociologist Neil Gross tries to settle the debate over liberal bias in academe. Using data, interviews, and his own experimental test, he confirms that, yes, professors identify as liberal more often than they do conservative, but the asymmetry is not as extreme as rightwing critics claim and it has relatively little effect on their teaching. Gross adduces that professors lean left more often than they lean right by about 2:1. In data from 2006, about 9 percent identify as radical (meaning they call for the redistribution of wealth), 31 percent progressive (less about wealth but keen on social and cultural issues), 14 percent center left, 19 percent moderate, 4 percent economic (but not cultural) conservative, and 23 percent strong conservative.

However, Gross also finds, from a set of extensive interviews as well as data and previous sociological studies, that the radical left has declined over the past thirty years and that professors' politics don't usually affect their teaching, with most professors declaring that they cultivate neutrality. In addition, Gross performed a slightly sneaky but intriguing experiment, sending dummy letters to graduate programs asking for information, in some noting that the prospective student had worked for the McCain campaign, in some the Obama campaign, and in some making no mention of political leaning. From the responses, he detects no bias at all. Most graduate programs are happy to take all applicants, regardless of party affiliation.

To explain why professors gravitate to the left, Gross turns to social psychology, speculating that it works through self-selection, similar to the process that results in most nurses or elementary school teachers being women. If you are left-leaning, you are more likely to consider going to graduate school and becoming a professor—especially in the humanities and in social sciences like anthropology and sociology. (Engineering and business tend rightward.) This seems circular—the stereotype reproduces the stereotype—but its significance is to dispel the charge that people experience indoctrination in college. Rather, most people develop their political orientation during adolescence and then gravitate to a profession according to their predisposition.

The liberal reputation of the professoriate stems from the late nineteenth and early twentieth century, according to Gross, when the research university first emerged in the United States. Professors in the early American college customarily were ministers, but in the period after the Civil War they increasingly became men of science. This new breed of more secular scholar prompted the first occurrence, according to a Google search that Gross relies on, of the label "liberal professor," creating "an enduring social characteristic" or "imprint" that continues today. Gross's development of the concept of imprinting is his contribution to the sociology of professions, and he theorizes that we choose professions based on such imprints.

There are a number of other professions that tack left, such as writers, artists, and social workers. (Medical doctors and clergy tend right—clergy by about two and a half times more than ordinary Americans, so I'm waiting for the scandal to break in the news that clergy are trying to indoctrinate us politically.) But conservatives have used college professors, over any other profession, as emblems to discredit liberalism, and the last section of *Why Are Professors Liberal?* examines this rather single-minded attention. Gross looks to the formation of the contemporary conservative movement, particularly to William F. Buckley Jr. and his founding *National Review*. Drawing on archival material, he shows how Buckley, though himself "only sometimes populist," deliberately tapped into populist rhetoric against cultural elites to forge "a strong collective identity" for conservatives. Gross aims to dispel the notion that the rightwing attack is a grand conspiracy, controlled by powerful puppet masters; rather, if not exactly bottom-up, it arises from "mid-level moral entrepreneurs" like Buckley or David Horowitz, engaged "in a war of ideas."

The value of *Why Are Professors Liberal and Why Do Conservatives Care?* is, as I have suggested, to leaven overwrought charges about professors. It is a polished book, leading through data and theory in a plainspoken style for a general audience—not a popular audience, but one versed in the rudiments of academic fields and likely to care about such debates. Sometimes we call this kind of work a "crossover" book, although the crossover is usually to those in other academic fields and journalism rather than those who might read books on a bestseller list. It is clear that the volume is Gross's bid to become a public commentator about intellectual matters and politics.

Yet, for all its various insights, the blindness of *Why Are Professors Liberal?* is toward the actual conditions of higher education. It takes politics entirely as a matter of discourse and exhibits the disconnect I mentioned, between the purportedly liberal views of professors and the neoliberal policies and practices that, over the past forty years, have remade the institutions of higher education that they inhabit. Gross seems to take professors' political views at face value, but one might question whether those views are in fact a facade, abandoned when push comes to shove (for instance, during the graduate student strike at Yale, when many proclaimed leftist professors threw the union overboard and sided with administration), or a form of false consciousness, a misrecognition of academics' true position (as many critics in the 1960s claimed of professors' complicity with the war state).

Another possibility is that the kind of liberalism contemporary professors espouse—focused largely on cultural diversity and sensitivity to racial, ethnic, gender, and sexual difference, and not so much on economic equality and the distribution of wealth—goes hand in hand with neoliberal policies.

In other words, professors tend to be what David Brooks calls "Bourgeois Bohemians," adopting the culturally liberal attitudes of the counterculture while remaining comfortably bourgeois, if not economically conservative. The trend away from radical views would seem to support this explanation.

Regardless of their views, the fundamental fact is that professors are disappearing, and the position they hold dramatically altered over the past forty years. The real issue, in other words, is not what views professors express, but the politics that have reconstituted their jobs. In 1970, the overwhelming majority of faculty had full-time professorial jobs, whereas now their labor has been largely casualized, with a stunning three-quarters holding contingent positions, as a 2012 American Association of University Professors study reports. Gross mentions part-timers only in passing (noting that they poll slightly less liberal than regular professors) and speaks about professors as if they constitute a continuous cohort over time. Moreover, rather than professors, the cohort now dominating higher education is administrators. According to Benjamin Ginsberg's *The Fall of the Faculty*, the proportion of administrative professionals in American colleges and universities has grown from roughly half that of faculty forty years ago to a majority now. In short, faculty no longer constitute the core of the university, as the classic image typically has it; they are more commonly service providers for hire, and the central figure has become the manager of the academic multiplex, who assures the experience of the student consumer.

The midcentury history of American higher education, I believe, provides a better account of the political reputation of professors. Gross underscores a direct line from the late nineteenth century, when professors became more secular. While this might be one link in their evolution, it is surely a distant one, and it is questionable how liberal professors were in that period (a Google search for mentions of the phrase hardly seems definitive to me). The much more substantial historical shift took place in the period after World War II, during the great expansion of higher education in the United States. A professor was a rare species of professional a century ago, only numbering about 24,000 in 1900 and 40,000 in 1920, about one-fifth the number of lawyers, but in the postwar era became a common one, with more than 300,000 in 1960 and 686,000 in 1980, about the same as lawyers. The postwar boom also changed the composition of the professoriate, opening it to a much wider demographic mix than in the early part of the century, when professors were typically WASPs hailing from the comfortable classes (there were few Jewish professors, for instance, before World War II). This suggests a better explanation for the right's attention to professors: professors represent the flourishing of postwar liberalism and the success of the new welfare state. Higher education was a form of social welfare that affected a wide swath of Americans and made the case for liberalism in a positive way, not just as a safety net in hard times but as a bridge to a better society, offering palpable steps up the class ladder. If there is a contemporary imprint of professors, it more likely derives from their apotheosis in this period.

The culture wars of the 1980s were a reaction to this period, marking a tipping point between postwar liberalism and neoliberalism. The same conservatives targeting professors for "liberal bias" also sought to delegitimate the legacy of the postwar welfare state during the Reagan-Bush years. Gross largely elides both this postwar history and the ensuing culture wars, and I think it shows the chief limitation of his approach. The editor of the journal *Sociological Theory*, he gravitates toward the general theoretical explanation of an imprint, which once established, is an "enduring characteristic" if not Platonic idea, rather than paying attention to the contingent and uneven texture of history. (He also emphasizes theory in his first book, *Richard Rorty: The Making of an American Philosopher*, published in 2008, which is an excellent and rich biography but overladen with a theory of "self-concept," not unlike his idea of self-selection.) It creates a gap in the book (it is amazing to me that, in a book on "liberal bias," there is no mention of D'Souza's *Illiberal Education* or similar texts) that abridge the actual history of the modern American university.

To me, it seems obvious that the recent spike of "liberal bias" is an echo of the culture wars, whereas Gross emphasizes it as a discrete event peaking in 2005 (from a LexisNexis search). This perhaps reflects a generational perspective—Gross remarks in the introduction that he was a junior professor at Harvard at the time and watched with chagrin the controversy over Lawrence Summers, then president of Harvard, who questioned whether women had inferior mathematical abilities to men, which spurred calls for his removal and his subsequent resignation. That event caused a spike in complaints about "liberal bias," and Gross fixes on it. Instead of the 1980s, he harks back to the 1950s and the founding of the *National Review*, in part because he wants to debunk the idea of a conservative conspiracy theory coming from those on the left. However, while charges of liberal bias might not result from a *Parallax View*–style scenario, they do often come from a small and concerted ring of conservative foundations and think tanks. For instance, American Crossroads, founded by Karl Rove, is funded by a small group of the superrich and supplies unprecedented amounts of money to conservative Republican campaigns. Such organizations might not finally win an election, but they do tilt the table, and let's not mistake their politics: they are plutocratic, not democratic.

By now, it feels as if the obsession with liberal bias in academe is a tired debate, occurring in an echo chamber. Gross tries to lend some reasonableness to the debate, but I don't think he leaves the echo chamber, and he effectively splits the difference, finding the charges of bias to be exaggerated as well as charges of conspiracy to be overblown. I doubt this will either settle the debate or help improve the conditions of higher education. What we need instead, I think, is a study of neoliberal bias, particularly since the rhetoric of neoliberalism has become ubiquitous, now the standard language of administrators and even many liberal faculty. In the 1990s, Bill Readings observed that the new rationale of the university was the amorphous, technocratic one of "excellence" rather than the traditional ones of reason or culture. "Excellence" no longer has quite the same currency; the new neoliberal mantra includes the buzzwords "disruption," "innovation," and "choice." Part of their force is that they seem self-evident goods: Who would be against innovation or choice? But I think they sidestep some of the crucial problems of higher education, especially regarding equality. According to all the statistical markers, college is subject to a steeper class divide than it was forty years ago, and academic jobs show a sharper stratification. This violates the best hope of the American university. What good is innovation if it brings us a more inequitable world?

TWENTY-THREE

The University on Film

At the end of an afternoon of committee meetings and office hours, it was strange to walk out of my office onto a movie set. During the fall of 2006, Groundswell Productions was filming *Smart People* at Carnegie Mellon University, where I teach in the English department, and for several weeks the hallway outside the faculty office suite was filled with heavy electrical cords, lights that looked like huge operating room lamps, and bustling young people carrying clipboards and telling us to please speak quietly while the cameras were rolling. There were also occasional sightings of the lead actors, Dennis Quaid, Thomas Haden Church, and Sarah Jessica Parker.

The film is about a crusty, fifty-something English professor (Quaid), and the production seemed especially concerned about verisimilitude: In preproduction the staff took pictures of professors to get the look of indigenous garb; they moved stacks of books on hand trucks from the English chairman's collection to the office being filmed; and they made ready use of the actual campus rather than a fabricated set. An occasional sign warned that if you walked across a lawn, you might be in the picture. It probably also helped that the screenwriter, Mark Poirier, is the child of a professor.

There is a common complaint among academics that films do not depict us correctly, and in some ways Quaid was accoutered by central casting, beginning the movie in a beard and corduroy jacket. My cohort is just as likely to wear DKNY, Diesel, or Armani, but this is an odd complaint from people who study the conventions of narrative representation. Of course such films draw on stereotypes, as do most films that represent other occupations and realms of life. Ordinary cops rarely draw their guns, even though from films you would expect that they're in gun battles several times a shift. It's like complaining that clergymen get a bad rap from *The Scarlet Letter*.

The more remarkable point, I think, is that universities are so frequently the setting of fiction and film, in novels by contemporary writers like Michael Chabon, Denis Johnson, Jonathan Lethem, Lorrie Moore, Tim O'Brien, Richard Powers, Francine Prose, Richard Russo, Jane Smiley, Robert Stone, and Donna Tartt, and in films by directors like Curtis Hanson, Amy Heckerling, Spike Lee, Tom Shadyac, John Singleton, and Gus Van Sant. Why this profusion? One obvious explanation is that the university is no longer an elite or extraordinary experience, but a central part of American life. If nearly 70 percent of Americans attend college at some point, the university is common experience, indeed more than high school was in the first half of the 1900s.

Fiction set in universities is usually divided into two subgenres: the campus novel, centered on student life, and the academic novel, centered on faculty. Films follow the same scheme. One reason for the prevalence of campus films probably stems from their foregrounding the formative moment of entry into adult life in our culture, similar to the way that Jane Austen novels focus on the buildup to marriage, the entry into adult life in her time. Novels often gravitate toward the bildungsroman; campus films present our updated bildungsroman. A secondary reason might be the American obsession with youth. The image of the college years evokes nostalgia as well as some prurience, since they are seen as a time of freedom to explore ideas, identities, and life choices, as well as to experiment with unencumbered sex, drinking, drugs, and rock 'n' roll. In reality, the average college age has risen to the late twenties, most students are part-time, and students at non-elite colleges work twenty-five hours a week on average, but the image of a space apart still holds power as an ideal.

The popularity of academic novels and films seems more unlikely—who cares about middle-aged teachers? But I think it stems from the charisma and authority attached to professors. They presumably dwell in the realm of ideas, similar to the image of preachers in the nineteenth century, who dwelled in the realm of the spirit. Stereotypes of the haughty, bumbling, or lecherous professor do not dispel the fascination with the life of the mind. A related reason is that the professor represents, as Stanley Aronowitz has phrased it, "the last good job in America," in which one has a good deal of autonomy to do the work of one's choosing. People might begrudge that freedom, but they might also envy it.

One additional reason, which I think is underestimated, is that colleges represent a little bit of utopia, or at least a genuine public sphere, where one can ponder and discuss ideas in more than sound bites, and in pleasant environs to boot. The word "campus" itself has far more pleasant associations than "office building" or "factory." Think of all the images of campuses: the green, parklike lawns of the typical quad (where else does one find a public square now?), students milling about flirting, talking, or reading while sitting under a tree, a professor staying after class to chat with students, and moments of excitement at ideas and discovery. Contrary to the utilitarian imperative of American culture, we still value the idyll of higher education.

Smart People advanced a new reason: advertising. Typically films set on campuses give them fictitious names—Faber College in *Animal House*, Wellman College in *The Nutty Professor*, and so on—and those that assign real names, like the Harvard of *How High* or *Stealing Harvard*, generally use them as a pretext, without much real contact with the school. In contrast, *Smart People* highlighted the fact that it was set at Carnegie Mellon, showing the campus, classrooms, offices, dorms, and even parking. The agreement with the university stipulated that there be two references to its brand name in most scenes. It was not so crass that Quaid wore a sandwich board; instead, it usually meant subtle product placement—maybe a Carnegie Mellon mug on Quaid's desk, or a Carnegie Mellon–embossed notebook on a student's desk, or an extra wearing a Carnegie Mellon T-shirt. And not "CMU," which is what most people here in Pittsburgh call it but could be confused with Central Michigan University—rather, the full appellation, Carnegie Mellon University.

Another stipulation was that the university had the right of refusal for scenes. (That is probably no different from films set on other universities as well as corporations or military bases.) A tricky moment came up about a scene in which Quaid's son in the film has drinks and, as night follows day, sex with his girlfriend in his dorm room, and Quaid, à la *American Pie 2*, arrives unannounced. It was tricky because the university does not condone underage drinking, nor would it want to spook more protective parents. But the people in the Office of Advancement who worked with the filmmakers decided to approve the scene. They reasoned that it was neither gratuitous nor salacious, but they also thought it would be good marketing because CMU is more likely to be in the Top 5 Nerdy Schools than the Top 5 Party

Schools, and it showed that, contrary to rumor, one might even have sex at Carnegie Mellon, not counting an intimate relationship with one's Power-Book.

In interviews I conducted, the Advancement staff did note that part of the benefit of filming was educational—some of the actors spoke to classes and some students worked on the set. But I doubt that equaled the university's effort to arrange for filming on campus. It was clear that the chief benefit for CMU was getting its brand out, which the Advancement staff member I talked to quite frankly stated as her primary charge. Being number twenty-two in the *US News & World Report* rankings of universities is nothing to sniff at, but, like any corporation, the administration aspires to crack the top twenty. In lieu of a major football team on TV every Saturday, a T-shirt on the silver screen gets the name out.

While the film represents a fairly innocuous means of advertising, the university has been hard at work developing subsidiary campuses bearing its brand in Qatar, Australia, and elsewhere. (In the English department office, we have two clocks, one giving Pittsburgh time, the other Qatar, where some of our grad students go to teach, and which brings in a good deal of money to the central administration.) This augurs a new idea of the university, oriented toward the bottom line, and one can imagine that, just as hospitals have consolidated into mega-HMOs, universities will consolidate into the strongest brands in the not too distant future. As Marc Bousquet has aptly described it, we are entering the age of global EMOs.

As a scholar of the history of higher education, I have to allow that from the late nineteenth century on the American university has negotiated a sometimes fraught and sometimes beneficial relation with business. Still, I think that the turn toward branding represents a new step in universities adopting the ways and means of acquisitive corporations, oriented toward accumulating funds, rather than retaining their traditional firewall from direct commercial enterprise. The problem is that corporations operate primarily to accrue profits for their owners; universities serve another purpose, one that cannot be tabulated in the same way. It is hard to quantify what it means to have a space apart from everyday getting and spending, and what value lies in the freedom to explore ideas.

TWENTY-FOUR

The Thrill Is Gone

Professors aren't what they used to be—at least in film, if not in life.

The professor has long been a staple in film, usually fitting a few types. One is the professor as snob, mocked in the Marx Brothers' 1932 *Horse Feathers* and recurring in characters such as the priggish business professor in Rodney Dangerfield's 1986 *Back to School*. Another is the bumbling but good-natured geek, made an archetype in the 1961 Disney classic *The Absent-Minded Professor*. A third, appearing since the 1950s, is the expert, who is a voice of reason about science, medicine, or history, like the Ronald Reagan character, in his 1951 *Bedtime for Bonzo*, who informs us about basic psychological behavior. Another familiar type, usually taking a comic hue, is the rascal or reprobate, for instance the Donald Sutherland character in *Animal House* (1978), who introduces his young charges to marijuana.

Of late, there is a new type: It seems as if professors have become depressed and downtrodden. For example, two well-regarded 2008 films, *The Visitor* and *Smart People*, center on aging, later-career professors who are disengaged from their work and exhibit obvious signs of depression. *The Visitor* depicts an economics professor, played by Richard Jenkins, who is going through the motions, teaching syllabi from years before and avoiding research. Around sixty, he is too young to retire but entirely detached from academic life. He is also a widower, which sets the tone of his life—he is alone, dejected, and hopeless.

The plot turns on his accidentally meeting a young man and woman who are illegal immigrants. He becomes caught up in their struggle to stay in the United States. In a climactic moment—the scene of recognition in an otherwise subdued film—the professor confesses, while having dinner with the mother of the young man: "I'm not busy, not at all. The truth is I haven't done any real work in a very long time. . . . It doesn't mean anything to me. None of it does."

It's hard not to wince at his words, especially if you're a professor, not only because of the pathos they express and their raw honesty, but also because they lend credence to the image a lot of people have of professors, particularly tenured ones, that we're privileged slackers. My cohort, who joined the professoriate around 1990, had to scramble to get jobs and, if anything, we are overachievers who can only wistfully imagine the days of the relaxed, leisurely, pipe-smoking professor.

As a type, the professor in *The Visitor* is remarkably similar to the professor in *Smart People*, played by Dennis Quaid. They are the opposite of Mr. Chips: Both are uninspired in class, plodding through old notes, and each stonewalls an earnest student who stops by his office. The Quaid character is a widower as well, and he has closed himself off. He seems to shuffle through life (according to the commentary on the DVD, Quaid worked on his walk for the film), disconnected from his profession as well as his family.

Though images of professors are not always positive, these represent a new turn. In *The Absent-Minded Professor*, the Fred MacMurray character, while bumbling, is a vital, young man on the rise, both professionally and in his personal life. The film takes the classic frame of a marriage plot—at the beginning the professor forgets his wedding but at the end it finally takes place—which exemplifies the springtime of life. Both *The Visitor* and *Smart People* tack to the opposite pole, depicting the winter of a career and life.

The earlier professor—good-natured, absorbed in his work, respected if sometimes mocked, and up-and-coming—is a fitting figure for post–World War II higher education, flooded with new students, new faculty, and new money. Around midcentury, the American university system saw, along with its steep climb in students, a parallel rise in faculty, from about 82,000 professors in 1930 to 247,000 in 1950. The rising professor was a byproduct of the postwar welfare state and its support for research as well as mass higher education. In *Bedtime for Bonzo*, the Reagan character is a quintessential postwar figure: he is a veteran, serious, hardworking, and ambitious. He is also the son of a convicted felon, which is a nub in the plot but eventually proves his thesis about nurture over nature; he himself shows the rightness of the meritocratic principle of postwar higher education.

If earlier films depict the rising professor, recent films portray a fall. One reason is simple. Though the university has continued to expand—student enrollments have gone up regularly through the past century—professorial jobs have receded, largely because a majority of positions have been reconfigured as casual or part-time rather than full-time, permanent slots. In my field, English, a Modern Language Association survey reported that 32 percent of jobs are tenure-stream, meaning that, for the first time in the past century, two-thirds of those teaching have impermanent positions. Professorial jobs are no longer secure but precarious.

This obviously has the harshest effects on those without decent jobs, but it has a side effect on those remaining with tenure-stream positions. With fewer new professors, in simple demographic terms, the permanent faculty is graying. We are no longer up and coming, but stagnating and shrinking. According to Jack H. Schuster and Martin J. Finkelstein's *The American Faculty* (2006), a majority of the professoriate (52 percent) is now fifty or older, whereas in 1969 more than three-fourths of faculty were younger than fifty. Not only is the majority of current faculty eligible for AARP membership, but there is very little new blood: Now only one in twelve is thirty-five or younger, whereas in 1969 one-third of faculty was thirty-five or younger. (Schuster and Finkelstein draw on a 1998 survey, so the ratios are probably steeper now.) Picture how these numbers play out in an actual department: In a department of thirty, ten professors would have been thirty-five or younger forty years ago, as opposed to only *two* now. One can only assume that it lent a different tenor to campuses to have a healthy dose of young faculty in classrooms as well as in meetings. Now, faculty members are more likely to be talking about their retirement plan than the latest band.

The situation is not much better for younger faculty in other well-regarded recent films, among them *We Don't Live Here Anymore* (2004) and *The Savages* (2007). In *The Savages*, one of the lead characters, played by Philip Seymour Hoffman, has a life as depressing as those of his senior filmic colleagues—he can't seem to finish his academic book on Brecht, he's schlubby and unshaven, his house is a mess (his sister remarks, "It looks like the Unabomber lives here"), and he lives in a perpetually dreary Buffalo, where it's always cloudy or snowing, compared to scenes in sunny Arizona.

He's also a widower-manqué, grieving a girlfriend's moving out. Part of the problem is that he won't commit, but, as he explains to his sister, his hesitance is rational rather than just typical male lack of commitment: "Do you have any idea how many comp lit critical theory PhDs there are running around this country looking for work?" And he adds, "Even if Kasha and I did get married, she could end up teaching at some university that's farther away from here than Poland."

The film portrays yet another side effect of the current job situation: It affects not only one's income but also where one lives and one's relationships. I have often thought that current professorial jobs are like being in the army: One might be stationed nearly anywhere, according to the orders that come down from an arbitrary academic puppetmaster.

We Don't Live Here Anymore taps into a different plot line, presenting an updated *Who's Afraid of Virginia Woolf?*, with a pair of couples pulling each other apart. One of the male leads, played by Mark Ruffalo, teaches at a small community college. He is the opposite of glamorous: We see him sitting at a side table in the living room slogging through a pile of student papers, and in one classroom scene he has trouble reaching a bored class about Tolstoy's *Ivan Ilych*. Like the Hoffman character in *The Savages*, he is unkempt, mumbles and stumbles around, and lives in a dark, sloppy house. The realm of expectations has shrunken: Professors are no longer privileged professionals but part of the downsized world of contemporary America.

One other type of professor has gotten some screen time in the past few years: the celebrity professor. For instance, *88 Minutes* (2007) and *Elegy* (2008) feature professors who might appear on CNN or *Charlie Rose*. In *Elegy*, the protagonist, played by Ben Kingsley, is an English professor but also has a television show, on which he comments on books and accrues fame as well as ready young women. In *88 Minutes*, the protagonist, played by Al Pacino, is a psychology professor but also testifies at high-profile trials and appears on TV. Both characters have enviable lives—successful, famous, and rich, with large, luxurious, urban apartments that the camera lingers over. And, instead of beat-up Volvos, they both drive new Porsches.

The celebrity professor might seem to counter the image of the downtrodden professor, but he is the flip side of the coin. He represents the "winner take all" model that governs businesses and, progressively more so, professions. Like the CEO who receives three hundred times what the person on the shop floor is paid, these professors reap the spoils while adjuncts do the clean-up work of teaching all the service courses on the cheap. (Actually, it would be administrators who take the lion's share and are the CEOs; perhaps celebrity professors are more like spokespeople advertising the university.) The celebrity professor exemplifies the steep new tiers of academic life, in a pyramid rather than a horizontal community of scholars.

Films, of course, are inexact historical evidence, but I think that this wave of them—all generally well made and critically regarded—reflects how changes in academic employment have affected professors. These films put some flesh on the statistics and get at not only the facts but also the feeling of what it's like to be a professor now. A professor is no longer an upbeat functionary of the post–World War II boom; now we are entrepreneurs of the mind, and it wears us down.

TWENTY-FIVE

Unlucky Jim

The academic novel typically centers on professors—as opposed to the campus novel, which depicts student life. But since the late 1990s there has been a rising number of novels that have displaced the professor from his customary starring role, focusing instead on those in marginal teaching positions or working in a peripheral realm of the university. They show a new academic world in which faculty no longer compose its core, replaced instead by temporary instructors and administrators to keep the money flowing.

This new wave coalesced in three well-regarded novels published in 2010, Sam Lipsyte's *The Ask*, James Hynes's *Next*, and John McNally's *After the Workshop*. In *The Ask*, the protagonist, Milo, works in the fundraising department of a New York university, although early in the book he gets fired and the plot turns on his trying to procure a donation to regain his job. In *Next*, the hero, Kevin, has a staff job in the publications program of an Asian Center at the University of Michigan. And in McNally's less well-known but funnier *After the Workshop*, the protagonist, Jack Sheahan, a graduate of the MFA program in writing at Iowa, hasn't managed to get a teaching job but works chauffeuring visiting writers around Iowa City. In a previous era they all would have been professors—Milo in art, Kevin in comp lit or philosophy, Jack in English—but that door seems closed; instead, they have service jobs a long way from a classroom and are hanging on by a precarious thread.

This trend had its first glimmers in the late 1990s, notably in Hynes's collection *Publish and Perish* (1997) and novel *Kings of Infinite Space* (2004). Hynes has been the leading portraitist of present-day, casualized academe, and the opening novella of *Publish and Perish*, "Queen of the Jungle," centers on a young academic, Paul, who fails to land a tenure-track position and works as a temporary lecturer at "University of the Midwest." *Kings of Infinite Space* is a kind of sequel, following up on Paul after his lectureship has expired, when he ends up in Texas working for the Department of General Services as a temp making $8 an hour. There he muses, "How had he wound up here? . . . He had a Ph.D. from a well-regarded university; he had won *awards*, for chrissake. . . . *He'd almost been a Fulbright!*"

This goes against the expectations of the genre. Sometimes the plots of academic novels revolve around tenure, which generates a tension to be resolved and implicates the other characters, for instance in Mary McCarthy's *Groves of Academe* (1952). But that is usually the conceit of the plot—the hurdle that the hero overcomes, or the problem that events comically resolve at the last minute. Even if a character does not gain tenure, he moves on to another job—perhaps at a less prestigious school but still a regular professorial position. For example, in David Lodge's staple of the genre, *Changing Places* (1975), there is a memorable minor character named Howard Ringbaum who has failed to get tenure at "Euphoria State University" in California. (He's memorable because he confesses during a party game that he has not read *Hamlet*, and that is the straw that precipitates his negative tenure vote.) In Lodge's classic sequel, *Small World* (1984), we meet up again with Ringbaum, who now is a professor at Southern Illinois University. This is offered with some humor and little sympathy since Howard is, as Lodge's blunt hero, Morris Zapp, puts it, a fink. But he is still a professor. Paul is a fink since he cheats on his wife and otherwise does questionable things outside school. But even finks might remain as professors. The hero of the new academic novel is a professor-manqué, thwarted from a professorial career, and the academic world no longer a path to middle class security.

———————

The academic novel is usually considered a minor subgenre, for a small-coterie audience, but it actually has become a mainstream genre in the past three decades, enlisting a good number of prominent contemporary novelists. In the first half of the twentieth century, the campus novel was the more dominant genre, and it naturally grafted with the bildungsroman, in classic examples like Fitzgerald's *This Side of Paradise* (1920) and Wolfe's *Look Homeward, Angel* (1929). The professor-centered novel was rarer, and often a stagey affair, set in the cloistered realm of a campus, most familiarly grafting which the mystery, in novels from Dorothy Sayers's *Gaudy Night* (1935) through the Amanda Cross "Kate Fansler" mysteries up to contemporary versions like *Murder at the MLA* (1993).

By midcentury, while the campus novel persisted, it transferred much of its momentum to film, and indeed each year delivers a number of films about student life. The academic novel started gaining more traction after World War II, in notable examples like McCarthy's *Groves of Academe*, Nabokov's *Pnin* (1957) and *Pale Fire* (1962), Bernard Malamud's *A New Life* (1961), and John Barth's *Giles Goat-Boy* (1966), and from Britain, Kingsley Amis's *Lucky Jim* (1954). Professors were no longer a rare figure, but for the most part the university was still depicted as a separate realm, with its own peculiar codes, engendering its own dramas.

The academic novel crested from the late 1980s to the mid-2000s. More than seventy academic novels were published from 1990 to 2000 alone, according to the standard bibliography (which doesn't include mysteries), and even more significantly, the genre enlisted a good number of well-known contemporary fiction writers, including Paul Auster, Michael Chabon, Denis Johnson, John L'Heureux, Jonathan Lethem, Lorrie Moore, Tim O'Brien, Richard Powers, Francine Prose, Richard Russo, Jane Smiley, Neal Stephenson, and Robert Stone, as well as a few older veterans like Philip Roth and Saul Bellow. Some of the novels are more distinguished than others, but they depict the academic as a main stage of contemporary experience—of midlife crisis, postmodern marriage, and middle class work. This profusion has gone largely unnoticed, and most discussion of the academic novel still gravitates to old standbys like *Lucky Jim*, *Groves of Academe*, and David Lodge.

The key to its rise to a more central literary position is the academic novel's grafting with other established narrative forms, particularly with the midlife crisis novel, the marital travail novel, and the middle-class-job novel, paralleling the campus novel's adapting to the bildungsroman. Don DeLillo's *White Noise* (1985) exemplifies if not inaugurates the contemporary turn. It is crucial that the protagonist, Jack Gladney, is an academic, and much of the satire depends on his commentary and interactions with colleagues. But *White Noise* goes after bigger fish, proffering a representation of the world we live in, one in which technology and media permeate our lives, and grafting with the marriage and family novel, so that it becomes an emblem of postmodern American life. Academe is not separate but a prominent theatre of that life. A good point of comparison is Lodge's *Small World*, which came out in 1984. *Small World* has attained standing as an archetype of the genre, but it is legible primarily to those who are familiar with academic conferences, reputations, and theory. *White Noise* transforms the genre from a sideshow to an allegory trying to capture the tenor of our era.

The new wave bears all the earmarks of the standard academic novel: the protagonist works in a university and his identity is bound with it; the plot concerns, in one way or another, his job; and the protagonist is often a hapless male in the midst of a midlife crisis. The haplessness sets up the humor, and the crisis pushes the action along. That is the pattern, for instance, of Michael Chabon's *Wonder Boys* (1995) or Richard Russo's *Straight Man* (1997), in which a likeable middle-aged male careens through his crisis, like Jerry Lewis through a room of delicate furniture (it is often a genre of physical comedy). It is also the basic pattern, without the humor, of more somber entries such as Francine Prose's *Blue Angel* (2000) and, outside the United States, J. M. Coetzee's *Disgrace* (1999).

However, the new entries tilt the axis of the university. The academic novel had revolved around professors and students, sometimes with a dean intruding as a foil, and its stage was the department, most often of English. They proffered the romance of academe, with professors the knights and departments their castles, and students commoners or wards. The new wave represents a world from which professors have largely disappeared, and it leaves the customary terrain of academic departments. If teaching, the protagonists have contingent jobs, as in Hynes's "Queen of the Jungle" or in Susanna Moore's *In the Cut* (1995), in which the main character is an adjunct teaching composition (she is one of the few women protagonists, caught up in a psychosexual thriller). Or the protagonists can't get teaching jobs, as in *After the Workshop*. They have affinities with other contemporary novels, like Joshua Ferris's *Then We Came to an End* (2007), that depict the drying up of professional, middle-class jobs.

In *The Ask* and *Next*, teaching disappears altogether and the novels revolve around characters who do support work. In *Next*, Kevin works at the behest of professors, who control the editorial decisions of the Asian Center, but his boss is the center's administrative associate and his job is isolated and invisible (at a departmental event, he recalls how one professor introduced him as an editorial assistant). Also, the novel turns on his trip for a job interview with a private company; the walls of the academic world no longer hold. Even more forthrightly, *The Ask* portrays the new, commercialized university, revolving around a fundraising office and its machinations. Clark Kerr, who presided over the expansion of the University of California in its heyday, famously quipped that the university exists for students to have sex and faculty parking; *The Ask* suggests that the university exists for the process of garnering funds and building monuments to wealthy benefactors. At one point during a meeting, a dean of development tells Milo, "We are not simply some heartless, money-mad, commercial enterprise. We are partly that, of course, but we are also a compassionate and, yes, money-mad place of learning." Professors barely exist in this cosmography, and students exist only in their relation to fundraising (the two students appearing in the novel do so because of their rich fathers, one precipitating Milo's firing). The romance is gone; the university is no longer a castle of reflection, or even of backbiting, but an expensive machine to keep fueled.

The new wave also switches poles from the reparative resolution of the comic academic novel to more corrosive endings. Typically, in novels like *Wonder Boys* and *Straight Man*, the protagonists are flawed but likeable; the resolution pushes them out of their ruts, and despite some questionable things they do, they end up well. For instance, in *Wonder Boys*, the protagonist Grady Tripp, despite having stolen a rare Marilyn Monroe jacket from a colleague and having an affair with the colleague's wife, the provost, ends up teaching at a small college outside Pittsburgh. He not only is still a professor, but he also gets the woman and family too. *The Ask* is not nearly so forgiving. The main character, Milo, ends up working on a scrappy construction job, separated from his wife and son, and living in a rundown basement apartment. In *Next*, the main character, after spending the first half of the novel following—if not stalking—a young woman who had sat next to him on a plane, ends up dying in a public disaster.

Even though they are comedies of a sort, the characters are distinctly unlucky, the opposite of the eponymous protagonist of Amis's postwar classic, *Lucky Jim*. *Lucky Jim* is taken as a quintessential academic novel, although Jim actually leaves academe; it is quintessential because it turns on the peccadilloes of academic life, and also, I think, because it displays the anti-academic strain of academic life. (Nothing is more natural to academics than criticizing academe.) Jim sets in motion a series of comic disasters—among other things, at the crescendo of the novel, he gets drunk and makes a stumbling public lecture about "Merrie England." Yet, things turn out well for him: he gets a coveted job as secretary to a lord and the most sought-after girl. Although Jim leaves academe, it is a decided success rather than failure; academic prospects, while secure, are unenviable, and he transcends the dull fate of university teaching and scholastic research. In contrast, Milo in *The Ask*, Kevin in *Next*, and Paul in Hynes's books are decidedly unlucky. Milo and Paul lose their academic positions and end up in minimum-wage jobs and dodgy apartments to boot, and Kevin, as I mentioned, meets his fate. Instead of gaining secure, middle-class toeholds, they are casualties of a Hobbesian academic world.

The academic novel has obviously followed the fortunes of higher education in the United States through the past century. If its previous protagonist was a beneficiary of the post–World War II expansion of higher education, the new protagonist confronts the entrepreneurial university and the reconfiguration of academic labor, from full-scale employment to casualization, which explains the tendency toward black or corrosive humor. The previous protagonist, for all his foibles, was on the rise, carried along the tide of upward mobility of the postwar United States, whereas now the characters are struggling against the draining of public institutions and have become emblems of downward mobility.

In 1900 it was rare to graduate from high school, much less attend college. Of about 76,000,000 Americans, there were only 95,000 high school graduates that year, 238,000 college students (about 1/319 of the population), and 24,000 college faculty (1/3,167), and not all were professors. According to the 1900 Census, there were nearly five times as many lawyers (115,000; 1/661) or clergy (112,000). It would have been rare for most Americans, especially outside the precincts of a college town, to encounter a professor, whereas each sizeable town probably had its parcel of ministers and lawyers. The novel, of course, does not follow demographics lockstep; even though college was a minority experience, the campus novel held a certain fascination through the early part of the century, probably because it showed the romance of privileged life, as in *This Side of Paradise*, as well as combined with the bildungsroman and featured tales of youth.

Through the century higher education became a progressively more prominent part of American experience. By 1940, high school had become much more common, with over 1,221,000 graduates that year. The accompanying table shows the climb of numbers of college students and professors over the next six decades. Contrary to the image of its being an elite experience, college has become mass culture, and the professor a common figure in American life.

Year	Population	Students	Faculty
1940	132,000,000	1,494,000 (1/88)	147,000 (1/898)
1960	180,000,000	4,145,000 (1/43)	300,000 (1/600)
1980	227,000,000	12,100,000 (1/19)	686,000 (1/331)
2000	270,000,000	15,310,000 (1/18)	1,113,000 (1/243)

As a point of comparison, according to 2008 census data there were 837,000 (1/347) lawyers in the United States. Lawyers have been a significant presence in the country since its founding, while the professor was rare before 1900, so it us remarkable that the professor has superseded the lawyer as a common professional—which provides some explanation for their increased appearance in fiction. The professor is no longer unusual but representative, especially of the white, male, professional middle class.

Genres are an alchemy of literary tradition and social circumstance. The academic novel still largely adhered to its traditional type through the middle of the century, casting academe as a cloister, but by the 1980s, as it drew a new generation of authors and a new audience who had experienced college as a natural part of life, it assimilated the less monkish and more common bearing of college-educated, middle America. It became a prime stage of suburban life rather than a world apart. *White Noise*, for instance, with its all-American blended family, bruited that professors might now live next door and shop at the mall. Over the next decade, the academic novel also became a prime stage of cultural tensions, with a number of novels depicting the culture wars, such as John L'Heureux's *The Handmaid of Desire* (1996), Francine Prose's *Blue Angel* (2000), Philip Roth's *Human Stain* (2000), and, in drama, David Mamet's *Oleanna* (1992). It was no longer a coterie genre like the locked room mystery, but a mainstream public forum.

Sometimes the rise of the academic novel is attributed to the rise of creative writing programs, and that probably has been a factor, but the salient issue is not that it represents the lives of writers, but that it draws an audience, an audience that sees college as familiar, and that understands the professor no longer as a kind of priest but a common, middle-class citizen. The academic novel resonates with the contemporary professional—of late, one who is beleaguered and anxious because he may not have a job next week.

The chief difference between the academic novel of the 1980s and 1990s and now is that the former assumed a stable world for the professor, whereas the new wave records its instability. Academic jobs have undergone a transformation over the past half-century, from relatively plentiful, full-time, permanent positions to a high proportion of part-time, contingent, or casual positions. In 1970, according to census data, about four in five faculty positions were full-time; in 2000, the number had shrunken to about one-half. The actual figure is probably much lower, if one factors in graduate student teaching labor (which was not commonly used until the 1970s), with the AAUP estimating it at about one-fourth. The professor is becoming an endangered species, and the new academic novel reports his anxiety.

At the same time, administration has increased over the past thirty years, comprising an increasing proportion of those who work in colleges and universities (from 1976 to 1991 administrative and professional staff grew from 15 percent to 22 percent of workers, and one can assume that number has grown to more than a quarter now). Milo in *The Ask* and Kevin in *Next* show this new face of the university and its corporate leaning. Rather than the humanities, administration and management are the new base of higher education, and they are oriented toward a consumer rather than learning enterprise. *The Ask* stages this new commercial ethos of the university in one of the few appearances, and the only speaking appearance, of a student. The student, whose father is very rich and a benefactor, comes to Milo to complain that she cannot get in a particular course. When he says that's not part of his job in fundraising, she encapsulates the new code: "My father taught me that the consumer is always right. I am the consumer. You are actually the bitch of this particular exchange." She's right, and Milo, a poor service provider, loses his job.

TWENTY-SIX

Academic Opportunities Unlimited

Academe is in crisis. Young academics have been left out in the cold: according to American Association of University Professors (AAUP) statistics, only about 25 percent of new PhDs find full-time, permanent jobs. We are wasting the talent of a generation.

There have been scattered proposals to redress the situation, such as cutting graduate programs, but none seems to have staunched the carnage. And it is unlikely to change in the foreseeable future; given current state and federal budget pressures, it will only get worse. Moreover, even if the situation turns around, professors, especially tenured professors, probably will not be first to gain increased public support.

Therefore, the best recourse is to solve the problem ourselves, taking matters into our own hands, as it were. To that end, I have recently founded an organization, Academic Opportunities Unlimited (AOU). Our motto is, "We can't guarantee you'll get the job, but we can guarantee an opening."

AOU is elegant in its simplicity, rebalancing an artificially skewed market. One of the effects of the job crisis is an aging professoriate. Since the 1970s, the scales have tipped heavily AARP-wards: while only 17 percent of faculty were fifty or over in 1969, a bloated 52 percent had crossed that divide by 1998. It is no doubt worse now, and strangling the air supply of potential new professors.

AOU would work to remedy this bias against youth. It would, through a rigorous screening process, pinpoint faculty clogging positions and select them for termination, or "extra-academic retirement" (EAR). While this might raise qualms from the more liberal-minded among us, we would argue that it is more humane, both to potential faculty who otherwise have been shunted aside and to those languishing in the holding pattern of a withered career, than our current system. The retirement would be efficient and quick, and strictly limited to those who, as the saying goes, have their best years long behind them.

In turn, AOU would enliven campuses with new faculty. It is widely acknowledged that faculty in most disciplines have their best ideas in the first flush of their careers, so a good part of their later careers are spent rewarming an old stew; AOU would encourage fresh ideas and innovative research, and bring some excitement back to campus. Undoubtedly, the changes would be visible: rather than looking like fugitives from a nursing home or a Rolling Stones concert, the faculty would be snappier, with better-fitting jeans.

A secondary benefit is that it would have a catalytic effect on those with tenure, who would step more lively when on campus or not hang on to their jobs until they had squeezed the last bit of ink from their yellowed notes. It would bring some concrete accountability to tenure and in turn help to recuperate its public image. Tenure would no longer be seen as a protection for lazy elitists, but be genuinely earned.

Though AOU might prompt arguments like those against euthanasia, I think that it is more fitting to see it like "Do Not Resuscitate" (DNR) orders in hospitals—no easy choice, but the reasonable one in many situations. One can envision administrators building such a codicil into academic contracts. While retirement might be sudden, consider how many times people say that, if they had a choice, they would rather depart quickly than decline over years in hospitals and nursing homes. Is not academe, given its current demographic, a kind of nursing home for the intellectual class? AOU would be more humane than most other ways of expiring, and it turns the tide from a drain on scarce resources to a more just and productive use of them.

We should stress that AOU is not predicated simply on age, which would be ageist, but on productivity. We are as yet undecided on the exact process—whether it should operate through nominations (a "three nominations and you're out" rule) or through a statistical assessment of productivity—although we will be conducting trial runs soon.

Foreseeing concerns that it might violate academic freedom, we should emphasize that AOU would not tamper with hiring; hiring should of course remain in the domain of the academic unit, as our motto indicates. AOU would clear the current logjam and create more openings, and then it would be up to particular candidates to demonstrate their excellence.

While AOU is an independent enterprise, we expect that university administrators will welcome the turnover of faculty. Cost-conscious provosts will embrace the reduction of salary lines from high-cost, low-yielding professors to beginning salary levels. Deans will welcome the infusion of new energy instead of old entropy into departments. At the other end of the spectrum, students will be enthused by more engaged faculty, with more contemporary popular culture references and the ability to text.

Among colleagues I have let in on the ground floor of AOU, there is some debate over whether we should employ independent contractors to perform retirements or whether we should keep the job in-house. The consensus leans to the latter, which would provide an excellent opportunity for PhD students or unemployed PhDs to serve as "Opportunity Interns" (OIs). Such an internship would have its own educational value. For one thing, it could apply the diverse academic skills that students learn in practical ways—those from physics could consult on ballistics, those in chemistry could advise about toxicity, and those in English could get coffee. It would be a truly interdisciplinary endeavor, and it would dispel the image of academics as nerds bound to the ivory tower, again building more public respect.

One way to think about it is that AOU would be a rational correction of the academic job market. The market has become distended in an artificial bubble; AOU would help to return the apportionment of faculty to a more natural range. Most scholarship shows that organizations work best if employees represent a breadth of youth and experience rather than clotting in one group, which, like sitting on one side of a rowboat, will swamp the organization. AOU would recover a more normal and productive range and revitalize the professorial ranks. We welcome both nominations for EAR and applicants for Opportunity Internships.

PART FOUR

The Personal and the Critical

This section enters more personal terrain. It includes several memoirs, although, as disappointing as it might be, there are no salacious confessions. Rather, several of the essays tell about jobs I've had, working as an editor, in a bookstore, and, a world apart from those bookish realms, as a correction officer. (Really, and not just as a metaphor.) I also include an essay about my mentor at Stony Brook, with whom I worked in graduate school and who died, far too early, in 1999, and a reflection on how I came to do criticism.

Several of the essays in this section are "imitations" in the sense that poets use—not exact replicas, but inspired by earlier examples. In previous sections, the writing might sometimes show the influence of other critics' moves or styles (for instance, I find myself occasionally channeling Rorty's plainspoken way of making a distinction or Louis Menand's short sentences to close a paragraph), but the essays here have more specific sources. The first is my transposition of George Orwell's "Shooting an Elephant." When I was young, I wanted to work at as many different jobs as I could to see what people actually did. And I was always struck with the different job experiences Orwell wrote about, as a dishwasher in *Down and Out in Paris and London* and as an Imperial Police Officer in Burma, which he did for five years when he was in his early twenties, in "Shooting an Elephant" and in *Burmese Days*. "Shooting an Elephant" dramatizes one particular moment, so the model is not exact, but I wanted to give a picture of what it is like behind the high walls of a max as he did of wearing the British uniform in Burma.

For the second essay, I had Orwell's "Bookshop Memories" in mind (he also has some telling descriptions of working in a bookstore in his novel *Keep the Asphidistra Flying*), as well as Benjamin's "Unpacking My Library," which ruminates on book collecting. For "Teacher," I looked to Susan Sontag's "On Paul Goodman," which captures Goodman's complications as well as the feeling of loss, not just emotional but intellectual. Paying homage to "Politics and the English Language," "Other People's Words" gives my rules of thumb for better critical writing, although its tone is admittedly a bit sarcastic.

The final essay, "Long Island Intellectual," was written for a collection of "credos" I gathered to conclude my editorship of *minnesota review*. It again looks to Orwell, this time to "Why I Write" (clearly I read too much Orwell at too early an age), although it is probably the nearest to a conventional memoir of my path, instead of *A Walker in the City*, presenting *A Walker in the Suburbs*. In some ways, these essays make use of the tools of creative nonfiction, although I remain committed to the possibilities of criticism over that genre. Still, I think that we should look more consciously to literary models to renew critical writing.

TWENTY-SEVEN

The Pedagogy of Prison

When I was twenty, I left college and took a job in prison. I went from reading the great books as a Columbia University undergraduate to locking doors and counting inmates as a New York state correction officer. Since I'm an English professor now, people never entirely believe it if it comes up, probably because of the horn-rimmed glasses and felicitous implementation of Latinate words. But I fancied I'd be like George Orwell, who took a job as a British Imperial Police officer in Burma and wrote about it in "Shooting an Elephant." I thought I'd go "up the river" to the "big house" and write "Shooting an Inmate" or some such thing. It didn't quite happen that way, although as a professor I've worked fourteen years in state institutions.

For the most part, I worked at Downstate Correctional Facility, in Fishkill, New York. (You can see it in a hollow along the north side of Interstate 84, just east of the Newburgh-Beacon Bridge.) Newly opened and still under construction when I started in 1979, Downstate was billed as a prison of the future. It adopted a "campus" style, with small blocks of thirty-six cells, the cells arranged in small, split-level, horseshoe-shaped clusters of twelve, rather than the traditional warehouse style, with long rows or "galleries" of thirty-six or so cells stacked three or four stories high. There were also amenities such as a shower for every six cells and a TV area in the center. The new style presumably created a more pleasant environment, or simply less chaos. Downstate was also threaded with electronic sensors that would supposedly indicate if a cell door was open or if someone was walking between the rows of razor wire encircling the facility. The electronics were bruited as a wonder solution to security, as well as more economical, since the old design of a maximum-security prison required a small island of cement, with walls not only thirty feet high but also twenty feet into the ground. The sensors, however, were moody, a sticky door registering locked and unlocked like a temperamental Christmas-tree light, and a raccoon, a bit of rain, or a poltergeist setting off the ones threading the ground between the fences. Though annoying, they kept you awake if you drew a shift on the berm overlooking the grounds.

Downstate was designed to replace Ossining Correctional Facility, better known as Sing-Sing, as the "Classification and Reception Center" for the New York state prison system. If you were convicted of a felony and sentenced to a sizeable term, you were shipped from a county jail to the state system. County jails are essentially holding tanks, mixing innocent and guilty awaiting trial, and eighteen-year-old shoplifters and forty-year-old murderers awaiting the next stop. State correction officers looked down on the jails as poorly run zoos, the elementary schools of the prison hierarchy; state officers had substantial training, and state prisons were the higher rehabilitation. Every male inmate in the New York system spent his first six weeks at Downstate (women, who at the time numbered less than 5 percent of the prison population, went to Bedford Hills Correctional Facility), taking tests and getting interviewed so correction counselors could decide where he would do his time. If he was young, maybe Elmira or Coxsackie; if a relatively short stretch, a minimum-security prison like Taconic; if a long sentence, behind the high walls of maximums like Green Haven, Great Meadow, Attica, or Clinton. Since most of those convicted came from New York City and environs, Ossining had earned the sobriquet "up the river" because it was a thirty-mile barge ride up the Hudson. Downstate continued the tradition another thirty miles up, although the present-day conduit is I-84 and the mode of transport a bus.

Before getting a badge, New York state correction officers had to do twelve weeks in the training academy in Albany. It was a cross between military and technical college, with calisthenics in the morning and classes all day. Wakeup was 6:00 a.m., with a couple of miles around the track; as in the military, your bed had to be made with crisp corners, belongings neatly stowed in your locker, hair short and clean-shaven. There were periodic spot inspections, and you got demerits if you missed a step. The academy held hourly classes, like high school or community college punctuated by a bell (lateness was one demerit). One class gave background on the taxonomy of New York's correctional system, so you understood the designations minimum, medium, and maximum, and where they were, so you got a tacit lesson on state geography, prisons dotting the state like community colleges. Another was on relevant law, defining necessary as opposed to excessive use of physical force (one might restrain an inmate from doing harm to himself or others, but should not hit him once restrained), or enumerating rights (if an inmate complained of a physical ailment, you had to notify the hospital even if you thought he was bullshitting). One course covered procedures, detailing how to do a count, how to keep a notebook (in part for legal protection, but mostly to pass on information to the next shift), or how to do searches (never ignore an inconvenient corner, even if you don't want to reach, but be careful of hidden pieces of glass or razor blades). And one course broached rudimentary psychology, or "Interpersonal Communication" (IPC), in which the instructors taught you how to deal with, for instance, an enraged inmate, by responding something to the effect of, "So you are telling me you're pissed off because . . ." Though it seemed mindlessly redundant, it was not a bad lesson in how to stop and listen. Prisons, like any social institution, run best when they respond appropriately to needs as well as misdeeds. Contrary to the popular image of sadistic prison guards, the motto the academy drummed into you was "firm, fair, and consistent."

Everyone asks if I carried a gun in prison, but the most severe weapon allowed inside the walls was a nightstick. You were always outnumbered, and a gun would more likely be a recipe for a takeover or escape. The only place you were issued a gun was on a perimeter post, at one of the gates or on the berm. At the academy, there were classes in weapons—back then in the trusty Smith & Wesson .38 revolver, with which you had to hit at least 270 of 300 to qualify (a key to shooting a handgun is not jerking your hand up in anticipation of the recoil); the Remington pump-action shotgun, which you just had to shoot without falling over; and a 30-30, basically a deer rifle, which granted a special qualification to work in a tower at one of the walled prisons. After you were on the job, you had to requalify with the .38 every year, and, like a field trip, we looked forward to the day that we got to go out to the shooting range. The one part we didn't look forward to was getting tear-gassed, deemed necessary so you knew what it felt like to have the rabid sting of CS or CN on your skin and wouldn't panic.

The lessons were usually reinforced with black humor, anecdotes, and morality tales. For example, you can use lethal physical force to prevent an imminent escape but not if an inmate is still on prison grounds. One quip was that if you shot an inmate scaling the fence, you had better make sure he landed on the outside, otherwise you'd end up inside. One story to remind us not to slack off on searches was about an escape a couple of years before from Fishkill Correctional Facility (actually in Beacon, across the highway from Downstate). The inmate, so the story went, had gotten a gun smuggled in the bottom of a bucket of Kentucky Fried Chicken because the correction officer searching packages had supposedly eaten a piece off the top and passed the bucket through. Another story, to reinforce the rule that you not eat state food or accept favors, however slight, from inmates, went like this: An inmate, who worked in the mess hall and prepared the trays that got sent to the blocks for ill or keeplocked inmates, regularly brought BLT's to the correction officer on his block. One day the kitchen officer happened upon the inmate using a bodily fluid as a condiment on the bread. I never knew if the story was true, but I always brought my lunch.

The first thing you learn when you get behind the walls or concertina wire is that prison has its own language. We received a glossary of terms at the training academy, but like learning a foreign language, the words didn't mean much until you got there. A prison guard is not a "screw," as in a James Cagney movie, but a "correction officer," or usually just a "CO." A prisoner is not a "convict" but an "inmate." A sentence is a "bid." A cell is a "crib." To calm down is "to chill." A homemade knife is a "shiv." "Motherfucker" is an all-purpose word taking many forms, from noun to adjective and adverb, defined more by tone and context than literal meaning.

Life in prison is punctuated by counts, three or four for every eight-hour shift. When I was in training, I spent time at Elmira Correctional Facility, which was an old prison with what seemed like mile-long rows of forty-odd cells three stories high. I remember walking down the narrow runway in front of the cells to take the evening count. There were whispered goads—"CO, you look gooood," "Who you eyeballing?" "Hey motherfucker"—or simply hissing, which was the worst. I didn't turn around to look, since you rarely knew where the voices came from, amid the echoes off the concrete, and to respond would only take hook to bait. It was a kind of initiation, and it didn't last long.

What makes time go by in prison is the talk. Talk was a constant buzz—about life, yesterday's mail, what happened in the visiting room, the food in the mess hall this morning, the lieutenant who was a hard ass and snuck around at night to catch you sleeping, if you were going fishing on your days off, if you were getting any. With inmates as well as other COs, although, as in a game of poker, you never let too much show to the inmates. The one time you worried was when the buzz stopped. You didn't have to know the literary definition of foreshadowing to know that something was about to happen.

I got good at finding things, as much to stave off boredom as from a sense of duty. Once I found a ten-inch shiv hung inside a cinderblock behind a fusebox door. It was fashioned from a soup-ladle handle purloined from the kitchen, filed laboriously on cement to a knife's edge, its handle wrapped with white bandage tape. I would periodically find jugs of homemade booze, made from fruit and fermented in gallon floor-wax jugs, wedged behind a clothes dryer to cook or stowed beneath the bag in a utility vacuum. Once I found a few joints taped under a toilet tank. The joints bothered me more than the rest, not because they were harmful—in fact, one way to still a restless prison population would be to hand them out, whereas booze, especially homebrews, tends to prime people for a fight—but because they came from outside. They could have come in through a visit, stowed in a condom, swallowed, and later excreted, or they meant a CO or other worker had a business they weren't declaring on their 1040. It violated the boundaries of the place, boundaries that you did not want to get fuzzy.

Prison carries its own set of lessons. One was about how life works, albeit life in a crockpot: mostly by repetition and habit, punctuated by sudden, sometimes scary, but strangely exhilarating moments that shattered the routine. Once when I was at Elmira, whiling away a shift after the inmates were locked in, except for the porters who did the cleaning on the block, I heard what sounded like a small stampede on the stairs. I looked over to see a porter, head dripping blood, running down the stairs, with another following a few steps behind him, carrying a piece of jagged glass in his hand. I followed to find the two officers on the first tier pinning the glass wielder to the floor. Danger raises your blood pressure, which isn't good for you over the long term, but a drug for the short.

Another lesson was "Do your job," which was a kind of mantra, repeated by COs and inmates alike. It meant take your responsibility, don't slough off, don't dump your job on someone else, or you'd be not very tactfully reminded on the cell block, in the parking lot, or at the next union meeting.

The ecological balance of prisons is probably not much more fragile than those of other institutions or there wouldn't be many prisons still standing, but its imbalances take a particular intensity. If an inmate had a visitor, for instance, you made sure that he got escorted to the visiting room right away, otherwise he would have a legitimate beef, which would make life harder for everyone. Especially in the summer, when cement holds heat like barbecue bricks and you didn't want any sparks.

A third lesson was "Don't back down." If an inmate didn't go into his cell at count, you had to confront him and write it up or be ready to hit the beeper you wore on your belt instead of letting it pass. Otherwise, the next day three people would be lingering at the TV. It was a different kind of lesson from what I had learned at Columbia. One might find it in the *Iliad*, but not, in my experience, in most academic venues, where aggression is usually served with the sugary coating of passive circumlocution. I miss the clarity of it and, as with single malt, prefer my aggression straight.

Another thing that prison taught me was a version of "There but for the grace of God go I." There wasn't much room for moral superiority inside the razor wire, and you quickly got over it if you had it. A case in point: I worked for a time in draft processing, which is where inmates first arrive after coming through the gates. They got a speech, a shower and delousing shampoo, a crew cut, and a khaki uniform cut like hospital scrubs, and then they were assigned to a block. To avoid bias, officers generally didn't have access to rap sheets, except in transport and draft, when the sheets were like passports that traveled with the inmates. There was a young kid, maybe eighteen or nineteen, who had escaped from a minimum and was being returned from Florida. He had gotten three-to-five for stealing—taking a joy ride in—a dump truck in upstate New York, and the escape would probably double his sentence. On his sheet, there was an entry that read: "Act Attributed To: Drinking a case of beer." It's been a few years, but I'm not making it up.

Prison gave me a kind of adult education that, as a scholarship boy, I had not gotten at Columbia. It gave me an education about people, how they get by and how they don't. One of the ways they get by is loyalty. The people I worked with, even some of the inmates, "had my back": If a lieutenant gave you a hard time, the union rep would be in his face; if you were out too late and took a nap in the bathroom, another CO would cover for you; if an inmate saw the superintendent coming while you were watching TV and he thought you did your job, he would warn you. The better species of loyalty is in fact not blind: If you screw up, someone you work with should tell you. The corruption of loyalty is when no one says anything.

It is always curious to see how colleagues react when they find out about my time—as I like to put it—in prison. Some are fascinated and quote *Cool Hand Luke*, but it's clearly just a fantasy to them. Some take a more serious cast and ask what I think of Foucault's *Discipline and Punish*, but then prison is a disembodied abstraction, something they know as much about as dairy farming, which, like most prisons, occurs a long way from any roads they've been on. Some curl their lip and look away, as if I had a swastika tattooed on my forearm, but they don't seem to realize that correction officers are of the unionized working classes, like cops, whom they wouldn't hesitate to call if they had an accident or their house was broken into. It is often said that literature expands your world, but it can also close it off.

It is also often said that the university is not the real world, but in my experience each institutional parcel of life has its own world. When you work in prison, just as when you work in academe, you experience a world that has its own language, its own training, its own hierarchy, its own forms of recognition, its own forms of disrepute, and its own wall from the outside. In some ways, prison is the flip side of the coin of meritocracy. Both prisons and universities originated from religious institutions and are based on the model of the cloister; both are transitional institutions; both house and grade people; and both deal primarily with the young. The difference, of course, is that the university represents the hope, and prison the failing, of the meritocracy. It's an unseemly sign that we invest more in the underside than in the hope.

TWENTY-EIGHT

Shelf Life

Bookstores, especially for the literary minded, have a kind of aura. Not the prefab chains, but the quaint used bookstore, with a tickle of dust in the air, piles of books crowding the aisles, and perhaps a cart of bargains out on the sidewalk. One might wistfully recall whiling away an afternoon leafing through this or that book, finding a hardcover you'd been wanting for $2.00, or the person you browsed with. The aura wears off, however, if you have ever worked in a bookstore.

While I was in graduate school at SUNY–Stony Brook during the late 1980s, I worked in one in Port Jefferson, an old harbor town on the Long Island Sound a few miles east of Stony Brook, that had not been gentrified yet and had a mix of funky shops. I needed the money—my stipend was around $7,000, which, even back then, barely covered the rent—and I thought it would be better than waiting tables. It was a serious bookstore—or "bookshop," as the owners insisted—that barred romance novels and textbooks from its shelves. The owners were a married couple who had originally moved to the area for graduate school, and they knew books, meticulously sorting through the bags and boxes people brought in, culling titles in fields from architecture to zoology, discarding dross like Harold Robbins and Tony Robbins, and separating current from outdated and clean from ratty copies.

When you work in a bookstore, you soon learn that books are indifferent commodities. The kind of people who are drawn to work in bookstores, like the kind of people drawn to publishing or to academe, especially in the humanities, probably started with a love of books, but sorting, shelving, and ringing them up dulls some of their luster. Like any other mass-produced object, they are plentiful, replaceable, and immediately priceable in dollars and cents. They might have personal value to you, like a keepsake or photograph, but they are rarely worth more than a few dollars for a hardcover, less for a paperback.

There is an ecology of books, and used bookstores serve as a leaching field for them. Every day people came through the door bearing bagfuls or boxfuls, some strutting in as if bearing a Gutenberg Bible, some shyly asking if you were buying that day. Although there were occasional finds—an early edition of *Ulysses* printed in Paris, or a Hogarth edition of Freud—most of the boxes held pulpy Reader's Digest volumes, yellowed Book-of-the-Month Club bestsellers two decades old, or musty college textbooks dredged from the basement. The finds survived to see renewed life on the shelves, while the latter were fated for landfill.

Some prospective sellers were affronted that their box was only worth $4, primarily for the copy of an art book that had somehow slipped in among an old set of encyclopedias. They were sure that, because "antique," their books were suited for auction at Sotheby's. Others quickly pocketed the cash and slipped out the door.

Any used bookstore, if it bought all of the books that people brought in, would quickly expand to Wal-Mart dimensions. Used bookstores are an effort to check entropy, to recover some of the flotsam, but even then they buy more than they can sell, and like libraries have to weed their shelves and dispatch once bright jacketed tomes to the trash.

———————

Used bookstores draw a motley collection of patrons. Contrary to myth, they rarely draw tweedy men with pipes who pore over calfskin-bound volumes, as George Orwell observes in "Bookshop Memories." Most people happened into the bookshop, some looking for a single book they'd heard about and were hoping to get for a good price, some seeking a gift for an uncle who likes sailing, and some just strolling the sidewalk, enticed by a book in the window. They were the book tourists, and they didn't stay long.

At the other end of the spectrum were the book addicts. Sometimes they were dreamy, literary types, with long thrift-store coats, who would stand transfixed in the corner where the philosophy section was and leave three hours later with an armful of inexpensive paperbacks by authors everyone praises but few people read. Another species of addict was the book missionary, who would make a beeline to a single section and later at the register intently tell you, with a gleam in his or her eye, about the truth of

Rudolph Steiner, sci-fi, or macramé. Though narrow in taste, they were dependable buyers and one of the lifebloods of such a store.

Professors generally weren't addicts. Not many professors came in, and if they did, they were often cheap about books, grumbling about the price of a $6.00 paperback or insisting on paying for $1.83 totals by check, much to the annoyance of my bosses, who had to pay a bank fee for checks. Perhaps the attitude of professors was like that of farmers who, after hoeing all day, find little charm in gardening.

And then there were the book moths, people who didn't buy books but gravitated toward bookstores. Some were friendly, popping in to pass the time and remark on the Yankees or village politics or the weather. Some were annoying, using the store as auxiliary daycare, letting their children run through the maze of shelves, then suddenly swatting them when they whined that they wanted to go home. (One way to encourage a child not to read is to subject him or her to long intervals in a dusty, library-quiet bookstore.) And some were disturbing, probably a dose short of their proper medication, muttering about the Jewish conspiracy or having an argument with a family member who was not actually there. One probably encounters a similar parade of humanity in parallel businesses, like antique shops or thrift stores. A used bookstore is a more civilized version of the pawnshop, but it still retains the incipient seediness of used things.

———————

Bookstores have their own rhythms. Rainy weather brings people in and makes them pensive, bright spring and fall days send them hiking, summer air conditioning bribes them to stay. December, with its festive air of people drunk with buying, is the month of redemption for many small businesses, tipping the year's ledger from red to black.

Time moves drowsily in bookstores. Even though there was always plenty to do as a clerk—putting newly arrived books out, straightening shelves, looking up prices in *Books in Print*, the Bible of the used bookseller before the Internet—afternoons could move with the speed of cold syrup. This is probably not much different for anyone who works as a clerk in a small office, although in a bookstore it seems etched in chiaroscuro, the light filtering through barely visible waves of dust. It didn't help that the radio was tuned to a classical station, which was a mellow way to start the day but by afternoon Pachelbel's Canon seemed like the Muzak most likely piped in to purgatory.

My grad school cronies sometimes expressed envy at my time amid book-lined walls, as if I were ensconced at the Huntington Library on fellowship. I confess I sometimes envied them because they could sleep in or catch up on seminar reading, while I had to be up and at the cash register. But it gave me a bit of structure usually lacking in grad school and a respite from the goldfish bowl that grad school can be. It also gave me an ersatz education in a breadth of fields and subjects outside literature. Sitting at the counter or shelving books, I could glance through C. Wright Mills's *Power Elite*, Eugene Genovese's *Roll, Jordan, Roll*, Alice Miller's *Drama of the Gifted Child*, or Rudolph Arnheim's *Art and Visual Perception*. And I got a sense of what was current in a field—there was a stack of extra copies of Mills languishing in sociology, for instance, but Edward Said's *Orientalism*, if one came in, stayed for no more than two days.

Used bookstores reveal, like an exposed rock face along a highway, a kind of geological record of our culture, the tenor of particular moments sedimented in the design as well as topics of books. The compact, serious, and subdued copies of Doubleday Anchor paperbacks, like Erich Auerbach's *Mimesis* or Kenneth Clark's *The Nude*, bespoke the post–World War II years, the buttoned-up and striving 1950s and early 1960s when Americans were hungry for culture and education. The band of shinier, more colorful paperbacks, from Bantam or other imprints, like Tom Wolfe's *Electric Kool-Aid Acid Test* or Norman O. Brown's *Love's Body*, signaled the unbuttoning of the late 1960s and early 1970s, their covers popping out like wide-stripe bell bottoms. The myriad copies of the black and red paperback of *The Culture of Narcissism* seemed a stoplight reproaching the 1960s, auguring the shrinking expectations of the late 1970s and early 1980s. When I worked in the bookshop in the late 1980s, it was the heyday of the so-called trade paperback, with glossy, high-design Vintage Contemporaries and their competitors starting to fill the shelves, befitting the good-looking surface encasing the yuppie pulp of the Reagan years.

Like other objects that one might collect, books reflect something of their owners. Just as some people keep their cars showroom-clean while others have a year's worth of Styrofoam cups strewn across the back seat, some people keep their books in a pristine state, the spines barely cracked and the pages clean, whereas others handle them hard, even if unread tattered and frayed at the edges, perhaps with a coffee stain like a liver spot on the cover, and marked throughout.

The French critic Roland Barthes distinguished between two kinds of readers, those who write in books and those who do not. Barthes favored the former, believing that only the "writerly" reader gave life to an otherwise mute text, but my bosses were allergic to marked-up books. Still, a few slipped through, and they exhibited their own hieroglyphics. Some were expressive, with exclamation points, a celebratory "right on" or dissenting "bullshit" in the margins; some were more scientific, with ruler-neat lines capturing key passages; some seemed arbitrary, with daft or incomprehensible jottings sporadically through the text; some bore full interpretive regalia, with commentary and summaries providing their own version of CliffsNotes along the way. Now, with the advent of highlighters, it seems that those who mark books don't write in them so much as paint them, in pink, lime, and blue pastels, forming abstract geometrical compositions.

Inscriptions are a paradoxical kind of marking, keeping a polite distance from the text and usually announcing the occasion of a gift. Some simply recorded a particular occasion, like "Happy Graduation" or "Merry Christmas, 1973." Some were more instructive, like one of my favorites from an author, "Please deconstruct kindly!" And some were closer to letters, professing friendship or love or memorializing a shared interest or experience.

One I came across in a copy of Schiller's *On Naive and Sentimental Poetry* bore a lengthy, florid pronouncement—over the front and back of the first leaf—of undying love. It made me wonder, were they college sweethearts? Did they part long ago, a college romance, or was the book the jetsam of a twenty-year marriage? Was the Schiller a gift that resonated with the person to whom it was offered or a sign of an eventual chasm between the couple (it is not one I would recommend for a sweetheart)? After seeing so many used books, I myself am reluctant to write in them.

Now, I try to limit the books I take in since they threaten to overtake my apartment, and I buy most of what I'm looking for online. But I occasionally wander into used stores, especially when I'm visiting someplace new. Though sitting behind the counter dispelled some of the mystique of books, I still like the sense of serendipity, and particular books bring me back to the places I found them. If I pull Said's *Orientalism* from my shelves, I remember whisking a first edition from the counter in Port Jefferson; there is the hardcover of Julio Cortazar's *Hopscotch* that I got during a fishing trip to Lake Placid; 20,000 *Years in Sing Sing* when I spent a year in Ithaca, New York; and last year I found an old collection of essays by Alfred Kazin on a trip to Santa Cruz. Instead of photos, books have become a kind of scrapbook of the places I've been, by now a long way from Long Island.

TWENTY-NINE

Teacher: Remembering Michael Sprinker

Michael Sprinker was a professor of English and Comparative Literature at SUNY–Stony Brook in the late 1980s and 1990s. Though he fought it against the odds for most of the 1990s, he died of cancer in 1999, at only forty-nine. He wrote several books, including "A Counterpoint of Dissonance": The Aesthetics and Poetry of Gerard Manley Hopkins *(1980),* Imaginary Relations: Aesthetics and Ideology in the Theory of Historical Materialism *(1987), and* History and Ideology in Proust: À la recherche du temps perdu and the Third French Republic *(1994). But his most prodigious scholarly work might have been his editing, as a commissioning editor for Verso, a series editor for Cambridge University Press, and for the journals* minnesota review *and* New Left Review. *He also put together several book collections, including* The Althusserian Legacy *(1993) and* Ghostly Demarcation: A Symposium on Jacques Derrida's Spectres of Marx *(1999). In addition, he was a tireless mentor, directing a record number of dissertations, including mine.*

To anyone who heard him in seminar, at the back of a lecture hall, or on the other side of a restaurant, Michael Sprinker's voice was unforgettable. A baritone with a Midwestern nasal tinge that pierced through even a crowded room, his voice carried. During a lecture, he would sometimes subtly raise it, with a concordant raise of his right index finger like a conductor's baton, so you knew where the italics were. An extension of his voice, his laugh was somewhere between a hearty chuckle and a staccato cackle that was unmistakably his own.

Michael's manner of speaking was both decorous and rude. He spoke with unusually precise enunciation, combining an exacting, learned diction with a relish for the profane. An honors philosophy major in college, he ranged effortlessly over the knotty terrain of philosophical concepts from

Aristotle to Kant to Derrida, and his phrasing was marked with literary tags, like Dickens's "in short" or Althusser's "in the last instance," and Britishisms like "at university." But also an erstwhile factory worker, he frequently parsed his favorite intensifier, "fucking," into a sentence, and was wont to begin a question, "I hate to put a turd in the punchbowl, but in the third critique Kant actually says . . . ."

One of the distinctive if not peculiar turns of phrase that he used was calling someone "my teacher." He never said "my professor in college" or "my mentor," but pronounced, "he was my teacher," with a certain formality. Some of the people that he accorded that status were Erich Heller, from whom he took classes at Northwestern, Edward Said, with whom he took a 1978 NEH summer seminar, and Paul de Man, with whom he took one in 1981. It was a designation that carried his respect not for academic position but for intellectual force.

When I first met him in 1985, when I was a first-year graduate student at Stony Brook, I recognized the cascade of his speaking as that of a working-class "lad"—another word he liked to use—who learned many of the words through reading and school, and held onto them with a relish that those to the manor born don't appreciate in quite the same way. It is not that he was uncomfortable with the words; rather, it was the payback of a smart working-class lad who has worked harder and thus knows more than anyone else, and who, with a seamless, muscular intelligence, takes possession of them and makes them his own. There was no falseness in Michael. Although he was a Princetoney graduate (as I liked to call his alma mater, usually rewarded with a cackle), he never forgot or desired to forget where he came from. Rather, he did not let the empyrean heights of academe forget.

Michael never abided the discriminations of class—and for him class encompassed the other discriminations we experience, whether of race or gender or anything else—as evidenced by the vast range of students he had, brown or white, men and women, with or without academic pedigree. That, probably more than any other trait, is what made him a great teacher and earned the trust and loyalty of his students. He treated people as he found them, whether the secretary at the Humanities Institute, his unpedigreed students at Stony Brook, or his colleagues. The other side of the coin was that he didn't "have time"—another of his phrases—for academic pieties and intellectual pretenders, and he made it clear that he didn't. This did not always endear him to his colleagues or to some of those he encountered in the profession at large, and he sometimes aroused as strong antagonism as he did admiration.

Michael's primary discrimination was who "did the work," and one of his mottos was, "At the end of the day, it's the work that matters." He had an unabashed respect for the intellectual tradition and reserved a certain decorum for it. One sign of his sense of decorum was that, though he didn't own a suit, he always came to class or to a lecture in a pressed shirt and tie. (This, too, I took as a sign of a working-class lad; as another of his students, Mike Hill, once observed, you can tell the rich kids because they dress down, whereas working-class kids dress up for school.) Another was the dedicated seriousness with which he approached the work, whether it was a neophyte question in a seminar, a three-hundred-page book manuscript, or a Jameson article. And he was tireless in doing the work, seemingly a force of nature, even when undergoing bone marrow treatments still writing, editing, and teaching.

A corollary to his belief in the work was that, when entering an intellectual forum, you should "leave your ego at the door." As he put it, "A lot of academics, they give a paper and everyone tells them it was 'interesting.' But your friends aren't doing you any favors if they don't tell you when you're wrong, because your enemies sure will." And he didn't hesitate to tell people when they were wrong, a code that not everyone appreciated and that bristled against some of the niceties of academic decorum. He didn't shy from a fight, and he sometimes saw the world in terms of friends and enemies. Like most people's, his strengths were his weaknesses, his rude bluntness inseparable from his integrity.

At the end of his life, Michael was drawn more and more to Benjamin and Brecht. (If he had a theoretical path, it went through de Man, then Althusser, leavened with Aristotle and philosophy of science, moving to Brecht; or his object of study moved from Victorian literature through Conrad and Proust to Ken Loach films.) Part of his polemic was recovering Benjamin's Marxist phase, not as a misguided infatuation with Brecht but as essential to Benjamin's thought. The essay that he foregrounded was "The Author as Producer," in which Benjamin corrects a leftist tendency to think that expressing our political views is enough; rather, our position in production determines our politics, so we have to change the relations of production. One way to understand Michael's life is that he took Benjamin's caveat to heart and worked relentlessly to change the relations of production.

He was "the teacher as producer," and particularly in his work with Verso, "the editor as producer," marshalling a range of left books, from those by Michele Wallace to Andrew Ross to Aijaz Ahmad. One can glean the extent of his work as producer in the dedications and acknowledgments in several shelves of books.

Under his tutelage, Michael made you want to do the work. His seminars followed a relatively traditional format, but were intense, heady, shot with adrenalin. He lectured for two hours, and I have often thought, while one can hear some of his inflections and decipher the coordinates of his thinking in his writing, that his brilliance shone most in his lecturing. After the lecture was our turn, and we—in my cohort students like the late Jim Paxson and Ron Phillips—would have combed through the third critique or de Man or Proust for the past week to launch a counterargument. One worked hard for him to say "fair enough" or, even better, "I take your point."

As a teacher, he paid the highest compliment that a teacher can pay to his students: He took us seriously, however inchoate or nascent our arguments were. While he was not always patient with his colleagues, he was almost indulgent with us. He obviously identified with his students, not the visceral identification of trying to stay hip—in fact, he was a lifelong Elvis fan capable of a spontaneous rendition of "Blue Suede Shoes," whereas we were Elvis Costello fans—but the deep political one, with the future and with those who don't have a full franchise. Yet.

He fought for his students, whether for an assistantship or a job, or a pass on comps, or some other nettle. In 1986 or 1987, we had a graduate student strike, and Michael characteristically showed up each day for the picket line. At one point he physically blocked the doorway—and, before he was ravaged by years of chemotherapy, Michael was a formidable physical presence, a brawny 6'1" who was not afraid to stand in someone's way—and berated a colleague for thinking of crossing the line. He fought for others, at one point for the secretary of the Humanities Institute to be granted a medical leave, at another for one of his junior colleagues to get tenure. He traveled from Massachusetts, where he was undergoing chemo, to attend the tenure meeting, by legend got into a shoving match with one of the old guard, and helped sway the vote for his postmodern colleague. Michael's rude loyalty came at a price, no doubt costing him some academic rewards.

For me, Michael was the kind of older brother you wished you had when you were growing up, the kind who, if in a ticklish situation, you would run down the street to get, and who would come back to "put paid"—again one of his phrases—to the argument. The other side of having an older brother who was fiery and larger than life was that you sometimes saw over his shoulder the antagonism he induced. But, like a younger brother, you had watched the other moments too, and you understood his code and admired its sense of justice, or simply its fearlessness.

Whatever his lack in the normal social graces, Michael was unavailingly generous. Though he had a strong personality, paradoxically he was surprisingly selfless, and he gave of his time, energy, and means. He went to lengths for people, whether students, friends, or someone who corresponded with him about an article or book. For students, he famously returned papers or dissertation chapters—at one time he was on over thirty committees— rarely after more than a couple of days, with long, single-spaced comments, or he made calls for jobs, or he set up publications. Likewise, for those whose work he edited, he combed through their manuscripts and put his finger on the problems, and ushered them into print. His favors were not always academic: more than once he lent his graduate students (including me) money, and I remember picking him up at the airport on his way back from a Verso meeting in London when he appeared with a baby in his arms, the child of one of his African students, whom he ferried to the States. When you are in graduate school, you tend to think that most professors act the way your professors do, and that's the way the profession operates. Of course, it doesn't.

Of all he gave, what I remember most, and most feel the loss of, is his conversation. Michael relished talk, and it is the places where we talked—in seminar, on the phone, in his flat in Boston, during a car ride, over dinner at a fancy restaurant, or over a beer at a seedy bar—that still frame my memory. I expect that anyone else who knew him will remember the various places too, where his voice pierced the air. He relished telling and hearing about the latest book in postcolonial studies, or a recovered eighteenth-century text by Schiller, or a recent conference at Duke. He relished stories about jobs or politics, about friends' and students' lives, about new TV shows or songs. And he relished jokes, on or off color, and usually moved conversation along with a string of barbs—like the dozens, again a working-class thing.

More often than not, conversation with Michael was also punctuated with advice. He liked to give advice, whether on an argument you were thinking through, a job, or buying a car ("After the revolution, we'll all drive hot cars"). He would listen for a long time to some predicament I'd lay out, whether on the phone or in person, waiting until I was finished, then start, "Look, ace, this is what you have to do." I especially remember one bit of advice he gave me, and I have often returned to it, sometimes repeating it to students and friends. It was just after I had gotten my first job at East Carolina University in the early 1990s, and I was embroiled in the PC wars. It seemed I'd been sent from central casting as a PC professor, because I was affiliated with leftist groups, on top of which I taught theory, plus I talked like a New Yorker (as one of my colleagues told me, "What's the difference between a Yankee and a damn Yankee?" "A Yankee goes home") and wore a high proportion of black. The conservative National Association of Scholars was then gathering steam and held an organizational meeting on campus. I went, I confess with intentions exceeding intellectual curiosity, and got into a heated argument with a history professor who made the claim, common at the time, that the de Man scandal was evidence of the wrongness if not totalitarian leanings of literary theory. I found it more than ironic that, claiming the platform of scholarly standards, he adduced an inaccurate, tabloid version of the facts of the de Man case, and from it employed the kind of syllogism that anyone taking an introductory logic class would debunk (de Man was a collaborator; de Man was a theorist; therefore, theory was corrupt). I told him so, in a few more words.

Michael listened, occasionally with a "yeah, yeah" to hustle the pace ("no wonder you like *Tristram Shandy*, you can't tell a story straight"), occasionally with his inimitable cackle, and then, when I'd finished, he said, "You were never on the debating team when you were in high school, were you, ace? When you're in a debate, you don't try to convince the other side; they're never going to agree with you. You try to convince the judges; they're the audience." I have often thought of that advice, for politics inside and outside academe, even if I have not always been able to keep it.

For those who do not know Michael's work, I fear that I have not done justice to his writing, his unpacking of Althusser's dictum that "philosophy is the class struggle at the level of theory." But I think the way he carried himself, the way he so vitally and indomitably was, is part and parcel of his work, and his legacy an example of how we should conduct ourselves as intellectuals, particularly if we are against inequality, oppression, and the tacit discriminations of class. Michael was against them "all the way down," in every facet of his life, whether in explicating the history of Marxist aesthetics or in the way he acted toward those without pedigree or position. We still have his writing, but there is a hole in the intellectual world without Michael. For myself, I can't get over missing being able to call him on the phone, or to have dinner with him and hear him cackle, and to have him correct me, praise me, and teach me something.

THIRTY

My Life as Editor

Nobody goes to graduate school to be an editor. When I was in grad school in English in the mid- and late 1980s, my cronies and I wanted to be great theorists, like Paul de Man or Edward Said, patenting the terms everyone used. Journals existed to publish us, not we to publish journals. We vaguely thought that journals were put together by elves, similar to the way that grocery store shelves got stocked at night.

So, two years out of grad school, I was hesitant when I was offered the job of editing *the minnesota review*, a small literary magazine that had published avant-garde poetry and fiction and left-leaning criticism since 1960. On the other hand, I was tempted by the chance to put on my own show. I didn't think I would edit it for long—maybe five years, which one friend joked seemed to be my limit for commitment. But, like most such expectations, that ended up being wildly wrong. I recently stepped down after editing it for eighteen years, from 1992 to 2010.

I did have a few models. Though I had never worked on the journal, the previous editor, Michael Sprinker, was my advisor at Stony Brook, and, before his untimely death in 1999, he was probably the most important editor of his academic generation. He did three people's worth of jobs, among them commissioning editor at Verso, the book arm of *New Left Review*, where he shepherded key books in cultural studies during the 1990s, by Aijaz Ahmad, Michael Bérubé, David Roediger, Andrew Ross, and others on topics ranging from the French Marxist philosopher Louis Althusser to whiteness studies. He brought boundless energy to the job and clearly relished being in the thick of the intellectual mix.

Awaiting my number in the great academic job lottery in 1989–90, I had also worked for a year as an editorial assistant at Routledge, which was the hottest press in literary and cultural studies at the time. There I saw how editors like William Germano, who spurred a good deal of work stamping postmodernism, cultural studies, gay and lesbian studies, postcolonial studies, and so on, went about their business. The people at Routledge were smart but distinctly unacademic in their mode of proceeding; they didn't hem and haw but followed their hunches, and they had a stethoscope to the pulse.

My time at Routledge was like a second graduate school, teaching me about the practical, institutional dimensions of our work, and I put it to use when I took over *minnesota review*. At the least, I knew how to file and write letters, and I didn't procrastinate, as I sometimes had on course papers. In the moment before full-scale email, I developed a healthy gratification in sending out a daily stack of letters and packets.

One way to describe the show I put on is that it combined the politics of Verso and the weathervane of Routledge, although my particular slant was to try to capture what was going on for my academic generation, those entering academe 1990 and after. Earlier generations had plenty of venues, and the 1960s crew seemed to have a monopoly on them, so I thought we deserved some airplay.

My cohort was marked by two factors: we were versed in literary theory, but it was something that our older siblings and parents had fought over and that we received secondhand. We were revising and reworking it, often taking up more explicitly public issues in more accessible ways, and *minnesota review* pushed in that direction. Another factor, coincident with our intellectual inheritance, was our material inheritance: We came of academic age when tenure-stream jobs were evaporating, so that also made us revise how we thought about the university. Thus, under my banner *minnesota review* became a home for writing on academic labor, often by the less enfranchised, and I wanted the journal to serve as a reminder to the more complacent wings of academe.

A form I made ready use of was the special issue. That points to one difference between a review and a standard disciplinary journal: A disciplinary journal might have an occasional themed issue, but its charge is to cover the array of work in a field, whereas a review is freer to follow its inclinations. The special issues also made editing more engaging for me, as they took up topics I thought important. Rather than a different "hat," editing *minnesota review* dovetailed with my own work and thinking.

I began with a bit of a flourish, with issues pitched toward the cultural politics of the time, such as the 1993 "PC Wars," which answered some of the attacks on the humanities. The cover of "PC Wars" had pictures of Beavis and Butthead, among other things, indicating the new phase of the journal and perhaps my professional adolescence—cheeky, with some attitude and a DIY sensibility.

The journal focused, more than anything, on institutional questions, and in the mid-1990s I launched a series on "The Institution of Literature." I had originally intended it to be one issue, but it grew like kudzu to four three-hundred-page volumes. Perhaps representing my professional early adulthood, the issues had an impossibly ambitious reach, for instance taking stock of "The State of Theory" and the turn "From Literature to Culture." The journal also became a home for work on the graduate student union movement, the job market, and other politics of the university, and during the late 1990s I organized or sponsored special issues such as "Activism in the Academy" and "Academostars." Continuing the tendency toward hefty volumes, they looked at facets of how the academic profession operates, exposing, I hoped, the vagaries of the academic world from the inside.

By the early 2000s I had given up the special-issue habit. Perhaps reflecting my professional midlife, I settled into a regular format, with sections like "Revaluations" and interviews, in slimmer, more frequent, single issues. At first I had included interviews on an ad hoc basis, but I eventually made them a major feature, with three or four in each issue. Looking back, they compiled a kind of oral history of contemporary criticism and academic life; over eighteen years I conducted almost fifty of them and published nearly sixty, with critics and writers from M. H. Abrams to Slavoj Žižek. Ironically, now that I have closed up shop, I feel that I have finally learned how to put out a journal regularly.

There are two kinds of editors: the diplomat and the autocrat. The diplomat is a manager who keeps the machine running, seeing that manuscripts are sent to readers and sorting their assessments. Such an editor is the linchpin of standard organizational journals, which represent the consensus of a field. The autocrat takes a more direct hand in stamping the work in a journal, deciding on topics, serving as a catalyst for some contributions, and peremptorily rejecting others. Such an editor tries to change the direction of things, or at least represent a direction not traveled. Though it sounds a bit dictatorial, I tended toward the autocrat.

I was a hands-on editor in cajoling and corralling people to write for the journal and suggesting what they might write on. I think literary studies suffers from a glut of mostly irrelevant readings, which appeal to a very narrow audience at best; as Bill Germano once remarked, if you have time to read something, are you going to read an essay on Joseph Conrad or Joseph Conrad himself? Instead of readings, I encouraged people to look at an author or topic in wide angle, to write a "provocation," to reevaluate an accepted figure or a forgotten one, or to call attention to issues that affect us everyday but often fell out of the normal discussion of criticism, like labor, the job market, and the plight of the underemployed.

Another way that I was a hands-on editor was in going over the sentences word by word, frequently cutting phrases or even passages. It always surprised me how often the real start of an essay was on page 2 or 3 and most of the opening was windup, so I would suggest that the author start there. I'm not sure if everyone always appreciated the blue ink on their pages, but I think they appreciated the results, and the writing in *minnesota review* tended to be brisker, livelier, and more pointed than that in most academic venues. The sad secret of most academic writing is that it receives little actual line editing.

Being an autocrat doesn't mean that you are narrow-minded. You have to keep your ears open, and editing was part of my continuing education in literary and cultural studies. I found out about new critics and theorists, new fields, political quagmires, and problems and solutions in higher education from the work I read and the people I corresponded with. Most of the time, after grad school, you pay attention to the field you work on but lose track of others. Editing kept me plugged in, and I'll miss that.

I'll also miss collaborating with all the other people who worked on the journal, primarily graduate students who did many of the day-to-day tasks that a journal entails, from opening and sorting through the mail to copyediting and doing proofs. I appreciated not only their hard work, but also hearing how they developed their own ideas and interests, for instance proposing and editing clusters on working-class studies and on animal studies. I am proud that several of them have become accomplished autocrats themselves.

Being an editor of a "small magazine" is like owning a small shop with an apartment over it. You might go upstairs at the end of the day, but you never leave it for very long. The continuous stream of work is like doing laundry or the dishes—not bad, almost therapeutic, if you keep up with it every day, but overwhelming if you let it build up.

Though at points I had fantasized about life after *minnesota review*, I was comfortable in the shop and it was running well. But I was prompted to leave the editorship a few years ago by my university landlord. The powers-that-be at Carnegie Mellon, where I had moved in 2004, decided to cut back some of the support they had provided and that I had received from my previous institutional bases, the University of Missouri and East Carolina University.

It seems strange that, after over a decade of backing from less highly ranked schools, a top-25 university was more penurious. It is tempting to see it as a sign of the economic times, but the pressure from Carnegie Mellon occurred well before the current financial crisis, and the new home for the journal, Virginia Tech, has agreed to support it generously. There may be no particular lesson except the idiosyncrasies of a place.

But I have also reflected that East Carolina, though known more for football than for English, provided a good deal of freedom—to take chances, to be naïve or cheeky, to be ambitious, and to do something new—in a way that a more highly ranked university, with more tenure and book pressures, would not. If you look at the history of criticism, the newest impulses often come from out of the way places, like the New Criticism from Kenyon College in the 1930s, or African American criticism from Garland Publishing in the 1970s, which are less constrained by established academic habits. The paradox of prestige is that it might lead to a narrowness rather than breadth of vision.

THIRTY-ONE

Other People's Words

It's good that people can't hear me when I edit their writing. "Blah blah blah." "Is this a garbled translation from the Cyrolean?" "Did you actually read your writing?" "I'm not your mother." "Urrrh." It wouldn't be polite. I've done a good bit of editing over the past twenty years, of the critical journal, *minnesota review*, of several book collections, and of students' writing, and sometimes it seems like I pay more attention to other people's words than they do.

Of course, some writing is as elegant as the drape of Armani, and one cannot expect everyone to write as well as Louis Menand. But if you pick up a typical essay in a critical journal, what happens? Does it put the ding in plodding? I think a chief culprit is that there is too little editing. I don't mean simple copyediting, standardizing the commas and making sure pronouns agree. I mean hands-on editing, in the manner of Max Perkins, who pared down Thomas Wolfe's novels from an ungainly box of pages to a novel, the kind of editing that engages the text at hand, kneads it, pares it, and makes it better. Nowadays there is little serious editing in academe. It is a scandal, and I think we should remedy it.

Editing, like sending thank-you cards, is one of those things that everyone acknowledges is a good idea but barely anyone does. It takes time, and you don't reap much reward, certainly not equivalent to the time. There is probably not enough attention to teaching how to write in graduate school, but at least there are plenty of models and plenty of chances to practice. Models of editing, however, are scarce—that is, unless you work with commercial presses or magazines. There, editors really edit. We think of those venues as shallow slaves to the market, but they often pay more attention to the words and ideas than those in academe. They never lose sight of their audience, holding the quaint assumption that writing is actually written for people—not for tenure or a C.V., both of whom are tone-deaf.

Editing can sometimes be overbearing, or twist what you want to say, but most serious editing is sympathetic. The best editing is like ventriloquism. It makes the edited text sound exactly like you, only better. Shorter, sharper, more orderly. It is like getting a transcript of a dinner party and cleaning up the things you said, keeping only the good things you intoned, or fixing the sentences that didn't quite come off. How many times do you wish that you hadn't uttered that line, or had thought of a better one? With editing you can!

Editing can occur, pen in hand or cursor on screen, only while reading a particular piece of writing, but there are several tendencies in critical writing that, like trans-fats, one should try to avoid:

GLOSSOMANIA, OR EXCESSIVE CITATION. Yes, we know you've been to the library, or at least Google, but sometimes it's too much of a boring thing. Or more likely masking insecurity in a fog of citation. Or simply being lazy, listing without distilling. Rarely do well-known scholars cite a lot. I was cured of the citational reflex by a philosophy professor, who commented on a course paper I wrote on Aristotle which was half quotations: "You have Aristotle almost letter perfect, although I don't know if I should give the grade to you or to Aristotle."

INDIRECTION. Some essays suffer from being excessively round about, taking longer to get to the point than Henry James. A common habit in critical articles is to start with a quotation or a description of a literary scene. In the essays of Stephen Greenblatt this can be a brilliant device, but it is sorely overused and often a false start, the real point being on page 5. Or the main points are buried, in the middle of a paragraph on page 12. A reader shouldn't have to be a detective to find the point. I don't always like his arguments, but I appreciate the mode of someone like Stanley Fish: You know what track the train is on, which way it's going, and it gets to its stations on time. Many academic arguments are more like a Kafka train, only without the irony.

FAUX DIFFICULTY. There is a common expression in the humanities that one "complicates" a topic. This is another academic habit, like excessive citation, of overcompensation. Shouldn't our goal be explanation rather than complication? Of course not everything is simple, and difficulty might go with the territory. But the reverse does not follow: A torturous explanation does not indicate difficult thought; it usually only indicates bad writing, its faux difficulty presuming its faux profundity. Think of Wittgenstein: He presents us with conceptual nubs that gnaw at us, but his sentences run clear.

SELF-INDULGENCE. Sometimes academic essays string together minor corrections or comments on small points, producing what Foucault once described as *"une petite pedagogie."* Reading such essays is like overhearing high school gossip, which endlessly dissects events and the intricacies of who said what to whom. The problem is not jargon, but the presumption of interest and more than a little self-indulgence. Who, other than one's analyst, should care about a minute chain of association? I am more interested in where a writer has gotten, and he should distill it before he tells me. "Reductive" has become a pejorative term, but most scholarly projects would be interminable and require slimming to make sense. Any kind of history, for instance, would take a rather long time to tell without reduction. A key to good critical writing is *distillation*.

LAZY LANGUAGE. Cutting cliched connectors has cost me boxes of blue pens—"in other words," "to put it another way," "in addition," are the lice of academic writing. Use them once and they might have some snap; use them eight times in an essay, and then they're tics and empty filler. Another glitch is announcing or narrating what you are doing, in phrases like "I would like to argue." Such metacomments might aid in moments of physical intimacy but are usually quite unnecessary during an essay—just argue it!

And then there are a slew of phrases that should henceforth be banned. "Always already" was striking at one time, but that was in 1972, and it's now an utter cliché. "Cutting edge" is a phrase that is anything but cutting edge. "Problematic" is just clunky, and really what people mean is probably "troublesome" or "contradictory." It would be asking too much to stave the tide of Latinates, as George Orwell advises in "Politics and the English Language," but a little more original phrasing would be nice, and straightforward is always in style.

Lest I seem a tad crotchety, I grant that editing does carry its share of gratifications. As most editors will tell you, probably the best one is publishing the first essay of a young writer and working with her to refine it. Many of us are teachers, after all, and it is always good to see tangible proof that the lesson took, even better if the result goes beyond anything you might have advised. It is also gratifying to work with a more experienced critic to whom you suggest a new tack, one in keeping with her leanings but that she hadn't thought of. It surprised me when I first started editing that younger critics were often more rigid and less open to changes, whereas experienced ones were often glad if you made concrete suggestions and helped them polish the piece.

Another gratification is having people tell me (I hope without their tacking my picture to a dartboard) that they imagine my blue pen when they go over what they write (red is too ninth-grade English teacher, black hard to distinguish, and I just like blue). Although "the editor with the blue pen" doesn't seem quite as elegant as "the reader over your shoulder," I think they realize that I value what they have to say, in fact so much that I pay attention to every word.

THIRTY-TWO

Long Island Intellectual

By the time I was fifteen or sixteen, I had decided I wanted to be a writer. It wasn't, as some writers report, an idea I had fixed on as a small child; then I wanted to be a cowboy or, a little later, a pro basketball player. When I got to high school, I would occasionally put "lawyer" in the box marked "future occupation" on official forms, because I had verbal skills and it seemed a natural default. I also saw the writing on the class wall—my father worked at a cement plant, but since I was a good student I was being boosted over that wall—and I had an uncle who was a lawyer, and who took me on fishing trips and drove a Lincoln. But I didn't have a passion for "The Law," as my uncle would pronounce it, whereas I did for books.

During my junior year in high school, I began reading. I had conscientiously slogged through my school assignments and picked up the odd novel or sports biography in the summer, but I started shutting the door of my room and reading for hours at a stretch every day. I found various lists of books, from classics to contemporary novels, and pecked through them. I kept a notebook in which I recorded the books I had read and copied out quotes that struck me. During a field trip to Teddy Roosevelt's house in Oyster Bay—I grew up on Long Island, in a town called Centereach, aptly if prosaically named since it was in the middle of the island, about fifty-five miles from Manhattan and five or six miles from each of the ritzier shores— I heard that Roosevelt had read a book a day, so I aspired to that benchmark. It prompted me to ferret out all the short novels I could find, although I abandoned it for special cases, as when I embarked on Will Durant's *Story of Civilization*, which one could get for a dollar if you joined the Book-of-the-Month Club. I got bogged down on volume six, going back to novels. They were more entrancing, and seemed to tell the secrets of the adult world. Now I am less patient with fiction and keener about history.

Taking a break one night, I remember wandering out of my room and telling my mother, who always seemed to be humming around the kitchen, that I wanted to be an intellectual. I'm not sure what she thought; she asked if I wanted something to eat. Though my parents always encouraged reading and education, I suspect "intellectual" had something unseemly about it. It was the 1970s, so it was probably better than saying I wanted to join a commune.

I have spent the time since figuring out what it means to be a writer and intellectual. George Orwell, in his credo "Why I Write," distinguishes four motives that writers have: sheer egoism; aesthetic enthusiasm; a historical impulse; and political purpose. I'm sure I started with a heavy measure of egoism: I didn't want to be a rock star, I wanted to have my picture on the dust jacket of a book on a table at the Dalton's or Walden at the mall near my parents' house. I confess I still like to see my name in print, I hope not merely out of vanity but to have the work it took, like that of any craft, recognized.

I am tempted to tell my story as an evolution from egoism or aestheticism to politics—which is Orwell's story—but that would not really be accurate. The truth is more fitful and, as Orwell observes, one's motives fluctuate. Alongside ego, from the beginning I had some sense of politics, perhaps because of the time I grew up, coming of age in the 1970s and seeing the crash and burn of the Nixon years, as well as Mao's red book on display at Dalton's. Or because of my class background, seeing my father going to work at 5:00 in the morning for a lot less than a lawyer made. Or perhaps because of my family's religious leanings, Congregationalist (evangelical but a bit more refined than Baptists), which I moved away from but which gave me a sense of righteous indignation at some of the ways of the world. Or simply because I was the youngest and watched all the transit around me, as my sister's friends filled the house or my father told stories about work. I had a sense that I wanted to tell their stories because they otherwise would not be told, and also to bring back to them what I had read and seen.

"Writer" seemed to cover politics as well as aesthetics. I had a vague idea that I would do different kinds of writing, as Orwell or Sartre did, ranging from philosophy to journalism, essays to fiction. I dabbled with fiction, though I liked the power of the essay to peg a point and to say what you mean, without a mask. I was drawn to the way a writer might engage one's own time, giving it words, chiding its excesses, pointing to a future.

At first I thought my path was laid out for me. I got a scholarship to attend Columbia, where Kerouac and Ginsberg had gone and Trilling had presided (he died a year or two before I entered, in 1976, when I was seventeen). For an intellectual-leaning lad, the great books sequence was like nip to a cat, plus it was a natural path for an ambitious Long Island lad to go to the glow of Manhattan. But a nineteenth-century novel might say that necessity impressed itself upon me, and an early marriage and child prompted my leaving college to get a job as a New York state correction officer. It was surely an unusual side step for a Columbia student, but I thought experience was fuel to fill the tank of the things to write about, and I had read Orwell on his time as a British Imperial Police Officer. I also thought it would be a short intermission, but it turned out to be three years before I went back to college, and then I went to SUNY–Stony Brook because it was practically free and near where my parents lived, which helped with daycare. I had declared, when I was first headed to Columbia, that Stony Brook was beneath me; for my hubris I was returned.

Scrambling to make ends meet, I quickly finished my B.A.—in 1984, four years later than my class, so I always felt as if I was behind and hustling to catch up—and went directly on to the Ph.D. I had considered getting my certification to teach high school, but the vacuity of the education classes I took dissuaded me, and I thought being a professor would afford me more time to write and pursue what I wanted. Though my graduate crew and I knew jobs were tight, those were the days, in the late 1980s, when predictions proclaimed that a flood of retirements would open the gate of jobs over the next decade.

Graduate school funneled me into the world of literary theory. I had taken a good bit of philosophy, so it was an easy step to make, and, during the 1980s, theory was where the action was. Though it was the sunset of theory, it was a colorful one, with the flaring of the culture wars, when it seemed that the "stakes" of deconstruction or postmodernism or the other isms could change the world. It sounds a bit inflated now, but it was a time when George Will could say that Lynne Cheney, conservative director of the National Endowment for the Humanities, had a more important job than her husband, then secretary of defense.

Credos are as much about what you walk away from as what you walk toward. In some ways, after flirting with it in graduate school, I walked away from the mainstream of academic literary criticism. My first article, which started in a graduate seminar and became a chapter in my first book, was a reading of *Tristram Shandy* that used Gerard Genette's structural notations to make sense of *Shandy*'s funky plot. It also wheeled out some deconstructive points about reflexivity to show how the novel was a "narrative of narrative." Looking back at it, I might dispense with some of the lines that channeled Paul de Man, but I think it is basically right about the plot of *Shandy*, and I still like my formulation of "narrative of narrative." However, I think there are more pressing issues that call our attention.

One of the things I've focused on has been the state of American higher education, particularly the advent of what I have called "the post–welfare state university" and its protocols of privatization, that have extracted greater profit from research under the public trust of universities, greater labor from its teaching force, and a greater pound of flesh from students, especially in the form of student debt. I feel there is a pressing need to expose the facts of the case of this institution within which many of us work and which runs through American life, to sort out the ideas and policies that inform its practices, and to assert its status as a public space, one whose best hope tacks toward equality. I can imagine a time when this would not be as pressing as it is now, but I find it unconscionable that, despite the radical claims of many theorists, few focused much attention or effort on the job situation their graduate students were facing or the draconian loan debt most of their undergrads were yoked to. Credos are not only about beliefs, since one can believe many things, but also about choices. The key is not the beliefs you hold or espouse but what beliefs you act on.

Of course, the university is not the only issue that might call our attention. But it points to another plank of my credo: that we respond to the politics and culture around us. I think that we sometimes suffer from an exoticization of politics: we look to Kuala Lumpur rather than the everyday politics in front of us, in our time and place. They don't seem as impressive academically, but, as anyone who has been in a union would recognize, politics start in one's workplace.

An adjoining plank is that we should extend our critical efforts to policy debates. In literary studies, we tend to spin out interpretations, spot contradictions, or "complicate" the typical view, but we rarely offer prescriptions or practical solutions. I think we should bring into our repertoire more pragmatic, practical proposals. One need not do this all the time, but sometimes it's called for: it is one thing to analyze the idea of the university, for instance, but another to propose ways to change it, which is why I have not only written on the historical roots and ideological consequences of student debt but also thrown my lot with proposals such as the Labor Party's FreeHigherEd, or suggested that we institute a graduate student job corps. To paraphrase Noam Chomsky's credo, "The Responsibility of Intellectuals," we have the training, time, and resources to research and write on these things, and I think we have an obligation to throw our hat in the ring of concrete policy alongside theoretical analysis.

Some might object that this is not literary criticism: it is fine to do it, but it is sociology, or union politics, or journalism. This view relies on the narrowest of nominalisms, as well as a historically shallow view of criticism. Just because it is called "literary" criticism does not mean that it must focus only on literature. Historically, literary criticism refers to a range of commentary on culture and society as well as on literature, and literary criticism has a special role in the public sphere. Added to which, the university is a standard topic in the tradition of the humanities. Moreover, it is literary criticism because of the form it takes, in the manner and mode of the essay, rather than in the form of an article in sociology or communication. Or, as a compromise, one might call it cultural criticism.

Still, this is not to renounce the way that I was trained. The concern with reflexivity informs my looking at the university, and my training in theory has led to my writing on the institutional and material vectors of contemporary criticism. Though I would probably now bill myself as an historian of criticism, it might be more accurate to say that I do a *reflexive criticism*, oriented toward examining its conditions of production—which carries out Antonio Gramsci's credo in *The Prison Notebooks* that "the starting-point of critical elaboration is the consciousness [that] one is . . . a product of the historical process to date, which has deposited in you an infinity of traces."

———————

The middle part of the twentieth century was known as the "age of criticism." I fear that our era will be known as an age of scholasticism. Sometimes accounts of contemporary criticism read as if we have made the kind of advances that they have in, say, medical science, assuming we have gone far beyond the leeches of the New Criticism to the sophisticated instruments of x theory. But our time might well be seen like that of medieval philosophy, when philosophers spent inordinate amounts of time on internecine debates and arcane issues, and were absorbed in nominalist questions—for instance, what constituted a sign. A good deal of contemporary criticism is circular, slavish to authority (isn't it odd that a criticism that puts all things in question relies so heavily on a fairly narrow set of authorities, whom it intones with genuflection, "as Derrida says," "as Butler says," and so on?), and pretentiously ponderous. Sometimes the goal of criticism seems to be to make endless minor adjustments—we "complicate" and "problematize" texts, once again—that has relevance only to a rarefied coterie and functions largely to keep the coterie going.

I believe that we have a modest but more consequential role to inform and educate. Over the past forty years, we have let that sense slip away, as dull and dutiful, causing us to neglect general education and to lose a good bit of our audience. Rather than sophisticated or complicated, I think we should strive for a *useful* criticism, one that helps give people ways to think about our culture and figure out our, and their, worlds. I think that we have gone down the wrong path to see criticism as "research," as if it were a technological advance, rather than a comment on our culture.

One way I think that we can be useful is to do more "intellectual reporting," explaining intellectual issues to a wider audience, making sense of and assessing them, and placing them in their histories. Intellectual reporting doesn't short on scholarship but eschews the pedantic or obscure; it reaches to a broader public but also eschews the superficial or facile; it combines intellectual seriousness with an ear to the ground. In some sense, it is like translation, taking issues from scholarly fields and intellectual history and reporting on them. Translation is not to dumb things down; rather, it is to make material available to people who do not speak the language that it's in, and to present it in a refreshed way to people who do speak that language. To that end, I have written a good deal on the history of criticism for both academic and journalistic audiences, and I have also conducted a great many interviews with critics that I hope fill out a more textured history of the past fifty years in criticism than we otherwise have. I have also reported on the history and vicissitudes of the university. I think that there is a need for this kind of reporting, particularly for students who are at swim in a sea of information, so there is a more accurate report than that offered on Fox News.

My migration since graduate school, or perhaps since my days of reading philosophy as a teenager, has been to see criticism as more pragmatic than idealist, shedding a Romantic image of imbibing and dispensing large, earth-changing ideas, to offering something more practical. Criticism should aim to reach people rather than reach the ineffable.

Another way to put it is that I have come to see criticism as a craft. It should simply be well made, which seems in short supply in much academic criticism, that piles on documentation and readings, without much regard for sentence and paragraph, or any real consequence. We need to digest and distill rather than complicate and problematize. It is not simply that criticism should be accessible, and in fact one can imagine a well-crafted criticism that is not, but it is frequently difficult as a result of carelessness or windiness. Criticism should renew its domain as the essay rather than the academic article.

One line that has stuck in mind since I first read it when I was sixteen is from the opening of Simone Weil's *The Need for Roots*: "The notion of obligations comes before that of rights, which is subordinate and relative to the former." I think that, rather than a right that we exercise at whim, criticism confers an obligation, an obligation to those with whom we live, in our time and place, and an obligation to the needs of that time. Otherwise what we do is a self-interested hobby. Criticism can do more than that: if history is what hurts, criticism is what tells us which parts of it hurt and why, and what we should do about it.